RFD THE CHANGING FACE OF RURAL AMERICA

WAYNE E. FULLER

☆

RFD

The Changing Face Of Rural America

INDIANA UNIVERSITY PRESS
BLOOMINGTON

Library of Congress Catalog Card Number 64-19374
Manufactured in the United States of America

To the memory
of my father and to my mother

CONTENTS

ILLUSTRATIONS

(following page 258)

FOREWORD

At the beginning of this century rural America lived, much as it always had, in its unhurried world of the small town, the country store, the one-room schoolhouse, the muddy, impassable roads, the horse and buggy, and certainly those who were living then thought that this world would go on forever. But suddenly along country roads appeared rural mailboxes and telephone wires and King road drags and gasoline buggies, and shortly, in less than a lifetime, old agrarian America, known and revered from the foundation of the Republic, was gone. What follows is the history of one branch of the postal service that promoted and reflected this transition from the old to the new rural America.

In the years this work has been in preparation, I have become indebted to many people whose help and counsel I wish to acknowledge. I am especially indebted to Dr. William N. Davis, Jr., of the California State Archives who first saw the possibilities of the study, encouraged me in its undertaking, and patiently read and criticized the work in its earliest stages. I am also obligated beyond the possibility of repayment to the officers and employees of the National Rural Letter Carriers' Association who permitted me to use the association's files of the *R.F.D. News* and *The National Rural Letter Carrier*. I especially wish to thank Mr. Charles Larson and Mr. Max Jordan, past presidents of the association, for sharing some of their experiences with me, and Mrs. Gwendolyn M. Aaberg, assistant editor of *The National Rural Letter Carrier*, whose interest in this study and prompt response to my many requests has been most gratifying.

I am particularly grateful to Mr. Arthur Hecht, sometimes referred to as "Mr. Post Office" of the National Archives, who worked patiently with me in the R F D material located in the Business Economics Branch of the Archives and to Mr. Harold T. Pinkett and Mr. Truman R. Strowbridge of the Agricultural and General Services Branch of the Archives whose help in running down obscure material was of great importance to me.

I wish also to acknowledge the very important help I have received in preparing the manuscript from Miss Jane Rodman, associate editor of Indiana University Press, and to thank the editors of *The Mississippi Valley Historical Review* and *The Journal of Southern History* for permission to use material from my articles which have appeared in their periodicals, the officials of the Rural Letter Carriers' Association for allowing me to quote from the association's magazines, and Miss Dorothy C. Chase, research editor of Publications Service, Cornell University, for permission to use material first published by the university's agricultural experiment station.

In addition to a grant from the Southern Fellowships Fund under the direction of Robert M. Lester, I was the recipient of research funds awarded by the Faculty Research Committee of Texas Western College of the University of Texas, all of which enabled me to complete this work. For these funds, for the help given by the Texas Western College librarian, Mr. Baxter Polk, and his staff, and for the comments and suggestions of my colleagues in the Department of History at the College, I am truly grateful.

Finally, and most importantly, I acknowledge the invaluable help of my wife who criticized and typed endless revisions of the manuscript and listened understandingly to the many reasons why it took so long to write about the R F D.

W.E.F.
El Paso, Texas

RFD THE CHANGING FACE OF RURAL AMERICA

1

BEFORE THE R F D

In writing to France, it is better and safer
To write on thin paper and seal with a wafer;
If the paper is thick, there's high postage to pay,
And wax can be melted to learn what they say.
Niles' Weekly Register, Aug. 9, 1845

THE United States postal system is a great machine. Into its hoppers billions of pieces of mail are thrown each year. Parcels, letters, magazines, newspapers—they come from everywhere and are bound for everywhere. Yet somehow, the machine takes them all, mixed and jumbled as they are, sorts them, and sends them on, neatly arranged even to the last circular, to their proper destination with seldom a miscue.

Americans take it for granted that the machine will always work: that it will take a letter for a few cents from New York to Truckee, California, carry baby chicks from Kansas City to Evergreen, Colorado, fill a money order, and deliver a new dress from Montgomery Ward to a private home. And usually the machine does work. But it was not always so. Over 200 years of experience, if one includes the struggles with the old colonial post office, have gone into making the postal service virtually foolproof, and the citizen of Washington's day stepping into the twentieth century would be as amazed at the change in the mail service as he would be at space flights. Certainly in 1796 when Washington was rounding out his last full year in office, there was no indication that the postal system would ever be anything but the clumsy, haphazard service it was.

As a matter of fact, in 1796, a committee had just been appointed in the House of Representatives to investigate the Post Office Department. Like many another committee in the years to come, its job was to find out what had gone wrong with the mail service. There had been a rash of complaints from the citizens of the young Republic about their mails. What had happened, they wanted to know, to their newspapers? With the debate over John Jay's treaty with England still raging, and everyone talking about Spain opening New Orleans to American flatboats, and relations with France growing worse by the minute, it was no time to be without the news. Yet from the South came grumbling—the newspapers had not been delivered; or, if they had, they were in such poor condition they could not be read.[1]

After a month of study a congressman from Massachusetts brought in the committee's findings. He admitted that the postal service had been negligent. Newspapers going a great distance had been thrown in the mailbags with the mail bound for nearer post offices. When the bags were opened at the early stops, the newspapers were thrown on the ground while the search for the mail to be left at the office went on. Temporarily forgotten, these newspapers had a way of disappearing among the news-hungry crowd that milled around the post office waiting for the mail.

But, the congressman continued, the newspaper printers were partly to blame. Anxious to get their papers off in the first mail in order to beat their rivals, they rushed their papers still wet from the press to the post office. Here they were put in the mailbags along with the rest of the mail, and because of their wetness and the roll of the stage or the jolting of a horse, they were torn and smeared beyond legibility.

The committee agreed that this was a serious situation. Some step should be taken to make certain that the newspapers would circulate through the nation with a greater degree of safety.[2]

The wonder of all this was not so much that the newspapers frequently disappeared from postal stations, or that they were torn and crumpled and smeared. The wonder was that the citizens of that infant, thinly populated nation should have expected anything else from their mail service. Here was a new government barely seven years old, short on funds, and possessed of a population that spread for more than a thousand miles along the Atlantic Coast and for almost another thousand inland. To handle the mail of nearly 4,000,000 people there were not yet 500 post offices. The 13,000 miles of post roads were seldom more than trails in the wilderness, often impassable except at great peril to the mails. To send a letter from the capital at Philadelphia to Lexington, Kentucky, and receive an answer took 32 days; from Philadelphia to Nashville 44 days.[3]

But all this made no difference to the people who wanted their mail. One of the first demands citizens made upon their government as they fanned out along the coast from Maine to Georgia and westward across the Appalachians was for mail service. For more than a century, from Washington's day to the first years of the twentieth century, the demands for postal routes, post offices, cheaper postage, and quicker service, would be repeated over and over again, and no branch of the government would be so intimately associated with the demands of the people as the Post Office Department; and none would be so twisted and shaped and expanded by the petitions and promptings of the people. In a way, the people themselves built the postal system.

There was reason enough for the keen interest Americans took in their mail service. In an era when days and weeks and even months passed with no news from farther away than the next clearing, loneliness was the rule and a trip to the post office an adventure. This was the world the early Americans knew, and many knew it still as late as the early 1900's. To these people, walled off from easy contact with the nerve centers of the world by forests and mountains, plains and rivers, the mails were their telephones, radios, and television sets. Only when the mail came did they learn the news of the outside world or hear from friends or perhaps an absent member of the family. Even the newspapers were dependent upon the mails. If the mails were late, and the exchanges from other newspapers failed to arrive before press time, it was a barren week for news for subscribers. The editors might curse the Post Office Department, but there was no help for it. The only thing to do was to print the local news and reduce the paper by half.[4]

If the people made excessive demands on their government and grumbled unduly about the mail service, it was only because for a lonely isolated people the mails meant so much. Besides there was no place else to turn. Only the government could legally bring them the mail.

Americans saw nothing strange in the government's monopoly of the postal system. The British had monopolized the mails during the colonial period, and the founding fathers virtually took it for granted that the new government would do the same. This might not have been altogether clear from the clause they wrote in the Constitution giving Congress the right "to establish Post Offices and post Roads," but when the new government went into effect in 1789 the postal service was taken over lock, stock, and barrel from the old government of the Articles of Confederation and given a new lease on life.[5]

The new nation profited from the government's monopoly of the new postal system, if not financially then certainly politically. New Yorkers and Virginians, Georgians and Pennsylvanians, were constantly reminded of their common country as they saw the United States postrider break suddenly from the forest and head into their settlement with the mail. Swinging along from post office to post office, his saddlebags stuffed with mail, he was a living symbol of national unity, a concrete evidence that the new government existed and served all the people.

The men who shaped the young nation's history were keenly aware of the postal service's value to a democratic government. If people were to govern themselves—something some Americans doubted could be done—then they must be informed. Only the mail could carry a regular flow of information. "Northing [*sic*] can be more fatal to a republican government then [*sic*] Ignorence [*sic*] among its Citizens . . . ," wrote Rufus Putnam to the Postmaster General in 1794. He was writing from faraway Marietta in Ohio, and he hoped that nothing would stand in the way of having the mails sent there, for "if it is considered in a Political light only . . . communic[a]tions with these remote parts of the American Empire may be of infinite consequence to the government."[6]

Putnam knew the temper of the people and knew that it was no certainty that they would always desire to stay in the Union. But the Post Office Department stretching out its long arms and bringing the tidings of the national government into every hamlet and mountain fastness, could bind the nation, West to East, and South to North, in one perpetual union.

And so, firm in the belief that the postal service had a great role to play in the destiny of America, the government did its best to keep up with the demands of the people for their mails. It was a monstrous task. With only a handful of men in the Department, there were postmasters to appoint and contracts for carrying the mail to let. There were accounts to be kept, dead letters to be opened and inspected, supplies to buy, and a vast correspondence to take care of.

Innumerable problems would arise. Postmasters would resign and contractors fail to keep their bargains; the roads would fill with mud and the rivers choke with ice. Regular schedules were impossible to maintain the year round, and when the mail was delayed the people would complain. The irregularity of the mails became a standing joke in western communities, and it was with malice aforethought that the Westerner with a twinkle in his eye would sidle up to the postmaster and casually ask him when he expected the eleven-thirty mail. One western traveler, waiting for the mail in Lexington, Kentucky, in 1807 was thoroughly disgusted. He was expecting an important letter, and the mail due at eleven in the morning failed to arrive until ten that evening. Such irregularity, he wrote, was the "cause of general complaint in this country against the postoffice department. . . ."[7]

Nor were the mails very safe. Mail robbery was a common occurrence, even though conviction of the crime carried the death penalty. At one time so bad was the situation that the Department was reluctant to have its own remittances sent through the mail.[8]

Against all these obstacles the Department struggled valiantly, but entrusting one's letters to the United States mail service in 1796 was still an act of faith. This was the day when letters were simply folded and sealed and mailed without envelopes. Postage varied, so much for the number of sheets in the letter, and so much for the distance it was being sent. Over 450 miles on land, the charge was twenty-five cents for a letter of one sheet in 1792. Because the government had not quite given up the old British idea that the postal service should make a profit, the rates were high and letters had a way of reaching their destination by private post without actually going through the mail in spite of the government's monopoly. There were no such things as stamps, and usually the one who received the letter paid the postage. Too often, it was the kindhearted postmaster who trusted his patrons to pay who was left to dig deep when his remittances came due.[9]

Once mailed, letters passed through numerous hands before their journey's end. Thrown into large portmanteaus at the place of mailing, they proceeded to the next post office where the local postmaster unlocked the padlock on the portmanteau, dug out the letters for his own office, put the rest back in the bag, locked it, and sent it on to the next post office. Here the process was repeated. In this way the mail going any great distance was handled by numerous individuals, and men of affairs soon learned not to disclose their secrets in letters. Both Washington and Jefferson complained of having their mail read, and Jefferson once wrote a friend telling him that the "infidelities of the post office" kept him from writing fully and freely.[10]

Such was the country's early postal system. Like the nation itself it was young and inexperienced. Years would pass before anything resembling the modern postal system would appear. In the meantime, the energies of the Post Office Department were absorbed in merely trying to keep pace with the fast moving nation.

In 1790, the nation's main post road ran from Wiscasset, Maine, to Savannah, Georgia. With reasonable luck a letter might make the journey in twenty days. All told there were 51 post offices on the main road. Here and there, jutting off from either side of the main road were crossroads running through forests and isolated areas to 24 widely scattered post offices. Neither Kentucky nor Tennessee had post offices and the mail went no farther west than Pittsburgh.[11]

But each year saw hundreds of families on their way West, and each year saw Congress hurriedly mapping out new post roads in answer to the people's petitions. Now the mails were sent over the Wilderness Road, through Virginia to Danville in old "Kaintuck"; and now from Pittsburgh to Wheeling, down the Ohio River to Marietta, Limestone (Maysville), and then to Danville; in 1797 a post road was approved to run from Moffat's Store in Tennessee to Danville, and another from Knoxville to Nashville and Nashville to Natchez in Mississippi Territory. By 1800 the mails had breached the Appalachian Mountains at several points, and a network of postal routes ran through the West. The Post Office Department had felt the surge of the westward movement sooner than many other government agencies, and the reality of that movement was written upon its ledger books almost before it was written any place else.[12]

Once past the Appalachian Mountains that for two centuries had barred the way into the interior, the westward movement took wings, and the Post Office Department worked furiously to keep pace with the rapidly moving settlers. Within a generation after 1800, the pioneers had crossed the Mississippi River and were spread out along the bend of the Missouri River. Then, leaping over half a continent, Americans found themselves at mid-century along the Pacific coast from Oregon to California. But even here came the mail from home: first by ship around the tip of South America, then by land and water across the isthmus of Panama, and then by overland stage. Finally in one last burst of speed, before the telegraph and railroad opened a new era of communication, the mail traveled overland by Pony Express.[13]

By the time the Department was fretting over the mail to the Pacific, the postal system had finally outgrown its colonial past. The mails moved with considerably more speed than they had two decades before, and the mail that brought the news of California's admission to the Union in 1850 to Springfield, Illinois, for instance, might well have traveled by any one or all of several conveyances which the Department now used to carry the mail.

At mid-century much of the mail was still being carried by horseback and stage as it had been since Washington's day. At first there had only been the postrider, carrying the mail through a wilderness of dim trails and unbridged streams, passable only if one walked or rode a horse. Then came the stage. Entrusted with the mails in 1794, it was soon seen in every populated section of the nation, sagging beneath its burden of passengers and mail and lumbering through villages and countryside wherever a road or suspicion of a road existed.[14]

Picturesque in retrospect, the mail stage was a comfortless conveyance for those who took passage in it in the bygone days. As

Mark Twain found on his trip to the West, one must be prepared to share one's seat with the mailbags, and if necessary even yield the right of way to the mail. Seated amidst the mail, and swaying with every twist and turn of the stage, it required a certain agility all passengers did not possess to stay atop the bags as they shifted positions from side to side. The English traveler, James Flint, traveling through Pennsylvania in 1818 came across a mail stage that carried twelve passengers and "was greatly encumbered by large bags . . . enormously swollen by the bulk of newspapers." In place of windows there were only large leather rolls to let down over the openings in case of bad weather. A clumsy vehicle, thought Flint; but clumsy or not, the stage became the Department's favorite means of transportation because of the greater protection it afforded the mails. During James Madison's first administration, the Department proudly announced that mail stages traveled over 51,000 miles weekly.[15]

Though the Department favored the stage, the postrider remained for years the mainstay of the transportation system. Even in 1834, according to the Postmaster General's report, more than half the country's mail was still carried in saddlebags. The year President Polk took office, 1845, Congress decided that the mail contractor might use any means of transportation to haul the mails so long as they were carried with "celerity, certainty, and security." The postrider, cheaper and faster than stage or buggy, was thus assured a place in the postal system for years to come. And wherever the mails were not too heavy to forbid it, it was usually the postrider who carried the mail.[16]

The contracts awarded for carrying the mail without designating any particular mode of transportation were marked with an asterisk in the records of the Department. This was the origin of the star routes so familiar to Americans of the late nineteenth century.

For a business organization, operated in large measure by congressmen and senators bedeviled by political pressures of every description, the Post Office Department remained remarkably buoyant. In spite of everything, it never became entirely immune to change, though occasionally change came slowly. Actually, though perhaps no one ever thought of the Post Office Department as being daring, there was often a boldness and imaginativeness in the conduct of the service that would have done credit to a Rockefeller. For example, the Department did not long hesitate to adopt steam transportation for its use on the country's rivers. Scarcely six years after Robert Fulton sailed the Clermont up the Hudson River, Congress was willing to let steamboats with all their perils carry the mails. There was more delay over the adoption of the railroads for postal use. Even so, it was only ten years after Charles Carroll broke ground for the building of the Baltimore and Ohio Railroad in 1828, that Congress declared railroads post roads and opened up a new era in mail transportation.[17]

Steam was carrying the mail faster than ever before in the East and up and down the rivers in 1855, but the old-timer who posted a letter in that year was probably more impressed with other changes a half century of experience had brought to the postal system and doubtless wondered why they had been so long in coming.

For one thing the letter he posted would be snugly enclosed in an envelope. The day of the folded letter sealed with a wafer was fast disappearing. More important to him perhaps was the fact that his letter could travel the magnificent distance of 3,000 miles for only three cents. He may have grumbled because he now had to prepay the postage and could not charge it up to the receiving end as he had in the past, but prepayment was now the law of the land. However, the Department had made it possible to prepay the postage with very little fuss. All one had to do was to buy a stamp. Such a simple thing, the postage stamp, but the American public had to wait until 1847 before the idea seemed practical to the men in charge of the Department.[18]

Thus on the eve of the Civil War, the outline of the modern

postal system had been drawn, and the service was growing by leaps and bounds. But time and growth brought new problems as well as conveniences.

Until 1825 there was no such thing as a mail delivery to private homes. When people wanted their mail they simply sent someone to the post office for it or went themselves. This was the time-honored practice, and no one thought much about it until the cities began to count their inhabitants by the thousands instead of hundreds. The problem of getting mail at the post office in a city of 150,000, the approximate size of Philadelphia in 1825, had become somewhat complicated.

Fortunately, the mails were small, but even so the problem was serious enough. The obvious solution was to have the mail delivered. The scheme seemed reasonable to Congress, and before the year of 1825 was out, it had authorized local postmasters to use mail carriers to deliver the mail. The carriers were to receive no salary but were to be paid by the people to whom they delivered letters. The going rate could be as much as two cents a letter. But there was nothing compulsory about the system, and the person who wished to avoid paying the carrying fee could still go to the post office for his mail. All he had to do was to indicate to the postmaster that he did not want his mail delivered.[19]

The delivery system that developed under these regulations lasted for nearly forty years but left much to be desired. Collecting the carrying fee was awkward and sometimes embarrassing if one did not have the right change or any change at all. It meant that letter must be delivered directly to some person instead of being left in a mailbox. And because of the voluntary nature of the system, the carriers worked in an atmosphere of perpetual uncertainty, not knowing from one day to the next what their wages might be. Worse still, private companies had cut in on the delivery of the mail, and many a letter that could have gone through the mail and been delivered by the regular carriers attached to the post office was delivered instead by private expresses.

The Post Office Department had always had trouble with express companies carrying letters outside the mails, and the reports of the Postmaster General long bemoaned the loss of revenues and complained about postal laws too weak to force the private carriers out of business. The practice of carrying letters outside the mails over post roads was illegal, of course, but fines for such violations were small; and, without the authority to search express wagons for hidden mail, the Department found it difficult to discover the violations. Repeatedly throughout the 1840's the Postmaster General asked for more stringent postal laws to correct the situation, but Congress stalled. The express companies were not without influence, and besides, a part of the nation's press was building a fire under the Post Office Department. The mails were too slow, said the press; the business clumsily handled. Private enterprise could do better. "What a purification of this government would take place," declared the *Boston Chronicle*, "if this great tumor, the post office department, were cut out and dried up."[20]

In this atmosphere the express companies had become brazen, so brazen they contemptuously advertised their mail services between Boston and Philadelphia in the pages of the newspapers and boasted that their service would beat the regular mail by half a day. There would be no charge for carrying the mail between cities: only a one cent delivery fee for delivering a letter to the home of the addressee.[21]

Express companies carrying the mail between cities was bad enough from the Department's point of view, but the private penny posts that had grown up in the large cities were even more of a menace to the welfare of the regular city carriers. No one seemed to know how many penny posts existed in the large cities, but one senator declared in 1851 that there were 98 places in the city of New York for the reception and delivery of letters. Probably many of these were private penny posts. Since the penny posts were privately operated, the Post Office Department had no authority over them, and New York's Senator William Seward complained that one never knew whether the letter given to one of the unknown hands ever reached its destination or not.[22]

Nevertheless, the penny posts were popular with the public, mainly because they were what their name implied. For one cent a letter would be delivered anywhere in the city, while the postage on an ordinary "drop" letter addressed to someone in the city and going through the regular mail was two cents—one cent mailing fee and one cent carrying fee. So, in spite of the possible uncertainty, people used the penny posts extensively, and the Department found its carrier service unused because of the competition. Yet President Buchanan's Postmaster General, Joseph Holt, hesitated to eliminate the private penny posts in the cities by making streets post roads, because it did not seem fair to make the people pay an extra penny for their "drop" letters.

Even with penny posts the system of mail delivery was inefficient. Moreover, the practice of having boxes in the post office for all those who wanted them had become obsolete. The Postmaster General reported in 1859 that the mail was delivered into the 4,000 boxes in the New York City post office only with the greatest difficulty. But if 10,000 more were installed, and this number would not fill the demand, the delivery situation would be impossible.[23]

The answer to this vexing problem, came in 1863, in the midst of the Civil War, when Congress accepted the Postmaster General's recommendation that the mail should be delivered to private homes free of charge and the carriers should be paid by the government.[24]

City people soon became used to seeing their mail carrier making his rounds on their streets. Gradually the population requirements were reduced so that in 1887 a town of 10,000 people was eligible for the service, and the demands for free delivery poured in upon the Post Office Department. After all, was not the man in uniform with his mailbag across his shoulder a mark of progress? No enterprising town with a future believed it could afford to be without free delivery.

But in 1890 the majority of people in America still lived on the farm or at least in rural towns. There were nearly 76,000,000 people in the United States in that year, yet scarcely more than 19,000,000 had their mail delivered to their doors by an obliging Uncle Sam. Elsewhere across the face of the land in the little villages and small country towns and throughout the farmland, the old mail service lingered on.[25]

Like spring planting and the autumn harvest, the old mail system was a part of the way of life in rural America. As far back as anyone in 1890 could remember the system had always been the same. There had always been the trip to the post office, a mile or so down the old dirt road to the first crossroad, a turn to the right and straight into the village. There was the methodic process of tying the horses to the rail in front of the post office, the call at the window, the slow unconcerned movements of the postmaster as he shoved a letter or two and the county weekly through the iron grating separating the public from Uncle Sam's official business.

Often there was a long wait. The star route carrier who brought the mail from the town where the train or stagecoach had left it was late. Perhaps the train was behind schedule, or the carrier's horse had thrown a shoe or the buggy lost a wheel. There was sure to be a good excuse. In the meantime, one could exchange pleasantries with a neighbor or poke around the store in which the post office was located and pick up the week's supply of merchandise. The storekeeper, who would be postmaster when the mail came in, bobbed about at one's elbow ready to make a sale.

At last the commotion at the door would announce the arrival of the mail carrier. The mail pouch was brought in; the mail sorted. Then with groceries, thread, articles of clothing, a jug of kerosene, and the mail, there was the trip back home. Altogether a morning might have been spent in getting the mail. Not all of it was unpleasant, but it was time consuming.

By city standards the old rural mail service was painfully unbusiness-like, and the urbanite vacationing in the country was likely to lose patience with it. A journalist of the early 1900's recorded the story of one such man who went to the post office when he thought his mail from the city should arrive.

> "No letters here for you," said the postmaster who was also the justice of the peace.
>
> "They ought to have been in yesterday."
>
> "Couldn't have got in yesterday as old Brown, who carries the mail, was drunk, and didn't go over to Basco after it."
>
> "And how about today?"
>
> "Well, he's sober enough today, but his old woman has cut her foot."
>
> "But there will be a mail tomorrow. . . ."
>
> "Skasely, sir. We don't have mail on Thursdays."
>
> "Then how about the next day?"
>
> "Friday is a sort of day off with the Basco Postmaster and he generally goes fishing. If he don't he sends the boy over. I never count on it, however."
>
> "You seem to have a slipshod way of running postal affairs in this country. . . ."
>
> "Waal, I dunno but we have . . . but as long as nobody but Uncle Bill Simpson ever gets any mail, and that's only a circular about how to kill cockroaches, we kinda take things easy and let the United States run along without worrying about the mails."[26]

Not all farmers, however, were as unconcerned about their mail as this village postmaster. In many communities they had arranged to have their own delivery service. In the summertime boys could be hired to carry the farmers' mail for very little. Or better still, the milkman would double as the mailman. He would pick up the farmer's milk in the early morning, take it to the creamery and while in the village drop around to the post office for the mail. On his return trip he would deliver the mail or hold it over until the next time he made his rounds for the milk. If he held it over, then the clanking of the cans down at the gate the next morning might indicate to the farmer that the mail was there as well as fresh cans for the milk.

For the most part, however, the farmers got along with the old system. They had always done so and could scarcely imagine anything else. There was even something to be said for going to the post office after the mail. It broke the monotony of farm life and gave the farmer an excuse to visit with his neighbors. But in the early 1890's when the inadequacies of the old system and the advantages of the new were pointed out to them, then nothing would do but that the old mail service must be replaced.

2

THE "FATHER OF THE RFD"

"I am a woman nearly 70 years old, running a farm of 75 acres. . . . To my mind . . . free delivery and collection of mail matter in rural districts would be an inestimable boon to every one. . . . Our men and boys would not so often be tempted to spend time and money in the billiard rooms and other similar places while waiting for the mail."

National Grange, *Proceedings,* 1891, 159

BACK in the late twenties John Stahl sat down to write his memoirs. He had had a long life as a newspaperman for America's rural press, and looking back on the achievements of a lifetime, he began to think that he had never been given proper credit for his part in the founding of R F D. "It is amusing, and yet annoying," he wrote, "that the credit for the victory has been persistently claimed for those persons and organizations not entitled to it. . . . At least seven public men have been anxious to be known as the 'father of rural mail delivery.' Not one of them was the least entitled to the honor. . . ." The truth, he went on, was that he was the real father of the service since he had suggested the idea as far back as 1879.[1]

At the time Stahl was writing rural mail carriers had been making their daily rounds for more than thirty years, and people were saying that R F D was the best thing the government had ever done for the farmers. So it was only natural that he would want to be known as the father of such a popular service. But no matter how hard he might try to exclude his competitors, the fact remained that the seven public men he mentioned all had valid claims to fatherhood, and upon whose shoulders the real title of the father of the service should rest was not nearly as clear as an old man's memory made it out to be.

Perhaps Stahl was the "father of R F D" in the sense that he originated the scheme. At least no one seems to have thought of it before he did, unless it was the little Grange woman who some Grangers believed was the originator.[2] But it was one thing to propose that the government carry the farmer's mail to him, and another to get such a service established. Thousands of people had to be enlisted in its support before Congress would consider such a plan, and until Postmaster General John Wanamaker began to agitate for rural delivery in 1891, few people had ever heard of it.

John Wanamaker was appointed Postmaster General in 1889, and it is doubtful if anyone around the Post Office Department then could remember when they had seen a more vigorous Postmaster General. Blessed, or maybe cursed, with unlimited energy and a titanic enthusiasm, he soon turned the staid Department upside down. In two years' time he had suggested more changes, tried more experiments, and tramped on more important toes than had all of his predecessors in the office since the Civil War. He had angered the express companies with his proposal for a parcel-post system, and roused the bankers with a recommendation for the establishment of a postal-savings bank. The gamblers of Louisiana were upset because he had led the fight to refuse them the use of the mails in conducting their lotteries, and the telegraph companies were enraged and his conservative colleagues in the cabinet shocked because he had suggested that the Post Office Department take over the telegraph and telephone companies.

In the spring of 1891 he began talking about delivering the mail to the farmers. Actually, he was already busily conducting a free delivery experiment in small towns and villages and calling it rural free delivery. This experiment had been designed to test the practicality of extending the free delivery system to farmers, and though the results were far from conclusive in 1891, Wanamaker was telling the American people that the test had proven the feasibility of carrying the mail to rural areas and that a rural delivery service should be started at once.[3]

Some people laughed and some sneered at this obviously fantastic proposal just as they had laughed at other Wanamaker schemes. The idea of sending a mail carrier trudging over hill and dale to find some farmer to whom a letter might occasionally be directed seemed ridiculous. The politicians thought it was just a trick to get votes, and others believed Wanamaker was planning to convert his stores into mail-order houses and needed rural postmen to deliver packages. Even a leading farm publication was critical at first: "*The Farm Journal* wants, and the people want, Mr. Wanamaker, 1 cent postage. We don't want our country roads overrun with half paid federal officials delivering 2 cent letters at a cost of 10 cents a letter."[4]

John Wanamaker took the jeers in stride. He was a pleasant looking, blue-eyed man, a little taller than average, and in 1891, at the age of 53, graying at the temples. After two years as Postmaster General he was used to the jibes directed his way, and not much could be said about him after he proposed rural free delivery that had not already been said before.

Wanamaker could easily have been the model for Horatio Alger's "rags-to-riches" stories. His birth was humble enough, and his virtues were ambition, hard work, and thriftiness. As much as any other of the nineteenth century's rugged individualists, he had raised himself by his own bootstraps. At the outset of the Civil War, he and his brother-in-law, against the advice of older heads, had dared to open a men's clothing store at the corner of Sixth and Market streets in Philadelphia. The store prospered almost from the start, and Wanamaker went on after the death of his partner to expand the business until he had built up the fabulous stores which had made his name one of the most widely known in the nation. Over this empire of merchandise, Wanamaker was ruling with a paternalistic hand in 1888 when he became involved in the political campaign of that year.[5]

A staunch Republican, Wanamaker was so anxious to see a man of his political faith return to the White House that he solicited funds for the campaign to be used to convince the people that Benjamin Harrison, not Grover Cleveland, was the man for President. The fund was large and effectively used, and when Harrison won the election and the time came to square accounts, he called Wanamaker to his home in Indiana and appointed him Postmaster General.[6]

The newspapers, or at least a part of them, pretended to be aghast at this shameful deal. Headlines shrieked that this was an outright purchase of a cabinet position, and Harrison was blasted for what he had done. The fuss went on for some time, and one might have thought that because of it, Wanamaker would have hidden himself in a corner of his office at the old Post Office building on Pennsylvania Avenue and passed his four years in office as quietly as possible. Instead he had scarcely taken office before he began changing things, and from then on until he retired with the Harrison administration in 1893, he stirred up one controversy after another.[7]

For the times and circumstances, Wanamaker showed a remarkable amount of courage or a surprising naïveté in making his proposals. To question the prerogatives of the express and telegraph companies in the 1890's was no little thing. Besides injuring good friends of the Republican party, this nineteenth-century businessman, turned Postmaster General, who might have been expected to know better, was invading the realm of free enterprise with his postal program. Whether the idea of turning the telegraph and telephone lines over to the government came from the mouth of a Republican Postmaster General or a radical farmer made no difference. It was still plain socialism to many prominent people. More than once the conservative President Harrison must have shuddered at his Postmaster General's suggestions, and it was no wonder that in later years Wanamaker could still remember the President asking, "Wanamaker, are you sure of your ground?"[8]

But not everyone disagreed with Wanamaker's efforts to reorganize the postal system, and this fact may have saved him from political ruin. Out in the farmland he had a host of supporters who liked his postal program and liked him for the enemies he had made. As far as the farmers could see, Wanamaker had just taken over their own ideas on the postal system. By 1891 their organizations were already demanding government ownership of telegraph and telephone lines and a postal-savings bank. And as for rural delivery, though this had not been among their early demands, they now agreed with Wanamaker that they must have that too.

In the autumn of 1891 the news of Wanamaker's town and village experiment had spread the country over, and his campaign to extend the free delivery service to the farmers was well under way. The Postmaster General himself was behind the publicity. For a man who had invented the advertising gimmick of the "money-back guarantee," publicizing R F D was easily begun. A word here, a letter there, and reams of free publicity began to flow from the nation's press.

The newspaper people had good reason to be interested. A successful rural delivery service would make it possible to put a daily newspaper within reach of nearly every farm family in the nation, and no one was quicker to realize the effect this would have on the newspaper business than the editors whose newspapers served the farmers. Regardless of what they might think of Wanamaker personally, they were enthusiastic about rural delivery, and they took up their pens to write dozens of favorable editorials until at last one exasperated congressman fervently hoped that Congress could be saved "from this newspaper advertising business and this invitation to rural delivery which is simply a piece of humbuggery. . . ."[9]

Just where Wanamaker got the notion of carrying the mail to the farmers is not clear. He might easily have picked it up from something Stahl had written. Or some clerk in the Post Office Department might have suggested it to him. Possibly he thought of it himself as he poked about in the Department's city free delivery division. He so obviously desired to extend postal facilities that there is no need to believe someone had to suggest rural delivery to him. Besides, he was well aware of the farmers' problems in these years, and when he said, "I try never to forget the country," he may have already decided without prompting from anyone that an extension of the mail delivery service to the farmers might soften the bitterness they felt toward their government. Regardless of where he got the idea, the significant fact was that he championed rural delivery as if it had never been thought of before, and while he was urging the newspapers to support it, he was doling out information on the matter to farm organizations.[10]

If one wanted the support of the farmers in the 1890's the most likely place to go was to the Grange and the Farmers' Alliance clubs. In these organizations could be found the most vigorous and intelligent of all the nation's farmers. Here were men who were vitally interested in their government, who knew a great many things about its operation, and who were ready to support any suggestions that might improve farm life.

To these people Wanamaker took his rural delivery plan, and as the winter of 1891 drew on, the subject was under discussion all over rural America. In little Grange halls across the land, Grangers met on cold, crisp nights, warmed their backs at the big stove in the main hall, smelled the coffee brewing in the kitchen, and discussed the pros and cons of having their mail delivered. And farmers riding along in the night on their way to and from their Alliance meetings pondered the matter to the accompaniment of the clip-clop of their horses' hooves on the frozen ground. They wrote and they talked, these farmers and their wives, at great length concerning the many things rural delivery would do for farm life, and their words were recorded in the minutes of their meetings and in their speeches and letters.

For the first time in their lives they could have the news of the world every day except Sunday. There would be daily market quotations and even daily weather reports. They would know when to sell their crops to the best advantage and when to wait for an expected rain to pass before cutting their hay. Important letters that sometimes meant dollars and cents to them or told of a sudden death in the family or of Aunt May's expected arrival would no longer lie two or three days in the post office because there had been no way of knowing they were there. Nor would they ever again make those trips to the post office to pick up the mail that never came in. And the time they would save! A man could cultivate an extra acre of corn or haul a couple of loads of hay in the time he had formerly spent going to the post office. And who knew but what rural delivery might increase the value of their farms, perhaps as much as $5.00 an acre. True it would be expensive. But added mail facilities usually meant increased postal revenues. At least so Postmaster General Wanamaker had argued.[11]

All these thoughts the farmers wrote down or included in their speeches, but to appreciate their deeper feelings, those they found difficult to put into words, one would have had to live on an average American farm of the 1890's. Only experience could reveal how it was not to know from day to day what the rest of the world was doing or how it felt to see the conveniences of life being adopted everywhere but on the farm. One would have to feel the tiredness in a farmer's bones as he harnessed the horses after a hard day's work to go for the mail, or know his disappointment as he saw his children leave the farm one by one because farm life offered so few of the comforts of life, to understand what the farmer meant when he said, "bring the post office to the farmers' doors and you will take more hay seed out of their hair, put more comfort in their homes and money in their pockets than any one thing purchased at the same expense." If one could know what it was like to be isolated by muddy roads in spring and snowbound in the winter, to feel the need to see a new face even if it were only the mail carrier's, if all these feelings could be experienced, then one would know why the farmers became so excited about the R F D.[12]

Before the year was out a number of farm organizations had announced their support for a free delivery service. The National Grange endorsed it at its annual meeting in 1891, and across the land local and state Alliances passed resolutions favoring it. It was remarkable how much enthusiasm had been whipped up in such a short time. Little out-of-the-way places never heard of before in the nation's Capitol began to show up in the *Congressional Record* as congressman after congressman presented rural delivery petitions from their people back home. The Greenwood Grange of Marshall County, West Virginia, Poplar Grove, Whitcomb, and Star of the West Granges of Indiana, Economy Grange of Mississippi, the Flat Rock Grange of Ohio, the Farmers' Institute of Connelsville in Lafayette County, Pennsylvania, the Elm Tree National Farmers' Alliance of Ohio, these and hundreds of other organizations, equally unknown but equally important, let their congressmen know that they wanted rural free delivery.[13]

The legislators had expected no such reaction as this when they had casually permitted Wanamaker to make his town and village experiment. Most of them, if they thought about it at all, had probably never really taken Wanamaker's talk about delivering mail to the farmers seriously. Now in their mail came all these petitions, in greater numbers than they ever had before, according to one congressman. From New York came petitions from over two-thirds of the farmers in one congressional district alone, and it was obvious to rural congressmen that something had to be done.[14] But what?

When members of Congress thought of rural America, they thought of miles and miles of country roads and dusty trails, of vast treeless plains and rolling hills; some thought of isolated areas where strangers rarely ventured and of rains and snows that alternately turned the countryside into seas of mud or mountainous drifts of white; most of all they thought of lonely farmhouses, and wondered how it would ever be possible to deliver mail to all of the nation's farmers. They were not being necessarily stubborn or stupid when they said rural delivery was impractical and impossible. Nor could they be blamed if they had a few unkind words for the man in the Post Office Department. After all, they reasoned, he had placed them in an embarrassing position.[15]

But the man in the Post Office Department was already going ahead with plans for a general rural delivery service. With the help of Congressman James O'Donnell of Michigan he worked out his ideas in a bill which O'Donnell presented to Congress.[16]

This bill was the first of its kind, and Congressman O'Donnell, a newspaperman in private life, ever after referred to himself as the "father of R F D." But the House Committee on Post Offices and Post Roads took one look at the price tag and promptly turned it down. Six million dollars was far too much money to spend each year just to carry the mail to the farmers. "The time may come," said a member of the committee, "when we shall have rural free delivery. . . . That time has not arrived."[17]

This was the reasonable view, but there were a number of congressmen whose desks were piled high with rural delivery petitions, who were unwilling to let it go at that. Their constituents were demanding rural delivery now and fully expected them to get it for them. Yet rural congressmen knew that to get Congress to pass a bill establishing rural delivery on a nationwide basis was impossible. There had to be another way. They began to argue that the least the government could do was to experiment with rural delivery to see whether or not it was practical. Possibly a little money could be set aside from the regular Post Office appropriation for the Postmaster General to use in another experiment.

Even this was not easy to arrange, and interested congressmen soon discovered it was nearly as difficult to bring R F D in the back door as the front. The first session of the fifty-second Congress adjourned in August 1892, and the lame duck session had come and almost gone before Congress finally agreed to permit the Postmaster General to use $10,000 to experiment in carrying the mail to the farmer. It was a paltry sum compared to the $6,000,000 Wanamaker had asked for, but this was 1893, the year of the great panic, and Congress was in no mood to be liberal. The farmers' representatives probably felt lucky to get that much.[18]

One congressman, at least, had reason to rejoice. He was Tom Watson of Georgia, a brash, redheaded young man serving his first and only term in the House of Representatives. He had made the proposal which Congress enacted into law, and time was to prove the advantage of being the author of this first rural delivery legislation. No one would make more of it than Tom Watson himself. The years would pass, and Watson's life would be bound up in one political controversy after another. There would be campaign after campaign, and he would one day be United States Senator from Georgia. But he would never forget, nor allow the voting farmers to forget, that it was he who had gotten them R F D. Time and again he would stand among them and, pointing with pardonable pride, tell them that he was responsible for "every rural free delivery box in Georgia and every other state from the lakes to the gulf, from sea to sea." Few politicians could boast of so many monuments commemorating their work as Tom Watson.[19]

In the course of time Watson was taken at his word and tradition has commonly credited him with being the real "father of R F D." This notion was firmly perpetuated in a monument erected in his honor on the fiftieth anniversary of the farmers' free delivery service. Whether he had done more than Wanamaker or Stahl or O'Donnell or four or five other men who helped to build the service, or whether he had done more than the Grange which has often claimed the credit for the establishment of the service, is doubtful. The truth was the R F D had, as Stahl ironically noted, a number of fathers most of them making such important contributions and at such crucial times, that the service was repeatedly saved from extinction only by their timely action.

Having set aside the money for the rural delivery experiment, Congress had done what it could for the farmers. The experiment was now left to the Postmaster General to work out. But now there was more trouble for rural delivery. The administration had changed hands, and President Cleveland was back in the White House for the second time, and with him he had brought an old friend from Buffalo, Wilson Bissell, to be the Postmaster General.

Postmaster General Bissell, like the President, had a conservative temperament and was in almost all respects the direct opposite of the man he succeeded. A brief glance about the Post Office Department convinced him that the mail service was in shambles, and he began to sweep up after his imaginative predecessor. He filed away the plans for a parcel post, and forgot the recommendations for a postal-savings bank and government ownership of the telephone and telegraph lines. More than that, he simply ignored the ten thousand dollar experiment in rural delivery. How the mail could be carried to the farmers every day he simply could not see; nor could President Cleveland. Bissell called in one of his subordinates, August W. Machen, the man who had been pushing the service and another "father of R F D," and lectured him sternly. Rural delivery would bankrupt the nation, he said, and he wanted to hear no more about it. Machen was to stop agitating the question.[20]

And this might have been the end of rural free delivery if conditions in rural America had been different. Life was hard on the farms in those days, more so than it had ever been; and the combination of hard times and angry, frustrated farmers produced, as it turned out, an environment well-suited to the development of rural delivery. In fact, the times themselves were almost as much the "father of the R F D" as the men who sponsored it.

In the second half of the nineteenth century fortune had not favored the farmers. Immediately following the Civil War, when farm prices were reasonably good, farmers, filled with hope, moved out onto the Great Plains to take up homesteads. Markets were good, the rainfall apparently plentiful, and the Great American desert seemed ripe for the plow. But the moldboards had barely broken the virgin earth before the farmers' troubles began. Their first rude encounter with what was always thereafter to be the "farm problem" came in the late 1860's when prices for their products fell sharply. They had not fully recovered from this when the Panic of 1873 came on bringing financial ruin through rural and urban communities alike. But even these disasters, sharp as they had been, did not stop the westward flow of farmers. For the lure of the land was great, and the railroads, eager to build up the country along their lines, advertised the new lands as a veritable heaven on earth. The farmers, some of them immigrants and many of them Civil War veterans, listened to these "Pied Pipers" and, always hopeful of a better tomorrow, continued to spill out into the nation's empty spaces until by 1890 they had virtually filled the choice lands and the frontier line had disappeared.

But the better tomorrow the farmers sought never really came. There were only interludes of prosperity, fleeting and deceptive. The old perplexities remained and grew steadily worse as the 1880's ran their course. Even nature periodically added to their woes. "It used to seem to us," wrote one man looking back on this period, "that the blind forces of nature and the malevolent powers of human greed had conspired against us. Every few years the grasshoppers would sweep down in clouds and devour all our substance. Every now and then, too, there would come a drought that would ruin our crops. I have seen corn as beautiful as eye ever looked upon—green and fresh and high as a man's head—burned to a crisp within 48 hours by the hot winds from the southwest."[21]

Misfortune piled on misfortune, and many a farmer surrendered to the elements and with his family made his way back to his former home. A pathetic sign, "In God we trusted, in Kansas we busted," sometimes written across their wagons, eloquently told their story. Others gritted their teeth and hung on and in time bent beneath the strain of the harsh life. Hamlin Garland, returning from the East to the farmland of his boyhood years, was filled with dismay as he shook hands with old friends he had not seen for six years. "The hard, crooked fingers," he wrote, "which they laid in my palm completed the sorrowful impression which their faces had made upon me. A twinge of pain went through my heart as I looked into their dim eyes and studied their heavy knuckles. I thought of the hand of Edwin Booth, . . . of the subtle touch of Inness, and I said, 'Is it not time that the human hand ceased to be primarily a bludgeon for hammering a bare living out of the earth? Nature all bountiful, undiscriminating, would, under justice, make such toil unnecessary.' My heart burned with indignation. With William Morris and Henry George I exclaimed, 'Nature is not to blame. Man's laws are to blame. . . .' "[22]

This was what the farmers thought. Man and man's laws were to blame, and in their frustration they began to attack those they considered responsible for their plight: the railroads that absorbed their scanty profits in excessive freight rates; the monopolists who controlled prices and charged dearly for the things the farmers had to buy; the middlemen who took their cut of everything the farmers bought and sold; and the moneylenders who charged exorbitant interest rates on the mortgages they held. "It has been said," wrote one who had lived through the period, "and I think with good reason—that more midland farmers' wives died of mortgage during those trying years than of tuberculosis and cancer together, and that more farmers' wives were sent to the madhouse by mortgage than by all other causes."[23]

Angrily the farmers turned to the government to redress their grievances. The government had always been the farmers' friend. It would curb the greedy trusts and force the railroads to lower their rates. But now the farmers found that times had changed. The nation hummed with business activity. There were rails to lay, oil to drill, refineries to build, steel to make, precious ores to mine, meat to process, and great fortunes to be made. Business was the talk in the Capitol's cloakrooms. There was no time for the farmer. When he asked for a law to control the railroads, Congress hemmed and hawed and finally passed a bill the Supreme Court promptly tore to shreds in favor of the railroads. When he asked for trust legislation, it was the same story.

The farmers watched these maneuvers with mounting indignation. They had always been told, and they believed it was true, that they were the backbone of the nation, the wellspring of democracy, and the source of the nation's real wealth and prosperity. Now they found they counted for very little in Washington. Before the Civil War they had been highly respected citizens. Now people looked at their ill-fitting clothes, their sunburned necks, and tanned cheeks, and muttered "hayseed."

Facing bankruptcy on the farm and lost prestige among the people of the nation, the farmers believed they could do one of two things: run or fight. They chose to fight, and when one of their women speakers in Kansas told them that what they needed to do was to "raise less corn and more Hell," they took her at her word. They would seize control of the government themselves and put it back in the hands of those who were the "bone and sinew" of the nation.[24]

Toward this end they had some success by 1893. They had organized a new political party and entered a candidate in the race for the presidency in 1892, and though their man had received only 22 electoral votes, the party had at least forced the older parties to try to placate the turbulent farmers. The Republicans had even promised them rural free delivery![25]

Still the election had settled none of the farmers' problems. Their situation was made more unbearable by the financial panic that struck the nation the next year. Farm prices skidded to new lows, and foreclosures on the farms fell thick and fast. Wheat prices now fell to an average price of 53 cents a bushel; cotton was 7 cents a pound. But these were average prices and individual farmers talked of 5-cent cotton and 25-cent wheat. Under the circumstances it was a grim Congress that met for its first session in December 1893.[26]

In a mood reflecting the bitterness of the people they represented, rural congressmen returned to Washington to find that Postmaster General Bissell had not even bothered to experiment with rural free delivery. There had not been time to do so, he claimed, because of "the pressure of more important questions." Besides, in his opinion, a successful experiment would cost $20,000,000 not $10,000, and he for one did not believe in burdening the people with such expense.[27]

Considering the temper of the lawmakers from farm areas, Postmaster General Bissell would better have kept his reasons for not starting R F D to himself. "There are thousands of people in this country who think this is an important question," thundered Georgia's Congressman Charles Moses. What were congressmen to say to the farmers who were demanding the experiment? "You appropriate eleven million dollars for free delivery in the cities and towns. It is expended. But they cannot find time to expend $10,000 to test the feasibility of rural delivery."[28]

And with this, Congressman Moses struck once more a theme that reverberated through the political debates of those years like the monotonous whine of a western wind circling the eaves of a house.

Nothing weighed more heavily on the minds of senators and representatives from the farm states than the belief that this government of the people had somehow become the government of the privileged few. Always it was the banker, the manufacturer, the corporation, the cities, that Congress helped. Never the farmers. In the words of one irate congressman from South Carolina, Congress was "ready and willing to go with the speed of the greyhound to appropriate money," if the banker or manufacturer asked for it. But let the "humble farmer" ask for the "least pittance," and there were certain to be great objections. "Discrimination" was the word congressmen used to describe the situation, and no word was so overworked. But in the opinion of the farmers no word better explained the policies the government had pursued since the Civil War.[29]

Governmental discrimination in favor of the business interests, was a convenient explanation for the farmer's plight but hard to prove. One could go round and round on such questions as the tariff and unlimited coinage of silver, and in the end prove nothing. But with rural free delivery this was not so. In this, at least, the farmers were sure of their ground. The city people had free delivery; the farmers did not. Here was absolute proof that the farmers were being discriminated against. Not only did the country people have no mail delivery service, but they must pay the same rate of postage on their letters that city people paid. As they saw it, they were actually being taxed so that city people might have free delivery while they must still go after their mail!

Was it just, the farmers asked, to carry one citizen's mail to his door and leave that of another miles away? City businessmen had their mail delivered not once but several times a day. Was not the farmer also a businessman? "Why should the machinery of government be used so largely for the benefit of the favored few?" asked a Granger. There was no doubt in his mind who had the greater need for mail delivery. "Since the farmer must necessarily waste more time to get his mail than the denizen of the city, he has the greater need of free postal service, besides his equal right." The farmers were not asking for electric cars and sidewalks, those things the cities pay for, wrote a farmer's wife, "but as long as the country pays its share toward mail facilities, certainly it is our right to have the same privileges afforded the cities."[30]

This, then, became the farmers' great argument, the burden of speeches in Grange halls all over the land, the point of countless letters, and the theme of hundreds of editorials. To the farmers already in revolt against governmental discrimination the difference in mail systems was as obvious as a windmill on the Kansas prairie. The First Assistant Postmaster General, Frank Jones, protested that the matter "should be considered as a business proposition, and not from prejudice and arraying one class of our citizens against those living in the large cities. . . ," but he might as well have saved his pen and ink. Neither the farmers nor their representatives were in any mood to listen.[31]

For another year Congress battled with the Postmaster General. Bissell was directed to spend not $10,000 but $20,000 in 1895 on a rural delivery experiment and, as if to make certain that something would be done, to report to Congress at its next session on the practicality of extending rural delivery throughout the country.[32]

Once more Bissell stood his ground and refused to try rural delivery any place, and the whole affair became a tug-of-war between the doughty Postmaster General and the embattled legislators. The jockeying back and forth might have gone on for two more years if the Postmaster General had not surrendered with a timely resignation, perhaps because he was tired of trying to keep the farmers from bankrupting the government.

One can easily picture President Cleveland breathing a sigh of relief at the resignation of his Postmaster General. Bissell had not only irritated the farmers but had also ruffled the feelings of loyal Democrats by a rather uncompromising stand on political patronage. The politicians were more than a little annoyed to discover that Bissell was actually trying to take the Civil Service law literally, and so many disgruntled partisans had expressed themselves that Cleveland could hardly have been greatly saddened by the departure of his old friend from Buffalo. At any rate, the administration was now able to take a more moderate stand on rural free delivery. To succeed Bissell, Cleveland chose William L. Wilson from West Virginia, and Wilson promised to begin the long deferred rural delivery experiment.[33]

Postmaster General Wilson was a statesman of unusual capabilities. A scholarly, quiet man, he had been a Confederate soldier and the president of West Virginia University. As a Democratic congressman from West Virginia he was one of the best-loved men in Washington. He had had the misfortune to be a low-tariff man in a high-tariff coal mining district, and in the election of 1894, the voters retired him from Congress. But West Virginia's loss was the administration's gain, for Wilson was an able administrator in the Post Office Department.[34]

He was no rural delivery enthusiast, though he has a claim to being another father of the service. He suspected that there was a good bit of politics and demagoguery behind the "free-delivery craze," as he called it, and like Bissell he thought it impractical. Still, he would not stand in the way. If the people really wanted a rural delivery experiment they should have it. Congress need only appropriate the money once more, and he would do his best to conduct a successful experiment. He may well have been thinking that the best way to end the "craze" was to let the experiment prove how ridiculous and impractical it was.[35]

Congress took him at his word, and at the insistence of Marion Butler, a Populist senator from North Carolina, and another "father of R F D," Congress once more set funds aside, $40,000 this time, for Postmaster General Wilson to begin a delivery service for the farmers.[36]

June of 1896 had come before Congress had made up its mind to appropriate the money, and the summer sped by while Postmaster General Wilson made plans to take the mail to the farmers. The site he chose for the first routes was the farm district near his home in West Virginia, and here he sent a postal inspector to lay the routes through the countryside and find men willing to carry the farmer's mail for less than a dollar a day.

No publicity attended the preparations being made. All eyes were on the political campaign and a young man from Nebraska who was preaching the virtues of coining silver at the ratio of sixteen to one up one side of the nation and down the other. Thursday morning, October first, when three mail carriers rode away from the post office at Charles Town, Uvilla, and Halltown, with mail for the farmers, even the Charles Town papers failed to see anything significant in the event.[37]

So it was that on the eve of the election of 1896, when the farmers were looking forward hopefully to the victory of William Jennings Bryan, the man they had pinned their faith on in their crusade against special privilege, the first steps were being made to end the discrimination between rural and city mail service. With a Postmaster General and a number of congressmen who disapproved of the scheme, rural delivery began under a cloud. But it had begun.

The election of 1896 proved to be a bitter blow to the farmers. Their man Bryan, with all his stouthearted courage and his silver tongue, was no match for the forces arrayed against him and the radical farmers he spoke for. William McKinley became President and the farmers' revolt collapsed. Years later many of the demands they had been making since 1892 would find a place in the nation's laws, but in the immediate aftermath of 1896, R F D was all that was salvaged, and it was to hang by a slender thread for another six years.

Bureau of Agricultural Economics

Overland Mail Stage loading up, Saratoga, Wyoming

Rural mail carrier at a mining camp on mountain route, Bingham Canyon, Utah

Farmers receiving their mailboxes, Delphi, Indiana

Patrons on Route No. 1 near Lafayette, Indiana, 1899

Library of Congress
Meeting of Grangers in Scott County, Illinois

3

EVERYMAN'S MAIL TO EVERYMAN'S DOOR

On one rural free delivery mail route an old farmer placed a note beside a crack in his fence which read: "Put the Male Hear."

R.F.D. News, 1 (May 1903)

MUCH of the excitement and spirit of adventure that made a saga of carrying the mail to the Pacific Coast in the 1850's were missing from the record of organizing rural mail routes fifty years later, and perhaps for that reason this latter-day achievement of the postal service is so little known. There were no Indians to fight along the rural routes and no Pony Express riders to race across the prairies. Mostly there were only muddy country roads and eager farmers, cranks, politicians, and fourth-class postmasters to provide what drama there was.

And yet the establishment of the farmers' free delivery service was not without its epic proportions. More money was spent, more men employed, and more paperwork done to lay out the rural delivery system than to establish any single extension of the postal service. And if there were no Indian ambushes to record and no great robberies, still the establishment of the farmers' mail service ranks as one of the Post Office Department's greatest accomplishments and merits its own particular place in postal history.

Rural delivery had just begun, and rural mail carriers were still a strange sight along country roads when an old-timer's complaint against the new service found its way back to the Post Office Department. "An' do you think," he was supposed to have said, "I'm goin' to drop my letters in a box out here for anyone to come along an' get? How'm I goin' to know they'll ever git to the post-office, or that some'n won't come along an' take the stamps off'n 'em?"[1]

Quaint as the old-timer's questions seem in retrospect, they were as practical in 1897 as the man who asked them undoubtedly was, and anyone looking back from the vantage point of the mid-twentieth century at what passed for rural free delivery in that first year of its existence, can easily understand the old-timer's apprehension about the new service.

Between the autumn of 1896 and the spring of 1897, 82 pioneer routes had been scattered through 28 states and the Territory of Arizona, and they were about as unlike one another as it was possible to be and still be called by a common name. Three were 35 miles in length, and three were less than half that long. Stretched out over nearly every kind of terrain in the country, they ran through regions where the roads were good to places where there were no roads at all. Routes were laid out in Arizona through farmers' fields and orchards, and in Kansas along the Missouri River over ground so hilly, that, as one man put it, a forty-acre farm had 160 acres of cultivable land. One route lay along a bayou in Louisiana, and three routes ran through a county in Kentucky that had no roads, no maps, and had never been divided into townships.[2]

The service on these pioneer routes like the roads over which they passed ranged from good to bad, and not more than a handful of mailmen would have won any prizes for delivering the mail with "celerity, certainty, and security." At Campbell, California, the roads were good, and not long after the route had been established a farmer reported receiving his mail as regularly as the clock. Similarly, at Loveland, Colorado, the roads were good enough to allow an enterprising mail carrier to use a buckboard wagon to deliver the mails and strike up a passenger and package service on the side. But at Climax, Michigan, mountainous snowdrifts plagued the service through that first winter, and in Sangamon County, Illinois, the mail carriers were forced to carry the mail on horseback and even then were delayed by muddy roads that had scarcely been improved since Abraham Lincoln rode the circuit there.[3]

Here and there poorly instructed mail carriers with only a vague notion of how the system should operate omitted parts of their routes and made no effort to keep regular schedules. A year or so after a route had been established at Gorham, Maine, for example, one carrier had gone so far astray from his original route he was regularly delivering the mail to only fifty of the one-hundred families he was supposed to have served.[4]

The "security" of the mails along the new routes was not much better than the "celerity and certainty" with which they were delivered. The farmers had been asked to put up their own mailboxes, buggy high, and within easy reach of the mail carriers. Most of them complied with the request but with boxes of such odd shapes and sizes and varying degrees of stability that the roads on which the boxes were located became a case study in individuality. The safety of the mails was left largely to faith, hope, and charity, and much in that order.

What this new service was like in that first year of its existence was nowhere better described than in the comments of an interested onlooker in North Yakima, Washington. "Nearly everyone within the district has his mail delivered," he wrote. "Some receptacle is fastened in a convenient place so that the carriers can drop their mail without getting out of their carts. Whenever a farmer has mail in his box which he wishes collected he displays a small white flag. This enables the carrier to drive on without stopping when there is no mail to take or leave, and as each carrier has with him a field glass he is thus often enabled to save himself a trip of a quarter of a mile up a lane and back. The 'boxes' are of sundry shapes, sizes, and colors. One man has a lard pail hung out on a fence post; three or four have nailed up empty coal oil cans, and a few have utilized sirup cans. . . . Old apple boxes, soap boxes, cigar boxes, and in one instance a wagon box, adorn the entrance to farms all over the valley. . . ."[5]

Perhaps no one should have expected a more efficient service in 1897. Rural delivery was a virgin field for the Post Office Department, and even if more effort and thought had gone into planning this first experiment, it would probably not have helped much. To have anticipated and prepared for all the problems that appeared as soon as the routes began to function would have been impossible under any circumstances. Nevertheless, not everything that went wrong with rural delivery that first year could be charged to inexperience. At least one cause of the confusion was the fundamental idea behind the initial planning of the experiment.

Before he left office in March 1897, Postmaster General Wilson had planned and established nearly all of the pioneer routes. His purpose, he had explained, was to locate them where weather, road, and population conditions varied as much as possible, and for this reason routes were planted in communities where there were no roads, where the population was sparse, and even where the people were not interested in having free delivery. Obviously, such routes could never be efficient and could only exist at great expense to the government.[6]

Wilson's motives in developing the experiment as he did were probably mixed. One of the purposes of the experiment was to find out how much it would cost to deliver the mail in rural America, and this could only be done if the new routes were laid out where conditions were both favorable and unfavorable for the service. At the same time, it was well known that both he and Cleveland frowned on free delivery for farmers, and possibly he had deliberately established routes where they would fail, or be hopelessly expensive, in order to prove to Congress the folly of trying to deliver the mail to all the nation's farmers.[7]

Whatever he had in mind, Wilson did nothing in the closing days of his administration to encourage the development of the experiment. In fact, the final report on rural delivery issued by his First Assistant Postmaster General estimated that it would cost between forty-five and fifty million dollars to carry the mail to every farmer's door, a sum scarcely calculated to win supporters, and probably if it had been left to Wilson and to certain influential congressmen, there would have been no R F D.[8]

As it was, Wilson left office with the Cleveland administration in March and the rural delivery experiment fell into the hands of two McKinley Republicans who saved it, nurtured it, and built the basic structure of present-day rural delivery. One of these men was Perry Heath, President McKinley's new First Assistant Postmaster General; the other was Heath's subordinate, August W. Machen, Superintendent of Free Delivery.

Perry Heath was a journalist with a flair for politics. His position in the Post Office Department had come to him not because he knew anything about delivering the mail to farmers, but because he had helped put President McKinley in the White House. On the other hand, August Machen had been in the Department since 1893, and knew almost all there was to know about rural delivery. Having become interested in the service in 1893 when Congress made the first rural delivery appropriation, he had studied the British rural mail system and corresponded with local postmasters across the country in preparation for launching the rural delivery experiment. His activities had been cut short by the opposition of Postmaster General Bissell who told him rural delivery would bankrupt the nation, but three years later, when Wilson established the first routes, Machen was on hand to help.[9]

Heath and Machen were a match for one another. Both were adroit politicians. As Republican campaign advisor in 1896, Heath had been closer to President McKinley than any other man except Mark Hanna. As well as any man, he knew the secrets of the Republican party, and from his post as First Assistant Postmaster

General he could be expected to keep abreast of the political situation.

As for Machen, no craftier politician ever set foot inside the Post Office Department. The very fact that he remained on as Superintendent of Free Delivery when the Republicans swept the Democrats from office was a tribute to his political agility. He had been a Democrat, and the Democrats had taken him in when he had come to Washington in 1893, debt-ridden and penniless. But after McKinley's election he skillfully defected to the Republicans who seemed only too happy to keep him on as Superintendent of Free Delivery. Just how he managed this is something of a mystery, but the chances are rural free delivery had something to do with it.[10]

What passed between Machen and Heath in the early days of the McKinley administration no one knows. But it would have been strange indeed if two such men had not discussed the political possibilities of rural delivery. By the summer of 1897 letters were pouring into Washington from farmers along the pioneer routes explaining how much it meant to them to have their mail delivered and begging the Department to continue the experiment. One enthusiastic farm woman near Loveland, Colorado, had even gone so far as to write that "those who established it [rural free delivery], will be remembered for all time as the farmers' benefactors." With letters like these before them, the wily pair in the Post Office would have been less astute than their records indicated they were, had they not considered the political rewards that might come to the party that delivered the mail to the farmers.[11]

At any rate, there was a meeting of minds between the First Assistant Postmaster General and the Superintendent of Free Delivery. For one reason or another the decision was made to support rural delivery, and toward the close of 1897 the Postmaster General's report included a ringing recommendation for continuing the experiment. At the time this official announcement was made, no new routes had been established since the previous April, nor were there plans to organize more. The experiment hung precariously between life and death, and Heath and Machen faced the problem of breathing life into it.[12]

As events proved, they were equal to the occasion. With the appropriation of $150,000 they received from Congress in 1898, the two men prepared to establish more routes. But unlike Postmaster General Wilson, they would organize no routes where there were no roads or where the people did not care for the service or where, for some reason, the routes seemed unlikely to succeed. Nor would they lay out routes in arbitrarily selected areas. Instead, early in 1898, they announced that if any group of farmers wanted a rural mail route, they had only to petition their congressman for it. If he approved their request, the Department would establish the route. The farmers were asked to send along with their petitions, descriptions of their community and their roads. Later on they were to draw a sketch of their proposed route and furnish a map of their county, but all the requirements were simple and took only a little of the farmers' time.[13]

These directions proved to be the turning point in the development of the R F D as Machen and Heath had probably foreseen. When word passed around among the farmers that all they had to do to have their mail delivered to their farms was to sign a petition, the rush was on, and every new route established brought a demand for a dozen or so more. Once this began, Congress could as easily have stopped an Oklahoma tornado as to have stemmed the demand for rural delivery.

There was always someone in every farming community interested enough to take the first step in getting a petition started on its way to his congressman. Sometimes a farmer or a farmer's son who wanted to be the mail carrier on the new route circulated the petition. Sometimes it was the local postmaster. More often, it was only some interested farmer anxious to receive a daily newspaper who took the initiative in signing up his neighbors. One of the favorite ways to circulate a petition was to have the farmer sign up on "Grange night," and many a rural route across the country owes its existence to some local Grange. But however it was done, signatures came easily, for not many farmers refused to sign a petition when their neighbor drove into their yards after the evening chores were done or met them after church and asked them if they wanted to have their mail delivered.

In a remarkably short time the petitions for routes piled up in Washington, and if all the correspondence that passed between congressmen, farmers, local postmasters, and the Post Office Department had been saved, it would probably have filled several rooms. But the Department has a custom of destroying what it calls "useless papers," and many rural delivery papers were so classified. Even so, enough remains to fill several shelves, and how the rural mail service was established is reasonably clear.

To build the system required the services of more men than the Post Office Department had ever employed for any of its past projects, and these Heath never hesitated to employ. Together, he and Machen hired men by the score—rural agents, route inspectors, and rural mail carriers—and soon erected an R F D bureaucracy that embraced eight rural delivery divisions with headquarters in every section of the country and at the height of its activity laid out more than 9,000 routes in one year.[14]

The unsung heroes of the R F D were the rural agents. They were the men who talked to the farmers and rode over the farmland, fighting the snow in winter, the mud in spring, and choking on the dust of country roads in the summer. Most of them were good Republicans put on the government payroll when Machen and Heath saw that the regular postal inspectors Wilson had used to map out the first routes could not be spared for extensive route organizing. For the most part they were friendly, intelligent men, and after they were trained, they handled themselves well in a job that required common sense and tact and everlasting patience.[15]

The heyday of the rural agents was the early twentieth century, and life on the farm in contrast to the terrible nineties was good. A wave of nostalgia for country life was sweeping the cities, and people spoke wistfully of going back to the farm. They seemed to be sweetly sad, remembering smokehouses and one-room schoolhouses and feather beds, knowing all the while that there was no going back. Perhaps this was why many of them forgot some of the worst aspects of the real rural America they had left with its drudgery and loneliness and why in the romantic glow of their memories they sang songs like "In the Good Old Summer Time," and "When the Harvest Days are Over, Jessie Dear."[16]

In the cities this sentimental mood persisted, but the rural agents, busily laying out rural routes, saw the farmland and its people not as they were remembered by the homesick urbanite but as they were. Never before had anyone investigated rural America as thoroughly as the rural agents did while they mapped out the farmers' mail routes. Almost nothing escaped them. When they had finished laying out a route, they knew the schedules of the trains or star route carriers that brought the mail to the local postoffice, the condition of the roads in the community, the number of houses along those roads, where the most important people lived, what the farmers thought and read, and what their avocations and backgrounds were. They even knew the local gossip, and, when special groups sought special favors from them and old sores were reopened, they learned of bitter personal feuds that sometimes split neighborhoods apart.[17]

What they learned, the rural agents faithfully reported to the Post Office Department, and when they were satisfied that conditions justified the service, they drew maps of the routes they approved and wrote detailed descriptions of them. In time, large blocks of rural America were recorded in Washington, where many of them can still be found in simple route sketches like the one that began at the post office in Homer, Illinois, and went "South to Brown's Corner 2 miles, West to Schoolhouse 2 miles, South to Hart's Corner 1 mile, East to Harvard's Corner 2 miles. . . ."[18]

The rural agents tried as best they could to follow their instructions. Routes were to be at least 25 miles long and serve 100 families. But there were always extenuating circumstances—politics, neighborhood quarrels, very important persons, and always the great pressure of the more isolated farmers to be included on the routes. The agents bent the regulations considerably, for it was hard to refuse the pleas of farmers to have the service extended to them even if it meant a route with less than four families to the mile. Nor was it easy to quibble with a very important person in the community or a politician about the location of a mailbox. There were no precise rules to cover many of these problems, and only the rural agent could really know the situation. They made their adjustments and the Department, at least at first, looked the other way. The rural agents were there to please the people, and when the routes were going in by the thousands, it was easy not to be too fussy about regulations.[19]

But even when they bent the regulations, when they traced and retraced their routes and worked over maps for hours to find the best solution to knotty problems, the rural agents soon learned they could not please everyone. Not that the farmers themselves complained so much. Usually they received the agents with the utmost respect, invited them into their homes for meals when they happened by, and listened attentively as they were told of the coming service and asked to keep the roads cleared for the mail carrier. Instead it was the businessmen in the small country towns, the fourth-class postmasters, and politicians who grew bilious about the way the routes were being laid out. Normally the agents were not to blame. There was simply no way to satisfy the numberless demands made by these people.

Yet there were times when the rural agents were rude and even arrogant. With so many people following them about and hanging on their every word for a hint as to where the new routes would run, the agents quite naturally sensed their power, and when their judgment was questioned they occasionally lost their heads. It must have been a particularly haughty agent, for example, who once planned some route changes in Georgia and ran afoul of Senator Alexander S. Clay. The senator was so enraged after he had talked with the agent about the changes that had been made he telegraphed the Department saying that the agent "thinks he is the Post Office Department," and that "he had boasted of his triumphs" over the senator's wishes.[20]

Such outbursts from prominent men against the rural agents were not uncommon, particularly when the agents mixed politics with business. Senator Joseph B. Foraker was once troubled with a "politicking" agent in Ohio. This agent had apparently taken the liberty of assailing the senator's character as he moved across the state setting up rural routes. The senator objected strenuously and would permit no more rural routes to be organized in Clermont County, where the agent had been holding forth, until the Department assured him that Agent Perkins had been removed from the area.[21]

Politicians though many of the rural agents were, one can hardly imagine how the farmers' mail system could have been organized without them. For they were the eyes and ears of the Department as they traveled country roads laying out new routes and checking old ones. They built up a wealth of information about rural delivery that was indispensable to the postal officials in Washington. Regulation after regulation based on the agents' reports and designed to take the kinks out of the service went out from the Department, until in a surprisingly short time, the farmers were receiving their mail every day on the hour with scarcely a mishap. When, for instance, the agents found that the lack of road maps hampered them in planning rural routes, the Department issued instructions that the farmers must include road maps with their petitions for new routes. And when they reported that farmers were using rickety, unsightly mailboxes which left their mail largely unprotected from wind and rain and snow and theft, the Department began issuing mailbox regulations that led to a long and acrimonious controversy with the farmers.[22]

At first the Department recommended that it buy the boxes and rent them out to the farmers. This proposal got nowhere in Congress. Then a postal commission, after advertising for sample boxes, selected the boxes of fourteen companies as suitable for the rural routes and recommended that the farmers agree to purchase their mailboxes from any one of the fourteen companies before their mail service would be given them. For a short time, this was the official policy, and farmers who failed to put up the approved boxes were likely to find this briefly worded warning in their mail: "The mailbox put up by you is not secure, not weatherproof. Within thirty days of this date you must supply one of the approved boxes enumerated on the reverse side of this card or your service will be withdrawn."

This policy only aggravated the Department's quarrel with the independently minded farmers. They and their congressmen cried "monopoly," a very ugly word in America in those days, and refused to abide by any such regulation. Finally, a congressional committee suggested that the Department set certain standards for rural mailboxes and permit any company to make them provided they followed the Department's specifications.

The Department agreed to this suggestion, set up its standards, and developed the present-day rural mailbox. So that everyone would know that the mailbox was authentic and protected by law, each one had to be marked "Approved by the Postmaster General," words that remain on rural mailboxes to this day.[23]

Today, the silver-gray rural mailbox is virtually the symbol of rural America, and no one would suspect it had once caused so much trouble. Through the years it has become a highly respected piece of property, and almost every country boy has learned about the sanctity of Uncle Sam's mailboxes. This has not always prevented him from stuffing the boxes with sand, rocks, and even an occasional possum as any rural mailman can attest, but on the whole, thanks largely to the work of the rural agents, the actual pilfering of mail from rural mailboxes is negligible.

Another of the rural agents' duties was to inspect the routes they had already established. In the earlier days of the service this was one of their most vital jobs since local postmasters and rural mail carriers were likely to forget or carelessly neglect their rural delivery instructions. The rural agent who checked the three pioneer routes at Cairo, Missouri, in 1899 found the mail carriers there had become their own masters, and one carrier did not even follow his prescribed route. When mail came for one of his patrons, he cut across forest and pasture and took the mail directly to the addressee's home. When the water in the creeks was low, he forded the streams. When it was high, he simply waited until it went down. Obviously, mail carriers and postmasters had a lot to learn about rural delivery, and it became the rural agent's job not only to teach them what to do but also to see that they followed instructions.[24]

But to lay out routes and inspect them too was more than the rural agents could manage, and so the Department added to the R F D bureaucracy another division made up of men whose principal duty was to inspect rural routes. Once every six months, or more often in case of emergencies, these inspectors rode the routes with the mail carriers to make certain the postal regulations were being followed and that the farmers were getting their mail on schedule and in the most efficient manner possible.[25]

There were a good many complaints in Congress about the increasing length of the R F D payroll and the number of politicians being quartered on government funds. But not until 1906, when the heyday of rural route organizing was over, was the rural delivery bureaucracy dismantled and the rural agents and route inspectors pushed into the regular postal inspection service.[26]

Until 1899 rural mail routes had been laid out through the countryside in a helter-skelter fashion, one here and one there just as the farmers petitioned for them, with no attempt to tie them together or to cover an entire county with free delivery service. But that year an experiment began in Carroll County, Maryland, which led in time to the laying out of rural routes on a countywide basis.

The Carroll County experiment owed its origin to the imagination of Edward W. Shriver, a clerk in the post office at Westminster, Maryland. His idea was to go a step farther than the collecting and delivering of the farmer's mail as was being done by the regular rural mail carriers. He proposed building a postal wagon to be used not only to collect and deliver the mail on a rural route but to perform all the usual functions of a post office as it traveled along. It was to be literally a traveling post office.

Eventually his scheme found its way back to the Post Office Department where Machen and Heath, always eager to try out new ideas, agreed to try it, and in the spring of 1899 a wagon—eight feet long and furnished with built-in drawers, counter boxes, and letter boxes—was built, and a rural route 30 miles long established. In addition to a driver, a postal clerk, authorized to perform almost all the functions of a regular postmaster, was assigned to the wagon.

The new post office-on-wheels made its first run, April 3, 1899, and after it had been in operation through the spring and summer someone thought of adding a few more postal wagons and auxiliary carriers and covering the entire county with rural free delivery. The plan was to have the auxiliary carriers meet the wagon post offices at various points along the way, pick up the mail from the wagons just as they would from a regular post office, and deliver it along carefully planned routes that radiated from the main wagon routes.

Machen and Heath saw in this new proposal a splendid way to test the new rural mail service against the old. They believed it could perhaps determine once and for all whether rural delivery could successfully replace the fourth-class postmasters and star route mail carriers. The experiment might also demonstrate whether the R F D really did increase postal revenues as its friends claimed or whether it was much more expensive than the old system as its enemies thought.

Before the system could begin, however, revolutionary changes had to be made in the county's old mail system. There were 94 fourth-class post offices in the county, and according to the experimental plan, 63 of these and 33 star routes had to be eliminated to make way for the new wagons and rural routes. But old mail systems were not torn up without turmoil as Machen and Heath had already discovered. So they took the precaution of asking the permission of William B. Baker, congressman from the district, before they made the contemplated changes. Once Baker had given his consent, new routes were laid out, new postal wagons were built, and December 20, 1899, was set as the date for the big change-over.

On the day before the experiment began, Perry Heath and a corps of rural agents arrived in Westminster to dole out postal equipment and give last-minute instructions to the postal clerks and mail carriers who would conduct the experiment. At the close of the business day, December 19, the 63 post offices and 33 star routes were discontinued. The next morning at 6:30 rural free delivery began from twelve distributing points throughout the county.[27]

Later it was said that the worst possible time of the year had purposely been chosen for the experiment in order to put rural delivery to its severest test. Whether or not this was true, a worse time could hardly have been picked. The mails, five days before Christmas, were heavier than they would be at any other time of the year, and no one knew but that the roads would be blocked by snow. It seemed almost certain that if this new experiment would work under these conditions, it must work anywhere. And the rural delivery people were determined to make it work.

The rural agents stayed on at Westminster for days after the experiment began, investigating complaints and making adjustments. Across the historic countryside where Confederate and Union soldiers had skirmished with one another and General Meade had had his headquarters on the eve of the battle of Gettysburg, the rural agents moved briskly about their business, altering the old routes, making new ones, and doing everything that seemed necessary to bring rural delivery to all the farmers of the county as efficiently as possible. Nothing kept the mails from going through. Even a spring blizzard that filled the roads from fence to fence with snowdrifts stopped the service only briefly, while gangs of snow shovelers, working furiously, cleared the roads for the wagons.

In spite of all the hard work, the Department was not satisfied with the efficiency of the service until February 1900. By then there were four postal wagons, 39 rural mail carriers, and four clerks in charge of distributing stations. The wagons and carriers were traveling over 833 miles every day and serving 19,336 people.[28]

That the fate of the R F D hung on the outcome of this experiment would be claiming too much. But Machen and Heath both regarded it as an important step on the road to nationwide rural free delivery, and gathered a mass of statistics which proved to their own satisfaction at least that spreading rural delivery over entire counties was practical. And probably most of the people interested in R F D agreed with the Department's statistics. The critics, however, remained unconvinced, and when all the furor had died, the experiment appeared to have been extraordinarily expensive and clumsy. For though the Department seemed satisfied in 1900, subsequent reports revealed that from then until 1906 constant changes were made in the routes which left the service in turmoil. Rural agents had come there so often to change the routes that they were a joke among the people of the county.[29]

The real importance of the Carroll County experiment, however, was not its financial success or failure but its effect upon the growth of the rural delivery system. For the pattern of rural route organizing from then on was shaped by what had taken place there. Hardly had the experiment begun before requests for similar county services began to reach Washington, and almost before anyone knew it, the Department was suddenly launched on a broad program of building county delivery systems over the nation.

At first, two corps of specially trained men were shifted from state to state to plan and install county systems on the Carroll County pattern. Then, after the postal wagons were found to be unnecessary for county service, every rural agent learned not only how to lay out single routes so they could later be dovetailed into others to make a county system, but also how to rearrange existing routes and to add a few here and there in such a way as to cover an entire county with the free delivery service. This was exacting work, and here if anywhere, as they honeycombed rural America with mail routes, the rural agents earned their pay.[30]

While the Carroll County experiment was going on, and the rural agents were busily planting routes across the land, rural delivery was still considered an experiment. More routes had gone in each year, and each year Congress had appropriated more money for the service, until one congressman was bold enough to say in 1900 that everyone knew the service was no longer an experiment. Yet Congress was unwilling to take the final step and make it a permanent part of the postal system.[31]

The truth was that many members of Congress were afraid to follow the logical course in the matter, because once rural delivery became permanent, it was assumed it must spread until every farmer in the land had his mail delivered to his door. This would be expensive, and though it was said the service would pay for itself in time, still there was always a chance it would not, and Congress would be faced with larger and larger appropriations each year. So Congress held back, and once in 1898 the Senate, led by Eugene Hale, even tried to kill the experiment outright.

Eugene Hale, senator from Maine and self-appointed watchdog of the United States Treasury, suspected, not without reason, that rural delivery was no experiment but a well-laid plot to "take everyman's mail to everyman's door." With a perception sharpened by long experience in practical politics, he could see that laying out of more and more routes would soon force Congress into a position where it could no longer refuse to appropriate money for the service, and he was anxious to cut the experiment off before this happened.

Hale found enough senators who felt as he did to strike the rural delivery appropriation from the Post Office bill for 1899, and only the timely intervention of the Grange and interested congressmen saved the service. Learning of the Senate's action, the officers of the National Grange raised an enormous petition of some 75,000 names in support of rural delivery and presented it to Congress. After this, when the Senate and House conferees met to work out their differences, the rural delivery money was restored to the Post Office bill.[32]

It was a narrow escape for the farmers' mail service, and a significant one. Had the Senate's action stood, rural delivery would have ended, and the farmers might soon have forgotten all about having their mail delivered. But when it was allowed to continue, there was no stopping it. Just as Hale predicted, the pressure to take "everyman's mail to everyman's door" became great enough to bind the service upon the nation. From this year on, no senator or congressman dared try openly to kill the service, and there was hardly a man in Congress who spoke on the subject who did not want to be known as a friend of rural delivery. Yet some men, fearful of the eventual cost of the service, did their best to change the structure of the system in order to make it less expensive.

Among those who tried was Eugene Loud, chairman of the Post Office and Post Roads Committee from 1893 to 1903. A Republican from California, staunch defender of the status quo and big business, Loud liked to pose as the friend of rural delivery, which, in fact, he never was. Haunted by the specter of what it would cost to cover the country with rural routes, yet knowing he could neither destroy the system completely nor keep it forever in the experimental stage, he lay awake nights, according to his own account, worrying over the future of the service. What he thought during these nightly vigils was made known in 1902 when he and the majority of his committee sponsored a bill to make R F D permanent, but to contract the rural routes to the lowest bidders rather than to continue the rural mail carriers on a salary basis.[33]

The friends of rural delivery in Congress reacted to Loud's plan as if they had been stabbed in the back. Raising old ghosts like the star route frauds of the 1870's when mail contracts were fraudulently awarded, they ran through argument after argument for a week as they pictured the terrible fate that awaited rural delivery if it were turned over to contractors. It would be the rankest discrimination against the country people, they argued, to change the structure of the R F D. While the city people would have an efficient service, the farmers would have to get along with a decrepit system that would prove to be as corrupt as it was inefficient. The man who would win the rural route under the contract system, said Virginia's Claude Swanson, would be "the man who is the least competent, the least capable, who has the poorest address, the poorest cart, the least equipped to perform the service. . . ."[34]

Swanson had a point. Like most congressmen from rural districts he knew the contract system firsthand. He had seen broken-down wagons pulled by scrawny mules poking along country roads with United States mailbags bumping around in the wagon bed together with a variety of other goods, and he knew the star routes were far from efficient. "Of all the disgraceful, damnable things that undertake to represent the United States," said one irate Georgia congressman, "this [contract] service is . . . the worst." There was nothing he was more anxious to rid Georgia's seventh district of than this.[35]

Not even Loud's argument that the mail could be delivered cheaper under the contract system had any effect. "Cheap! Cheap!" shouted an Indiana congressman who already had a large number of rural routes in his district. "I insist that the brand of cheapness be not placed upon this promising service. . . ." He knew it would cost, but this was all right with him. "I want this service to cost more each year for I know that it is increasing and spreading its blessings in a wider circle. . . ."[36]

Eventually the debate came around to that old question of

whether the postal service should pay its way or not. It was a problem as old as the mail system itself, and sooner or later every great debate on postal matters returned to it.

In the early days of the Republic, it had been taken for granted that the mail service would pay its own way and perhaps show a profit. Probably this was why the Post Office was first attached to the Treasury Department. But the constant cry for better postal facilities and the belief that the mail service was the good right arm of democracy, led men in public life to look upon the Department more as a service than as a business. They began to demand better and cheaper postal service even if it meant that the Department must go in the red and be bailed out with congressional appropriations. The intentions of Congress were clear enough in 1851 when it reduced the postage on a letter going 3,000 miles to three cents and declared that if there were a loss of revenue resulting from this act, there was to be no reduction of services. Obviously the deficit was to be made up from the public treasury.[37]

From that time on, the Post Office Department has rarely paid its way, but there have always been those who have insisted it should unless they faced the necessity of reducing some vital service such as the franking privilege for senators and representatives.

Congressman Loud was a firm believer in a postal service that paid its own way, and this belief was behind his desire to let the rural routes out to contractors. But the farmers' spokesmen could see no difference between the Post Office Department and the Army and Navy, in this respect. All three performed services, yet no one expected the Army or Navy to pay their way. Why, then, should the Post Office be singled out for special treatment? They were for economy in government, of course, they said, but not false economy, and if more money must be saved, let it be saved on something other than rural free delivery. Their favorite target was the growing fleet, and if every congressman who wanted to cut down on battleships in this period had had his way, the great white fleet would have never have weighed anchor.[38]

When the debate was over, the friends of rural delivery had won the day. Congress voted to make the R F D a permanent part of the postal system without the crippling contract provision. There would not be one kind of service for city people and another for farmers, and to the present time, in spite of some subsequent attempts to change to the contract system, the structure of rural delivery has remained much as Heath and Machen had built it during its experimental stage.[39]

No one could have been more pleased with the outcome of the rural delivery fight than Machen. He had stayed on as Superintendent of Free Delivery after Heath had resigned as First Assistant Postmaster General in 1900, and for six years, all told, he had been the key figure in the development of rural delivery. More than most men who claimed the title, he deserved to be called "the father of the R F D." "I have tried to make the development of the rural delivery system the great work of my life," he once said, "and I am content to accept it as the only monument I can possibly care for when my life shall have closed." Now, after nursing the service beyond the experimental stage, and with petitions for new routes pouring into the Department, he could begin to organize rural routes in earnest. The day he had been looking for had arrived.[40]

But, alas, in May 1903, just when the great organizing program was beginning, Machen's past caught up with him and he was removed from his office. He had been too clever for his own good. He had long before learned there was money to be made in negotiating contracts for departmental necessities, and he had begun to take advantage of such opportunities as there were. Eventually his negotiations even involved the rural delivery service. In 1900 he had made a contract with Maurice Runkle, a New York clothier, for small leather cases in which rural mail carriers might carry their registry books. The Department paid 90 cents apiece for the cases, but Runkle had had them made for one third of that amount. In February 1902, when Machen had ordered another shipment, there were 11,000 rural mail carriers, but the Department already had over 21,000 cases. All signs pointed to the fact that for this lucrative contract Runkle had bought from Machen $2,450 worth of mining stock which he, Runkle, admitted was "not worth a d——."[41]

The Runkle contract was only one of the lesser deals Machen had made for his own profit. During the spring and summer of 1903 Joseph Bristow, President Roosevelt's special investigator, uncovered a nest of misdeeds in which the Superintendent of Free Delivery and other men in the Department and even members of Congress had been involved. Unbelieving senators and representatives who a short time before had thought so highly of Machen they had voted him a $500 increase in salary soon learned the worst. According to Bristow's report, the story of Machen's official record "had no parallel in the history of the postal service." Investigation revealed he had interested himself in ten different kinds of graft, and in the words of one inspector, sat in his network of fraud "like a fat spider watchful and expectant."[42]

In time, Machen was indicted on fourteen counts, convicted of his crimes, and sent to a federal penitentiary. The rural delivery service was then transferred from the First Assistant Postmaster General's bureau to that of the Fourth Assistant Postmaster General. Two separate free delivery divisions were set up, one for the city and one for the country, each with its own superintendent.[43]

So the system Machen had organized was built by other hands, and after his imprisonment, his name rarely, if ever, appeared again in connection with the R F D. But there remained the rules and regulations which he had drawn and the rural delivery structure which he had fashioned, and all that was left to his successors was to lay out the mail routes. And this was done on a gigantic scale. For the next three years, the countryside fairly sprouted rural mailboxes. Congressmen were swamped with petitions, and rural agents seemed to be everywhere. In 1902 there were not many more than 8,000 routes in the nation. Three years later there were over 32,000. But these were the boom years of route organizing. After 1906 routes were laid out more slowly, and some were even discontinued. Until 1926, however, new rural routes continued to be organized. There were 45,315 rural mail routes in the nation that year, the highest number ever reached. After this, the routes steadily decreased as routes were lengthened and consolidated, until in 1960 there remained just 31,379.[44]

4

POLITICS

"We ask that the Rural Mail Carriers, who will daily penetrate every part of this county, may be Republicans, each and every one. . . .

"The political effect of such appointments upon the Republican party will be instantly felt and appreciated from one end of the county to the other. And as for the service which will be rendered, it will be of the same high class which from time immemorial has been required by Republican administrators from the Government's public servants."

W. B. C. Brown, Republican congressional nominee, and others, to Postmaster General Charles Emory Smith, Nov. 2, 1901. County Rural Delivery Records, Jackson County, Mo., National Archives

THOUGH often discussed in Congress and sometimes reported in the newspapers, there was much about the connection between politics and the organizing of the nation's rural mail routes that the farmers never knew. Some of them may have surmised more than rumor and report revealed, but even they would probably have been surprised had they known the extent of the political tug-of-war that went on backstage at the Post Office Department to bring them their mail routes.

Because American politicians have always had a particular interest in the postal system, it is reasonable to surmise that rural free delivery would have become involved in politics regardless of the methods used to build the service. But from the day the Post Office Department decided that the farmers must petition their congressmen for the new mail routes, politics and the establishment of the R F D were inseparable, and representatives of rural districts, as anxious as the farmers to see the new mailboxes go up along country roads, became the catalytic agents that hurried route organizing to its conclusion much faster than it would ordinarily have gone.

Nowhere on the political landscape of the early 1900's was there a greater opportunity for a politician to increase his value in the eyes of his rural constituents than to lend a hand in bringing them their rural mail routes. One route planted in a community might remind 100 families every day of the congressman who had sponsored the route; two routes, 200, and so on until the possible political rewards trailed off into infinity when one considered the prospect of covering an entire congressional district with rural routes. Beyond this, every rural mail route must have a mail carrier. To find good, solid men with the right political faith to carry the mail to their neighbors for a monthly paycheck would be reasonably easy, and only twenty such men, someone once estimated, making their daily rounds among the people, would make an excellent political machine for the congressmen who helped them get their jobs.[1]

Happily all these political plums could be gathered legitimately and in accordance with the government's rural delivery policy the congressmen themselves were fashioning. "Of course," snapped the *Philadelphia Press* in 1903 in refutation of the charge that rural delivery was being used for political purposes, "Members of Congress helped themselves by helping the people get free delivery . . . but the service was legitimate." So it was, and seeing this and knowing there was political ore to be mined, congressmen, and senators too, were drawn to rural delivery like metal to a magnet. Many of them would never leave their names on a single piece of national legislation, but they would at least secure a kind of immortality by being remembered as the men who brought the R F D to their communities. And they would be twice blessed; once when they gave the routes to their districts, and again when they received the votes of grateful farmers.[2]

With the promise of great rewards in the offing, congressmen, overburdened with stacks of rural route petitions, hurried off to the Post Office Department in the early 1900's to get their rural routes. But here they found that if they followed the rules of the Department, none of them could immediately have as many routes as their constituents wanted. For the rules stipulated that rural mail routes would be installed only where roads were passable the year round and where 100 families could be served within a 25-mile limit. Along with these rules went a policy, announced in 1901 when rural route petitions began to backlog in the Department, that only one half of each congressman's petitions would be immediately answered. Theoretically, these basic requirements put rural route organization on an orderly basis. But only theoretically. The stakes in rural delivery were high, and congressmen tried in every possible way to get as many routes as they could in spite of the rules.[3]

One of the ways to play the game was suggested in 1903 by James Hemenway, congressman and later senator from Indiana, when he advised his colleagues in the House of Representatives to be active route seekers, for it was, he said, the "active member of Congress" who got the most routes. This advice he and many another congressman faithfully followed in those years when rural delivery was young. Hat in hand they waited to catch the ear and curry the favor of August Machen, Superintendent of Free Delivery and the first dispenser of rural mail routes. After Machen was dismissed, they sought out the men who subsequently took charge of the service—Joseph Bristow, William R. Spilman, and Peter V. DeGraw—until before the end of DeGraw's administration in 1913, the lavish days of route organizing were over.[4]

Members of Congress used every imaginable argument to induce the Department's authorities to set aside the regulations and establish more rural routes in their districts. Old promises of routes were recalled, and political pressures they endured were pointed out. The number of routes in their neighbor's district, they would say, was greater than their own, and they only wanted justice. At times they would bluntly ask that the regulations requiring 100 families on a route be waived; their constituents, they would explain, were above average in the amount of mail they received and this would compensate monetarily for the lack of families. When the Department would object that the roads over which routes were desired were impassable, congressmen would reply that this was only a temporary condition. Their people were working their roads all the time and spending large sums of money on them. ". . . I do not want the Department discouraged by reports of bad roads . . . ," wrote Iowa's Senator Jonathan Dolliver to DeGraw in 1907. "At the time the Inspector was here he had a rather bad opinion of our roads owing to the continuous and unprecedented rains. But that is all over."[5]

To those who were active and adept at playing the game, rural routes came thick and fast. In 1903, Hemenway himself had approximately 100 routes in his district, but he had gotten a late start. At the same time, his colleague from Indiana, Charles Landis, had been so busy bagging routes he could boast of having 37 more than his nearest competitor. He did not say how many this was, but it must have been over 200, for "Uncle Joe" Cannon, who was just then being elevated to the Speakership of the House, had more than 160 routes in just four of the six counties in his district; and influential William Hepburn, chairman of the highly publicized Committee on Interstate and Foreign Commerce, had something over 190—"not as many as I want," he said, "and not as many as I intend to have, if it is possible to get them." Like Hemenway, Hepburn also admitted he had been diligent in seeking rural routes.[6]

It was obvious to anyone who could add up the totals of rural routes in each state that diligence had its rewards. But there were those in Congress who doubted that diligence was the only prerequisite for securing mail routes. Henry Clayton of Alabama had another explanation for the fact that Congressman Hepburn could have 190 routes in his district in Iowa while there were only 129 in the entire state of Alabama. "I have been exceedingly active," he said in reply to Hemenway's criterion for success, "but did not happen to be a . . . Republican." And here Clayton touched on a vital point in establishing the R F D. Indeed there was no escaping the fact that in winning rural routes for their districts, Republican congressmen had the inside track.[7]

As long as the administration of rural delivery remained Republican, which it did throughout the most active years of route organizing, Republican congressmen facing Democrats in crucial elections could put their hurried pleas for routes before the Department on the basis of political necessity. But Democratic congressmen opposing Republicans could scarcely hope for a shower of new routes that might strengthen their position among their constituents. And in the South where Democrats faced Democrats in primary elections and Republicans were not involved, it was always possible to establish routes with less haste and in closer conformity to regulations.

Southern Democrats, like Clayton, who charged that Republicans were using rural free delivery for political purposes, buttressed their claims with statistics. In 1906, when the days of hasty route organizing were nearing a close, South Carolina's Congressman Asbury Lever, declared that "the records of the Department will bear me out in the statement that this [rural delivery] service has been administered in a sectional and partisan manner." He pointed out that in the Southern states having a total population and density of population equal to certain Northern and Midwestern states, there were less than half as many routes. Fifty per cent of the adverse reports on route petitions came from the South, he said, while other sections had less than ten per cent of their petitions for routes rejected. "The state of Kansas," said he, "as rock-ribbed and everlasting in her republicanism as South Carolina in her democracy . . . had in operation 1,555 routes, as against 532 from South Carolina—a difference of over a thousand routes in favor of Republican Kansas."[8]

The Midwest—Ohio, Indiana, Iowa, Illinois, and Kansas, in particular—was the specific target of the Democratic charges. As early as 1903 one disgruntled Southern congressman had told his colleagues to go take a look at the map in the Post Office Department indicating the areas where rural agents were installing routes if they wanted proof of discrimination. "They have a little pin with a flag on it," he said, "and they will take that with the agent's name and set it out in the different States all over the country. Out there in the Middle West . . . it looks like a dense forest. . . . Then look over this vast territory, which many of the gentlemen on this side represent, and you will see what looks like an occasional cottonwood on a bald prairie."[9]

From the Department's own statistics, that map must have appeared much as the congressman described it. So rapidly had rural routes been organized in those five Midwestern states, that by June 30, 1906, they had 11,794 rural routes, while the eleven states of the old Confederacy and Kentucky, had only 9,126. At the same time 74 per cent of the petitions from these five states had been approved for routes, while but 51 per cent of all petitions from the South brought routes.[10]

To these charges of political favoritism, the Republicans always had the answers. If more petitions were approved from the Midwest than from the South, politics had nothing to do with it, they argued; conditions in their states merely conformed to departmental prerequisites for establishing routes. Their roads were better, they would say, their people more literate, their population larger, and their communities more thickly settled.

These arguments were not entirely unsupportable. The differences in the roads and the density of population between the two sections might not be so marked, but certainly the South had fewer literate people than the Midwest. In 1900 21 per cent of the South's people above the age of ten were illiterate, in the five Midwestern states only 3 per cent were illiterate. There might be some question concerning the propriety of withholding routes from citizens who could neither read nor write, but this was the practice, and the Department defended it on the ground that to give this service to people who would neither receive nor send much mail would be too expensive. Consequently, rural agents discounted those illiterate families in the South when estimating the number of families to be served on any proposed route. When this was done Southerners were obviously handicapped, for it was then hard for them to plan routes where the required number of families could be found within a 25-mile stretch.[11]

Even so, Southerners like Lever could not understand why Kansas, with a density of population in 1900 of 18 persons per square mile, should have one rural route for every 1,300 of her people in 1904, while at the same time South Carolina with a density of population of 44 persons per square mile should have but one route for every 4,500 of her inhabitants. It was equally hard to believe that the differences between the roads and literacy of population in Kansas and South Carolina were enough to account for the fact that only 39 per cent of South Carolina's petitions for routes had been approved while 72 per cent of those from Kansas had brought routes.[12]

Or take Oklahoma. In 1906 it was not even a state, but it was represented in Congress by Bird McGuire, a Republican delegate. Said Lever: "Republican Oklahoma with a population of only 398,000, has in operation 594 routes—62 more than in my own State, with a population four times as great." Such comparisons as these, he remarked, could be carried on endlessly and all "demonstrate the fact that the service has been administered in a partisan and sectional manner that is disgraceful to any government."[13]

Lever and others who opposed the Department's rural delivery policy, based their charges primarily on the Department's statistics, and these were certainly revealing. If they could have gone behind the scenes at the Post Office Department to watch the building of county rural delivery which accounted for so many of the routes established in these years, they would have found ample proof for their suspicions. For, at first, before so many troublesome problems arose over their installation, county rural delivery systems were pearls of great price to each congressman, and their establishment teemed with partisan politics.

County rural delivery first became a factor of political importance in 1902. Until the middle of July of that year only twenty county systems had been established though the Carroll County experiment had been conducted a year and a half before. The Department had not pushed the service, partly because the procedures adopted at Carroll County, and only later simplified, were expensive and required the use of a large number of rural agents. Then, too, until 1902 rural delivery was still an experiment with an uncertain future. But in that year Congress had made the R F D permanent, and the Department was free to build the service as rapidly as appropriations would permit. And as fate would have it, 1902 was also an election year. In the budding campaign the political possibilities of county rural delivery first dawned on the members of Congress, and the intimate relationship between politicians and rural free delivery was sealed.[14]

From an administrative standpoint there was much to recommend the county rural delivery systems. They could supplant haphazard routes that had been established singly and laid out in all directions across the county. Some routes could be altered, some added, some eliminated, and most duplications ended, thereby increasing the efficiency of the service. But as far as the congressmen were concerned, the political advantage of county free delivery far outweighed the administrative. County service could be established upon their request without the necessity of waiting for petitions from every corner of the county, and when it was installed it brought the daily mail system to the county with a flourish. At one blow the old system was out and the new in; hundreds of farmers were simultaneously grateful. A congressman would be remembered for having secured county rural delivery when he might otherwise be forgotten if he had only scattered routes throughout his district to his credit.

Once aware of this advantage, Republican congressmen and senators hurried to have their counties covered with rural routes. In a prosperous year when issues like tariff revision and antitrust legislation scarcely stirred the blood of the average farmer, congressmen could build a political campaign around county rural delivery and many did. Indiana Republicans, the most seriously challenged of all Midwestern candidates of the Grand Old Party in that first midterm election of the Teddy Roosevelt era, led the way.

In April, not long after he had helped defeat the proposal to let the rural routes out to contractors, Congressman Edgar Dean Crumpacker—Judge Crumpacker to almost everyone who knew him—dropped in at the rural delivery headquarters in Indianapolis to chat with the man in charge of the office, S. B. Rathbone. What the Judge wanted, it developed, was the installation of county rural delivery in Tippecanoe County in his district.

Rathbone was cordial and anxious to cooperate. He had already taken soundings and knew what was in store for his branch of the service in the coming year. "It seems there will be a great demand during the coming year, for County service . . . ," he wrote his chief in Washington in reporting Crumpacker's visit. But he might have spared himself the trouble of prediction, for the man to whom he wrote was well aware of the situation in Indiana.[15]

In 1902 August W. Machen, Superintendent of Free Delivery was ruling over the fortunes of rural delivery in the grand manner. His power over this new service which he had nourished from infancy was complete, and its secrets were his own. How many promises he had made for county service in the spring of that year only he knew. But when Rathbone wrote him of Crumpacker's request in April, it was significant that the spadework for county delivery in two counties in Congressman James Hemenway's district, where one of the bitterest political fights in Indiana was expected, had already been done. Obviously, he was already prepared for the demands that would be made for rural routes before November.[16]

Not long after Crumpacker's visit to the R F D headquarters in Indianapolis, "Charlie" Landis, whose district was soon to be heavily crisscrossed with rural routes, wrote confidentially to Machen asking for county service in Hamilton County. "It will do me lots of good *personally* if it goes into operation not long before election," he wrote. "I want it humming along *when I canvass the county*. Please do me this additional favor. Send me a telegram that it goes into effect October 1st and I'll have it published."[17]

Landis's district was the ninth. Not far to the north of this was the thirteenth, and here the Republican incumbent, Abraham Lincoln Brick, found himself in trouble as election day approached. By October, he hastily telegraphed to Machen: "Order rural county service in Kosciusko and Marshall counties. Can't you do this for me? I need it badly." There was obvious need for action. The Democrats had boasted they would carry this county as well as several others held by Republican congressmen.[18]

While Congressman Brick fretted over the impending election in his district, Senator Charles Fairbanks, the state's senior senator, was worrying about the possibility of losing the state legislature to the Democrats. To be returned to the Senate he had to have a Republican-dominated state legislature. In county rural delivery he saw a golden opportunity to pick up votes in a Democratic district.

In the spring, he and the state's junior senator, Republican Albert Beveridge, had both requested county service in Bartholomew County. Later in the year they both made a similar request for service in Jefferson County. The novelty of these appeals was that both counties were represented in Congress by Marion Griffith, a Democrat who had been in the House since 1897. Under ordinary circumstances Griffith might have been expected to ask for rural delivery in these counties himself. Now he found himself outmaneuvered by the two United States senators.[19]

Back in Washington Machen worked to satisfy all these pleas for help. Plans were made to draw a rural agent from Illinois to lay out the service in Tippecanoe County for Judge Crumpacker. Hamilton County was investigated for Landis; Jefferson and Bartholomew Counties for Senators Fairbanks and Beveridge. For Abraham Lincoln Brick, who had telegraphed too late for work to begin in his counties before election, Machen did the next best thing. "Impossible to put county service in Kosciusko and Marshall Counties by November Sixth," he wired Brick. "If you want an order for some date beyond November fifteenth same may be issued at once." Upon Brick's assurance that he did, the Department sent word that orders would be issued to investigate those counties for rural free delivery service on January first or soon thereafter.[20]

Almost all these matters had been accomplished throughout the summer of 1902. But autumn approached and the routes were not yet in. Crumpacker wrote in August to express his satisfaction with the work being done. He only hoped the service would go into operation "by the first of Oct.," as it was a "matter of much importance to us that this be done." Charles Landis was more uneasy. Mid-September had come, and there had been no announcement of the appointment of the rural carriers. With the starting date so near he thought the carriers should be appointed so they could get their wagons. "Do not, as you value your life," he wrote Machen, "fail to get this service started Oct. 1st. It would cost me hundreds of votes if it did not go in according to promise."[21]

As it turned out the service started neither in Hamilton or

Tippecanoe Counties on October first. But two weeks later, October 15, 1902, rural delivery began on a countywide basis in both counties. The elections were still three weeks away.[22]

In Congressman Griffith's district where the Republican senators had asked for county service, there was more delay, and Republicans in both counties were becoming anxious. The postmaster at Madison in Jefferson County, wrote Senator Fairbanks in October that he had been informed it would "make a good many votes in this county if the announcement can be made at once in Washington that our new rural routes will become effective upon a certain date." The postmaster cared less about the date than the announcement. "Democrats & perhaps others," he continued, "are saying the institution of these routes will never be seen, it is only a play to help the legislative ticket. . . . Good friends in the county tell me it will help to have the announcement made at once." In Bartholomew County the situation was much the same. Fairbanks was urged by a constituent from the county to have the Department rush the announcement of the establishment of county delivery and warned that it should "under no circumstances be later than October first in order to get the expected benefits."[23]

Senator Fairbanks sent the letters he had received from his friends in Bartholomew and Jefferson Counties to Machen with the request that appropriate action be taken. Nothing could be done about county service in Jefferson County until April of the following year, but Machen gave orders that the Bartholomew service was to go into operation on November first. The matter seemed settled and all going well until October 17, when Fairbanks wired Machen that there was dissatisfaction over the appointment of the carriers at the town of Hope in Bartholomew County. He asked Machen to "withhold the announcement of the other carriers until after the election," if he could and "to postpone the establishment of the rest of the service until November fifteenth."[24]

Machen found he could do this. The entire service in Bartholomew County was postponed until November fifteenth. The carriers appointed at Hope would have to stand. But the examinations of the other carriers, Fairbanks was informed, had all been lost, accidentally perhaps but certainly conveniently, in transit, and there would have to be a new examination. In the meantime, the appointment of the carriers, other than those at Hope, would have to be withheld, presumably until after the election.[25]

In the election that followed close upon this backstage maneuvering for county systems in Indiana, the Republicans swept the state. Senator Fairbanks was returned to the Senate, and the nine Republican seats in the House were saved though the party made no gains there. Judge Crumpacker and "Charlie" Landis won easily. In three of the four Republican districts claimed by the Democrats before the election, six county services were established or publicly promised. James Hemenway in the first district had two; George Washington Cromer in the eighth had two; and Abraham Lincoln Brick, the other of Indiana's heroically named congressmen, had two promised.[26]

All in all, though it was by no means the only state where county systems had been established or promised with an eye on the political situation in 1902, Indiana came out of the election with fourteen counties in which complete rural mail service had either been put into operation or where open assurances had been given that it would be at an early date. Illinois, its nearest competitor had ten county services, evenly divided: five for "Uncle Joe" Cannon's district which was now completely covered with rural routes on a countywide basis, and five scattered among the districts of the other twenty Illinois congressmen.[27]

But the South was not entirely overlooked in all this. Eleven county systems had been established in the Southern states in 1902 or shortly thereafter. Eight of these were in Tennessee. Of that eight Republican Richard Gibson had one, and Republican Walter Preston Brownlow had six. Cobb County, Georgia, home of the ranking Democratic member of the Senate's Post Office and Post Roads Committee, Alexander Clay, also had one.[28]

The year 1903 promised to be a busy one for building county rural delivery systems. Many assurances that the service would be established had been made in the preceding months, and more requests for county rural delivery were reaching the Department almost daily. Postal authorities seemed prepared and willing to install them as rapidly as possible. But in May 1903 the work came to a standstill when August Machen was removed from office and the Free Delivery Division was transferred to the Bureau of the Fourth Assistant Postmaster General, then headed by Joseph Bristow. A young man, educated at Manhattan College in Kansas, William R. Spilman, became Superintendent of Rural Free Delivery. But he was to wield no such powers as Machen had. This was no longer possible. Henceforth rural delivery policy was to be made largely by the Fourth Assistant Postmaster General himself.[29]

Joseph Bristow was also from Kansas where he had been engaged in newspaper work. He had been appointed Fourth Assistant Postmaster General by President McKinley for his services in the election of 1896. Detailed in 1900 to investigate the scandal in the American administration of the Cuban postal system, he had thoroughly exposed the situation there. Two years later when evidence of corruption in the Post Office Department itself was discovered, President Roosevelt assigned him to an investigation of the situation which resulted in the conviction of several postal officials, including Machen, and made lasting enemies for Bristow among members of Congress. Tall and gangling, his upper lip concealed beneath a heavy black mustache and his body habitually attired in a black frock coat, he was an ungainly looking man. But he was believed to be fearlessly honest.[30]

When rural delivery came under his official roof, over 10,000 petitions for single routes were awaiting action besides many insistent demands for county service. With characteristic energy and directness, Bristow set about reorganizing the system of laying out routes. He gave orders that after June 3, 1903, the old rule requiring that each route established serve 100 families would be strictly enforced thereby admitting, of course, that this had not always been done. Furthermore, routes would be parceled out on the basis of 50 per cent of the applications made from any one congressional district and established in order in which the petitions had been filed. The building of county rural delivery systems was to be restricted until the individual route petitions had been taken care of.[31]

What Bristow meant by the "restriction" of county service, is not altogether clear. If he had hopes, as he seemed to have had, of stopping the establishment of these systems completely, those hopes were shattered by the sheer weight of political pressure. Such a policy might have been possible the year before. In 1903 it was not. Shortly after the first of July when he began cancelling orders for county services already in the process of being investigated by the rural agents, an avalanche of protests engulfed him. If he had not known before, these protests must surely have enlightened him on the political realities behind the organizing of rural delivery.

The situation was particularly uncomfortable in Indiana where so much had been promised. In Steuben County, where months before Senator Fairbanks had requested county rural delivery and where by early summer the planning of rural routes was already in progress, the rural agent in charge of the project was suddenly ordered to drop his work. Since this was another of those counties for which Fairbanks had gone over the head of the district's Democratic congressman to ask for county delivery, and since he had been given credit in all the local papers for having got it, he was understandably upset by the order cancelling the work. Indiana's Lieutenant Governor Newton Gilbert felt certain it would not be pleasant for the senator "to have the people feel that after all nothing was to be accomplished under it." He told the senator that the county chairman was trying to keep the matter quiet, but urged him to take it up with the Department. Almost without choice in the matter, Fairbanks dashed off a note to Bristow asking him to let the order for county service in Steuben County stand.[32]

But no one was more indignant over the new policy than Judge Crumpacker when he learned that the work of establishing a county system in Benton County was to be discontinued. It was not fair, he wrote Bristow, "to put certain other districts on the same basis as mine, beginning on the 30th Day of June last." He told Bristow of long-standing promises for county service, of work begun and left undone, of routes laid out but never put in operation. Agents for rural mailbox companies had long ago sold the farmers boxes on the supposition that the routes mapped out would soon be activated, but there was no service. "Boxes were put up on a route out in Idaville in White County over two years ago and no service has been established on that route yet . . . ," he wrote. His repeated requests for service in the last year, 1902, were all put off except for Tippecanoe County. "I was informed that in view of certain conditions, that I need not express, my district would not receive attention until after the election, but that special agents and inspectors were being used at that time in certain other districts in this and other states."

But even after the election the routes had not come. "The districts surrounding mine have on an average twice as much service as my district has," his letter continued. "My constituents know this and it has given me a great deal of embarrassment. There are some things in connection with this service that I would like to say to you, but I do not care to put them in writing."[33]

Under the circumstances, Bristow's problems mounted, and his lot was probably the most unenviable one in official Washington in these years. How was he to reply, for example, to the personal appeal of Jesse Overstreet, chairman of the Post Office and Post Roads Committee, asking that his home county in Indiana—

Johnson County—be quickly given county rural delivery before it was transferred, as it was soon to be, from his district to one represented by a Democratic congressman? And in subsequent months how could he refuse the requests for county service of such men as Senator Shelby Cullom of Illinois and Ohio's Senator Joseph Foraker? Politically it seemed impossible. Bristow's honest restrictive policy had run afoul of his rural delivery inheritance, and he found, as he wrote Crumpacker, that "everybody seems to claim their districts have been neglected and . . . they all refer to long deferred promises and so on." County rural delivery was a treadmill to the men of his party. When county systems sprang up in one district, it became imperative that the neighboring district be given the service, and there was no way to hold back the tide.[34]

Despite his best intentions Bristow, the competent investigator, was gradually forced to give way to Bristow the politician, a role he seemed to fill much less comfortably. While he continued for a year to answer requests for county service with noncommittal responses and with the reminder that this type of service was being deferred, still within that year in which the restrictive policy was theoretically in effect, over 70 county systems were installed, principally in the Midwest. This was more than double the number previously established.[35]

Toward the early part of 1904, however, Bristow began considering a change of policy, and in July, almost six months before the presidential election, he removed the restrictions from the building of county service. Later, he explained this could be done because Congress had authorized the employing of more rural agents to lay out routes and because the backlog of rural route petitions had been greatly reduced. There is no evidence that President Theodore Roosevelt himself was behind this change of policy, but no doubt he was anxious to include continued rural route organizing among his campaign promises. Angry at the attacks Judge Alton B. Parker, his opponent for the presidency, was making on his policies, the President wrote William Howard Taft and George Cortelyou, chairman of the Republican National Committee, in September urging them to promise the voters that the Republicans intended to maintain rural delivery where it was already established and to extend it.[36]

Whatever lay behind it, Bristow's new policy came at a propitious time for Republican office seekers, and insofar as rural delivery was concerned, the election of 1904 was a repetition of the one held two years before. The same pleas were made and the same promises given. Here was a congressman in Indiana to whom it was "Positively necessary to have solid delivery in Decatur and Shellby [*sic*] counties"; and one in Iowa who asked for county service in Washington County because his constituents in that county thought he had not "urged their claims with enough strenuousity." Another from Ohio begged Bristow to establish rural delivery in Montgomery County as "per our talk" and reminded him that just before leaving Washington he had explained to him "the importance."[37]

Senators, too, were pulling strings to secure county services as they had in 1902. Charles Dick, senator from Ohio, having been assured by the Republican county chairman in Shelby County that rural routes reaching some of the county's best citizens "would greatly strengthen us in the coming campaign," bypassed the district's Democratic Congressman, Harvey Gerber, to ask for county service in Shelby County.[38]

Early in the year the Republicans of Allen County, Indiana, hoping to outmaneuver their Democratic Congressman, James Robinson, asked Senators Fairbanks and Beveridge for county rural delivery. The postmaster at Fort Wayne wrote Fairbanks that "it would give us splendid ammunition for the coming campaign, and greatly help the entire ticket." And another prominent Republican from the county gave the senator an even more important reason for obtaining the service. "We want to forestall," he wrote, "any effort on the part of Robinson or his friends to steal the honor." There was need of secrecy, the letter warned, "because if he [Robinson] should discover that such a move is being made, he will use every effort to get the benefit."[39]

Goaded by such pressure, Bristow hurried the building of county systems as rapidly as possible. The investigation and planning of these services had by now been worked out in great detail, and in one year, 134 more counties were covered with rural mail routes. Among the 134, as might have been expected, was Allen County, Indiana, where the requests of Senator Fairbanks—soon to become the Vice President—and Senator Beveridge, had stirred up a bitter political fight with both sides claiming credit for having brought rural free delivery to the county.[40]

In all the confusion, the postmaster at Huntertown tried to straighten the matter out once and for all. Just a few days before election he wrote the Department demanding to know to whom the promise of county delivery was first given, what date it was given, and when the rural agent was first notified of the Department's intentions. The Department's reply to the postmaster is missing from the Allen County file, but on the back of the postmaster's letter was a note indicating that Senators Fairbanks and Beveridge had been responsible for rural delivery in the county.[41]

Though many Republicans were running scared in the election and even President Roosevelt was apprehensive about the outcome in such states as Indiana, the Republicans, from a political standpoint, really had less need than they imagined to cover their counties with rural mail routes. When the ballots were in, their party had won easily and probably would have, even if no county systems had been established. In such an overwhelming victory, James Robinson might well have lost the seat he had held through four Congresses to Newton Gilbert anyway. Still, he could scarcely have been blamed if he felt he had been defeated by the machinations of two United States senators who got the official credit for the establishment of county rural delivery not only in a county he represented in Congress, but, to add insult to injury, in the very county where he had lived all his life.

This political maneuvering for rural routes which still in 1904 had not run its course, left its mark on the farmers' mail service. Because of it, so rapidly were rural routes built in the Midwest and in such states as New York and Pennsylvania that within a decade from rural delivery's inauguration, the system was virtually complete in those areas. Over 11,000 routes had been planted in Ohio, Indiana, Iowa, Illinois, and Kansas by 1907 to round out the service in each of these states except Kansas. But to lay out the system in the Midwest, many rural route petitions from the South had to be ignored, and in 1907 all the states of the old Confederacy and Kentucky combined had only 9,305 routes. To make matters worse for the South, just as the Northeastern and Midwestern states were becoming saturated with rural mail routes and Southerners might have expected that more would soon be organized in their region, the Post Office Department began to curtail the program.[42]

For some time before 1909 there had been talk about the possibility of a deficit in the Treasury. Some said it was because of the building of new battleships, and others believed it was because of increases in the pay of government employees. Everyone had a theory, usually partisan, but very little information to support his conclusion. At any rate President Taft was alarmed enough about the situation in 1909 to order all department heads to cut expenses "to the quick," as he said, and it was clear he expected drastic cuts to be made in the R F D. After this it became increasingly difficult to get new routes established.[43]

For a number of years Southern congressmen belabored the Post Office Department for curtailing the organization program and even tried to force the establishment of more rural routes. Every year when the Post Office appropriation bill came before Congress, Southerners led the fight to appropriate more money than the Department asked for so that new mail routes could be established. But each year the Department, showing how easy it was for the executive branch of government to thwart the will of the Congress, turned the additional money back to the Treasury while new rural routes, already inspected and approved, went begging. Even when the Democrats came into office in 1913, the freeze on new rural routes remained, and Southerners found themselves fighting their own administration to get more routes. Beginning in 1915 and continuing for four years, they were able to raise the rural delivery appropriation to $53,000,000, four to five millions above the amount sought by the Department. But in no case was the full appropriation spent and all the while rural route petitions went unanswered.[44]

Finally, in 1916, Senator Thomas Hardwick from Georgia, supported by many Southerners in Congress, tried to compel Albert Burleson, President Woodrow Wilson's Postmaster General, to lay out more routes by writing into the Post Office appropriation bill a declaration stating it was Congress's intention that "rural delivery be extended to serve as nearly as practicable the entire population of the United States." This, too, was ineffective. Hardwick and his friends had formulated a basic principle for route organizing to which Burleson and succeeding Postmaster Generals paid lip service but moved slowly and reluctantly to implement. Through the years rural route extensions were made and occasionally a new route laid down, but compared with the earlier period, the growth of the system was tortoise-paced. By 1920 rural mail routes extended over 1,151,832 miles of the nation's roads; thirty years later only 341,533 additional miles had been added to the system, and most of these only because of strong pressure from Congress.[45]

True, many of the new routes and extensions made in these years were located in the South while the overcrowded service in the Midwest was readjusted and duplications winnowed out. Altogether, between 1907 and 1930, Illinois, Iowa, Ohio, and Indiana lost 1,000 mail routes while the South gained 3,335. But even so, the South had missed out on the golden days of route organizing, and in proportion to the number of people living in the South and in the Midwest who could benefit from the service, the South never did achieve equality in the rural delivery service with the Midwest. In 1950 five Midwestern states had 7,047 rural routes while the entire South had 10,242. In both sections each route averaged 47 miles in length, but in the South there was only one route for every 2,038 rural inhabitants; in the Midwest there was one for every 1,278 persons in rural areas.[46]

PATRONS, POSTMASTERS, AND IMPORTANT PEOPLE

"The whole matter is, that the business men of Kalida, aver that the Rural Free Delivery, hurts the town, as it keeps people away since they do not have to come after their mail, they even claimed that the saloon business had fallen off and that additional [R F D] service from other offices would make the business situation worse than it was."

Supplementary Report of Special Agent Charles Murphy, Apr. 12, 1905, County Rural Delivery Records, Putnam County, Ohio, National Archives

NO governmental service ever belonged more completely to the nation's farmers than the R F D. They had been responsible for the service's establishment in the 1890's as they were in the 1900's for its expansion. They had initiated and circulated the petitions for the rural mail routes that brought the mail to their farms. They had even planned their own routes, drawn sketches of them, and plotted them on maps. So busy were they with their new mail service in the first few years of the new century that within a decade after the first mail routes were installed farmers by the thousands had scratched their names in big, stiff-knuckled scrawls across countless petitions and sped them on their way to Washington. In the nation's capital they filled congressmen's desks and eventually found resting place in the files of the Post Office Department, testimonials to the fact that the service belonged to the names attached. And in return the routes came, nearly 40,000 of them in the first nine years of the 1900's.

Yet the process was not as simple as this. Forty thousand mail routes had not been strung out through the heart of the nation's farmland without difficulty. Organizing the rural mail system brought dissensions to rural America as well as gratification, for with the coming of the rural routes old neighborhood quarrels were reopened, jealousies flared, misrepresentations were made, and angry protests went winging their way to Washington.

Soon enough the farmers learned that not everyone in their communities welcomed rural delivery as they did. Some among them did not want it at all; others would tolerate it only if the new mail routes began where they wished and ran where they said; still others were swayed this way and that, sometimes supporting and sometimes opposing whatever was done to bring the service to the farmers.

This clash of interests left its abiding imprint on the structure of rural free delivery. It helped determine the location of the routes and the course they followed. It influenced the shaping of rural route regulations, and it delayed the completion of routes in some localities for years. Moreover, the stormy controversies that swirled about the farmers' new mail system forced the Department to operate the old mail service side by side with the new long after the old was unnecessary and so increased the cost of establishing rural free delivery.

All of the men who had helped organize rural routes, Perry Heath, August Machen, Joseph Bristow, and others, had had their innings with the troublemakers. But the man who inherited the lion's share of turmoil was Peter Voorhees DeGraw. Large, rugged, and mercurial, DeGraw was a journalist and widely known in Washington where he had been one of the founders of the Gridiron Club. During the election of 1904 he had been an aide to

George Cortelyou, Roosevelt's campaign manager. After the election, when Cortelyou became Postmaster General, DeGraw was brought in to replace the unpopular Bristow as Fourth Assistant Postmaster General, and found himself in the middle of the route organization program at the very time when community quarrels over the new service were raging. Here, berated and bedeviled on all sides, he remained seven unquiet years.[1]

Like his predecessors, DeGraw was troubled by the politicians' demands for county rural delivery systems. Yet as the days passed, he found his official life more upset by the congressmen and senators who begged him to quiet the tumult stirred up by the establishment of county rural delivery than by requests for new services. Congressmen like Charles Landis and Abraham Lincoln Brick, who in an earlier day had been so eager for county systems, were in 1908 urging the Department to proceed with caution in laying out the service or asking that tactful agents be sent to their districts, and finally requesting that nothing at all be done until after election.

One could see the dilemma these men faced over county rural delivery in a letter Congressman Pleasant Thomas Chapman of Illinois wrote to DeGraw just before the election of 1906. The Department was preparing to establish county delivery in Edwards County when Chapman asked that no changes in the mail service be made. He had learned that certain influential people were opposed to the changes, and, on the eve of the election, he felt compelled to bow to their wishes. But fearing that the farmers who wanted the service established might discover what he had done, he prudently asked that "no one in Edwards County be informed of" his request to cancel county delivery.[2]

Organizing rural mail service was never free from the interference of people whose interests were not those of the farmers. This meddling was bad enough when routes were being laid out one at a time, but it was magnified many times over in the organization of a county system. As old routes were altered to fit the new pattern, and a dozen or more new ones were laid out, as new mail carriers were appointed and scores of fourth-class post offices and star routes were discontinued, rural communities were sometimes torn apart at the seams. Town was set against town, village against village, postmaster against postmaster, and neighbor against neighbor. And the key figures in all this were the rural postmasters.

In the rural America of the 1890's and early 1900's, country postmasters were virtually institutions. With their little combination stores and fourth-class post offices, they had been the heart of the old rural mail system from George Washington's day to the beginning of rural free delivery. For their services they received the rentals from post-office boxes and fees for stamps canceled, but the actual money they made from their post offices made none of them wealthy. In 1899 no fourth-class postmaster made more than $1,000 a year from his postal business and the average annual salary was only about $200.[3]

But the post office drew trade to their stores, and the postmastership had a value not measured by money. For in rural communities few people were more important than the local postmasters. The very life of their communities pulsated beneath their fingertips as they sorted out the day's mail and flipped it into the post-office boxes. A return address on an envelope, a penny postcard, even a magazine subscription could reveal a world of information to the postmasters who already knew so much about the people to whom they were sent. Better than most people in the community they knew the secret lives of their neighbors, and by this knowledge their position in their communities was enhanced.[4]

Because of these more or less intangible rewards inherent in the postmasterships, country storekeepers all over rural America were almost as attached to their post offices as they were to their right arms, and when the rural free delivery service began to encroach on what they had always considered their postal prerogatives their hostility was immediately kindled.

It took no great foresight on their part to see how the new rural mail routes would affect them. Anyone could see that the farmers' trips to town would be reduced when they no longer had to come in for their mail, and the trade at the store would suffer accordingly. As for the post-office boxes, the farmers would have no need of them, and, since their outgoing mail would be picked up by the mail carrier, only those post offices from which the rural route emanated would get the cancellation fees. Worse than all these probabilities, was the announced intention of the Department to abolish all those fourth-class post offices that duplicated the new mail service.

Because their post offices were so important to them, the fourth-class postmasters spent little time sitting on their cracker barrels philosophizing about this assault on their vested interests. They had already given notice of what was in store for the future organizing of county rural delivery in 1899 and 1900 during the Carroll County experiment in Maryland. Angered by the abrupt closing of over 60 post offices they had raised a huge petition of 2,000 names and sent it with a delegation representing their interests to Washington. There the postmaster's delegation confronted a rival group of farmers supporting the service, and the first large-scale fight between country postmasters and farmers was joined. The postmasters lost this battle when their congressman sided with the farmers, but their attacks had been so strong that the character of rural delivery in Carroll County long bore the scars they had made, just as it would all over the nation where the interests of the postmasters and rural delivery clashed.[5]

The postmasters' first line of defense as they girded for battle was in Washington where their friends sat in the House and Senate. The origins of their connections with the men in the Capitol stretched far back into American history. Traditionally the United States Post Office was the "political plum" of victorious political parties. It had more offices to give to loyal party workers than any other department of the government, and of these positions the fourth-class postmaster, numbering more than 72,000 in 1900, were the most numerous. Until President Taft completed Theodore Roosevelt's work of putting these postmasters under civil service, each change of political administration in Washington brought great upheavals in the rural post offices as wholesale dismissals and resignations were followed by the appointment of members of the victorious party.

From 1885 to 1889, for example, Adlai E. Stevenson, Cleveland's First Assistant Postmaster General, won his place in history as "the headsman" by turning out of fourth-class post offices more than four fifths of the "Republican rascals." But when the Republicans returned to office in 1889 with John Wanamaker as Postmaster General, the wheels turned once more, and Republican postmasters again filled the fourth-class offices. Of a total of 56,315 such post offices, there were 16,953 removals and 31,902 resignations during Wanamaker's administration.[6]

New appointees to these offices were nearly always made on the recommendation of congressmen who, by giving some loyal party worker a post office, strengthened their positions at the grass roots. Obviously these appointments in such strategic places were important to members of Congress, and the postmasters knew how to take advantage of this fact. Threatened by the loss of their post offices, they importuned both senators and congressmen to intercede for them at the Post Office Department. In this way they put their congressmen in the unenviable position of having to choose between their post offices and the new rural routes since it was the Department's policy not to have both if they duplicated one another.

Unable to decide one way or another, congressmen hesitated over this unpromising situation. Many of them instinctively felt as Richard Bartholdt of Missouri did when he learned that if St. Louis County was to get county delivery, numerous fourth-class post offices would have to go. To his good friend, Robert Wynne, the First Assistant Postmaster General, he wrote that to consent to the discontinuance of those post offices "would be equivalent to committing political suicide" in his district. He thought neither he nor "anyone else could outlive the resentment of the men who would thus be deprived of their annual income."[7] To relieve themselves of this embarrassing situation, congressmen often induced the Department to establish the rural routes and close its eyes to the little post offices that stood in the way.

The result of this indecision was that the Department needlessly maintained duplicating mail services throughout rural America for years. Partly to protect the little post offices, for example, the Post Office Department had a rule that no rural mailbox was to be set up within a half mile of a post office, and a rural mail carrier was not to deliver mail to any farm within this zone even if his route ran by such a farm. But in Madison County, Illinois, where rural routes had been built close to a number of such post offices, farmers within the zone set up their boxes anyway, and when a rural agent investigated the county in 1905 he found over forty mailboxes established in violation of the rule. At Fosterberg he located six boxes within half a mile of the post office, at Wanda two, and at Grantfork four. Even the married daughter of the postmaster at Melville had put up her box within a half mile of the post office.

To the rural agent it was clear that the people, even the postmaster's daughter, favored rural free delivery over the old system, and his solution to the problem was to discontinue the post offices rather than compel the people to take down their boxes "in order," as he wrote, "that the adjacent store-keeper may oblige them to come to the store for mail that he may derive some financial benefit thereby." But even after he recommended that the post offices be done away with, the power of the postmasters was so great he was more than half afraid his recommendations would never be followed.[8]

Though it often continued duplicating services to stop the complaints of congressmen, the Department was never happy about the situation, and as early as 1901, William H. Johnson, the

First Assistant Postmaster General announced that from then on, mail routes would be withdrawn where congressmen insisted on keeping the little post offices in their districts open.[9]

Johnson's gesture was more threat than promise, yet it was true that the growing rural delivery system continued to chip away at the fourth-class post offices. This was particularly noticeable in the establishment of county rural delivery systems where so many small post offices were wiped out simultaneously, and it was principally for this reason that organizing county rural delivery had become so troublesome in DeGraw's time.

Country postmasters, sometimes pictured in the American past as genial, easygoing men, revealed another side of their nature as they fought to maintain their post offices. They were a resourceful group of men, and many of them never hesitated to use underhanded tricks to save themselves. "The animal instinct of self-preservation is strong in the postmaster who has a store in connection with his post office," wrote one rural agent, and so it proved. They did not necessarily wait for help from Washington which sometimes came and sometimes did not. They had their own devices to defend themselves. One was the petition, the most time-honored method of getting a hearing in democratic America. With this the postmasters sought to prove that their post offices were preferred to the rural routes.[10]

Harper, in northern Illinois, was a little village of eight houses and ten families in 1905 when Rural Agent Alex Charles passed through in the process of laying out rural delivery in Ogle County. Finding that the post office did a very meager business and that all the people there as well as those living on the roads immediately around it could have their mail delivered by the mail carrier from Forreston, Charles recommended that the Harper post office be closed. Immediately, the Department received a formidable petition of protest from the Harper postmaster. Agent Charles was forced—as rural agents always were when protests were received—

to make a supplementary report to the Department explaining the reason for his recommendation.

Charles made his explanations, and wrote, "Mr. Jacob Buss, the postmaster at Harper runs a store and his idea when I was there was, that the discontinuance of the Harper Postoffice would ruin his business." Then Agent Charles turned a critical eye on the petition itself and found what other rural agents across the country were discovering: "Ed Burt one of the signers of the petition lives in Shannon . . . Ill.," he reported, "and receives his mail there, F. G. Laing . . . lives in Forreston, Illinois and receives his mail there. J. Geiger lives in Baileyville, Illinois . . . , George Bumgarden receives his mail at the Forreston Postoffice. John Newman Co., is a firm doing business in Elgin, Illinois." Many of the names on the petition, he discovered, were farmhands and children. "Take the case of John H. Diehl," he wrote, "which is followed by Ida, Effie, Clara, and Fred Diehl . . . all members of the same family ranging in ages from five to sixteen years of age."

Fraudulently signed petitions were a common enough weapon in the fight against R F D. But even when they were signed by the proper people, postmasters' petitions were always suspect in the eyes of rural agents. In rural communities where relationships were open and intimate, it was a simple matter to get signatures on a petition. Friends of the postmaster, all too unaware of the implications of their actions, would often sign the petitions as a neighborly gesture. "Mr. Buss," Agent Charles had written, "is a very nice and popular fellow and I am not at all surprised that he should be able to procure and forward to the Department the petition. . . ."[11]

As often as not, however, the postmasters deliberately tricked the farmers into signing their petitions. When the installation of a rural route and the discontinuance of a post office were imminent, tales emanating from that post office were spread abroad in the community, prophesying widespread hardship and inconvenience from the new mail service. Rumors flew that county taxes would go up or that each farmer would be assessed so much money every year for their mailboxes. Very often at such times the people heard that the new mail routes were unworkable and that their mail would be delayed. A petition was raised against the closing of a post office in Osborn, Illinois, in 1905 on the plea, contrary to the rural agent's opinion, that rural delivery would never work there because the Rock River overflowed the road for a part of each year making it impossible for the rural mail carrier to make his rounds.[12]

To help them thwart the attempts of the Post Office Department to install the new rural routes, the fourth-class postmasters had the help of the star route mail carriers and contractors, who, from 1845 on, had composed the other arm of the old country mail service. The jobs of these men who carried the mail from some distributing point to the smaller, isolated post offices were also threatened by the new delivery system, and they were no more anxious to see themselves supplanted by another service than the fourth-class postmaster.

The star route carriers performed their services on the basis of a yearly contract. Usually the actual carrier did not make this contract directly with the government but rather with a contract speculator who had bargained with the government for a number of routes. Once he won the contracts, the speculator subcontracted them to the star carriers. This arrangement was often made profitable by combining with it a passenger or freight service which would of course also be seriously impaired by free delivery.

As far as the mails were concerned the contract system was wasteful and inefficient and often reduced the pay of the actual carrier to a mere fraction of what the job was worth. Yet the carriers, and particularly the contract speculators, clung tenaciously to the old system, and, since their interests were linked to those of the postmasters, they fought side by side with them against the establishment of rural routes.[13]

Like so many places in rural America, Gallia County, Ohio, along the Ohio River, by a steady accretion of small post offices and star routes throughout the years, had become finely covered with these instruments of the old mail service. The star route carriers had built up profitable hack lines carrying "passengers, freight, whiskey in Jugs and bottles," along with the mails. Yet the demand for rural delivery among the people was strong enough in 1905 to prompt Congressman Henry Bannon, to request that county rural free delivery be established there. The Department acknowledged Bannon's request, dispatched a rural agent there to investigate the county, and was prepared to install the service in December 1905.[14]

In the meantime it had become known throughout the county that great changes in the mail service were impending. Agent William F. Heck had recommended that 17 star routes and 37 post offices be discontinued. Word then "leaked out that the star carriers were going to knock out the rurals," and two months before the new service was to begin, Congressman Bannon was relaying to the Department the urgent letters he was receiving from postmasters and star carriers. They assured him the service at the post offices was satisfactory and begged him to assist them in "preventing the wrong" they were "threatened with. . . ." Rural routes, they said, would greatly delay the mails and cause great dissatisfaction. The postmaster at Bush's Mill wrote that if the star route to his office were abandoned the mail would be delayed twenty-four hours in the winter, because it would have to be ferried across the Ohio River at Bladen.[15]

The Department tried to allay Bannon's uneasiness by pointing out that it simply was not true that the mail at Bush's Mill would be twenty-four hours late. Nor would the mail by rural route be delayed at Mercerville where other complaints had originated. Bannon was assured the rural carriers would leave Gallipolis at 9:30 A.M. after the principal morning mails, including the daily papers, had arrived on the Baltimore and Ohio Railroad and return in time to dispatch their day's collection. But all in vain. The pressure was too great, and the proposed county service was cancelled in November 1905.[16]

The farmers of Gallia County who wanted rural delivery were deeply disappointed at this turn of events, and one angry farmer, still fuming over the situation a year after the service had been cancelled decided to write to President Roosevelt. "the carriers made Preparations and was ready to go to work," he wrote. "also the people bought and put up the Boxes and was rejoicing what a grand thing it was, but all at on[ce] there came a Notice to carriers that their appointments was rescinded, and routes was cancelled. . . . I wish you knew how all the people are feeling over it. its a Shame. Now what made the Department change its colors so quick. was it just because the Star route carriers made a kick because they were running Hacks carrying mail and Passengers and the fourth-class Postmaster to help them. . . ." Roosevelt's correspondent indicated he thought it was, and he concluded by asking the President to "Please take some thought in this Subject and help the people if in your power."[17]

This conflict of interests in Gallia County had so muddied the waters the Department was unable to determine the real wishes of the majority of the people. On one hand it had been assured the mail service in the county was satisfactory, yet requests for new routes continued to be made. Eventually, by 1916, the county did get the number of routes Agent Heck had proposed in 1905, but new routes were only added gradually. No single, sweeping change was ever made.[18]

As in Gallia County, so in rural communities across the nation, the fourth-class postmasters delayed and disrupted the establishment of rural routes. Even so, they often troubled the Department less in their efforts to stymie the laying out of new routes than did that great body of postmasters, first-, second-, third-, and fourth-class alike, who left no stone unturned to grab as many routes for their post offices as they could when the county rural delivery services were being laid out.

Ever alert to profitable enterprise, these men saw in the new rural routes a way to enlarge the territory tributary to their post offices and increase their revenue. Content to let the smaller offices fall by the wayside, so they could absorb their business, they had to make certain the new mail routes were located where they would bring them the most returns. To secure this objective they had the ready support of the businessmen of their towns and villages.

The merchants in America's little rural towns, like the fourth-class postmasters, had feared rural delivery from the beginning. Visions of deserted streets and empty stores and ruined businesses danced before their eyes when they realized the farmers living on rural routes would no longer be forced, or have an excuse, to come to their post offices for their mail. But since rural delivery was a fact, they were determined, as were many fourth-class postmasters, that the new routes should emerge from their towns. This, at least, would give them something, for the farmers' trade centers would normally be the same as their post-office address. If their trips to town were interrupted by the rural routes, trade with them could still be carried on through the rural mail carrier. This idea led them to associate themselves with the postmasters of their towns who, for their own reasons, wanted as many rural routes to emanate from their post offices as possible, and together these two groups of influential citizens turned the installing of county rural delivery upside down.

The postmasters and their friends in the villages and towns began their attempts to arrange the rural routes to their own advantage on the day the rural agent first set foot in the county to plan the service, if indeed they had not begun before then. Often, they would drive the agent about the area adjacent to their post offices in their buggies, showing him the roads, filling his mind with pertinent bits of local history, and making suggestions. If they did not do this they might invite the agent to dinner or wait until he visited them at their post offices to advise him on the best plan for their vicinities. Or if they missed him altogether when he came to their communities, they would call upon him at the countyseat where he usually maintained his headquarters.

If the agent carefully followed his instructions, the postmasters never knew at the time the effect their cooperation was having on the agent's report. Consequently, rumors flew thick and fast, and the Department was accustomed to receiving scattered protests even before the agent's report was filed. One postmaster at Little Falls, Minnesota, for example, without having seen the agent's full report but hearing he was to lose one route under the new system, enlisted the help of Congressman Charles Lindbergh and for over six months he and the congressman made life miserable for DeGraw trying to get from him the agent's report and maps, so they might see what recommendations had been made and put themselves in a position to draw up a more "suitable" plan.[19]

The Department had learned to expect complaints when they released plans for a new county service and automatically withheld the starting date of the new arrangement for several weeks after the announcement, so the protests could be made and answered before the service began. But often the allotted time was not enough to answer all the indignant grievances of postmasters who, like rejected suitors, found their courtship of the rural agent had not helped them much. Where they had hoped to get at least one route, they frequently had none. Or if they had one route before the reorganization, even that might have been taken from them. Those who had expected several routes or extensions were sometimes similarly disappointed. Their old routes might be torn up and changed, valuable territory would be lost, and some rival town or postmaster would be left to gloat over them. "When Mr. Nevens [*sic*] came here to institute County service," wrote an angry postmaster at Owaneco, Illinois, upon learning the plans for the new service, "in some way he gave Millerville and Taylorville all they asked for, when I asked something from Mr. Nevens [*sic*] he gave me to understand that I would be luckey [*sic*] to retain two Routes from here, so it proved that he gave away Territory that by Honest and Fair means belongs to Owaneco. . . ."[20]

In their bitterness the postmasters would lash out in all directions to locate the sources of their troubles. Political pressure, ungrateful rural carriers, collusion between the rural agents and rival groups, the list of the people who had wronged them ran on and on. The Postmaster at Bernhard, Wisconsin, knew exactly why the Helenville post office two miles distant from him had gotten a rural route and he had not. "There is no question but what political pressure is brought to bear on this subject and an Investigation should be made," he wrote. In Marion County, Illinois, the postmaster at Brubaker who had lost his one route was sure it was the fault of the rural carrier who wanted the route changed to Salem and was using "his patrons as 'cat's paws' to gain his ends," and he wrote Senator Albert J. Hopkins asking him to see "that justice is done."[21]

Then there was always the problem of the unjust rural agent. The Brubaker postmaster complained that he had been unable to see the rural agent to discuss the matter before his route was taken from him, and the postmaster at Bernhard, Wisconsin, had succeeded in seeing the rural agent only after repeated attempts. According to the postmaster, when he did talk to him, the agent was rude and kept him standing while he went on working. When he suggested that the route he had petitioned for two years before had been given to Helenville because the postmaster there was a friend of the county chairman of the Republican party, the agent became so enraged, the postmaster reported, that had he not kept his temper the agent would have struck him.[22]

The postmaster at Owaneco had a similar experience. "I asked Mr. Nevens [*sic*] to consult the Business Men and Patrons that were making the complaint," he wrote DeGraw. "His answer to me was, 'I know to[o] D—— much now.' " And he left the office, as the postmaster remembered, in a very discourteous fashion and "in close communication with the carrier," from the rival town of Millersville.[23]

Rural Agent Nevins' retort if blunt had nonetheless been exact. He knew without talking to the businessmen of Owaneco what they would say, for wherever county rural delivery had gone into effect it was much the same. In Owaneco they had already raised petitions, which he had probably seen, claiming that "every grave injustice had been done the business interests of Owanico [*sic*], Illinois, and the people of Locust Township and the surrounding County." L. F. Danford, one of the town's businessmen found space in the *Owaneco News* to complain. "Why is it," he asked, "that in place of having an additional rural route that the two we have have been cut down. . . ? I think we are entitled to more territory. . . . I don't think it right that some man from Washington City and a postmaster from Taylorville and Pana should undertake to cut down our territory in the rural mai[l] service." Owaneco with its population of 250 was not to be belittled. "Owaneco is no suburb of either Taylorville or Pana, but stands out as the metropolis of Locust township and as a town we claim to be able to look after the best interests of the people living within a radius of 5 or 6 miles in either direction."[24]

This position was the common stand of many businessmen in the little hamlets and towns throughout the country wherever rural delivery threatened their interests. Coupled with their desire to maintain and improve their businesses went an intense pride in their towns. It was as though they must be forever defending and improving the spot where choice or fate had placed them, in order to prove that their choice had been wise or that fate had been kind.

No matter how small a village, the loyalty was the same. Marietta, Kansas, in 1905 had one general store, one blacksmith shop, and two elevators. Its citizens were proud and objected strenuously when the town failed to get a rural route after county rural delivery went into effect in Marshall County. "I believe that every man in the town has been to . . . see me upon this question of Rural Delivery," wrote the rural agent who was laying out the service, "every man pointed out with pride the advantages of Marietta over Oketo . . . ," the rival town. Similarly, the patrons about the little town of Newton, Indiana, in Charles Landis's district, became so angry when the rival town of Mellott got the route, they refused to patronize it although it ran directly through their village. According to the rural agent, the residents prided themselves "over having far the best inland town in that section of the country," and deeply resented being overlooked.[25]

The time spent by the Department's officials in answering the protests of postmasters and their friends, the businessmen, was enormous and the delay in establishing county service ran anywhere from weeks to months to years. Sometimes complaints even reached the Department before the agent had left the county. If so, the agent could immediately investigate the trouble and write a supplementary report to his chief. More likely, however, the agent had to be taken from another project and returned to the county to iron out the difficulties. It was tiresome and annoying for the agents and their supplementary reports reflected their exasperation.

A biting report from the agent who investigated the complaints of the postmaster at Brubaker, Illinois, for example, denied that the route there had been moved to Salem because the rural carrier had wanted it so. Rather, according to him, it had been done at the almost unanimous request of the patrons who were "worn out with the uncertainties and meagre mail facilities frunished [*sic*] from Brubaker by the Chicago & Eastern Illinois Railway." There was an equally vehement denial of the postmaster's contention that he had been unable to see the rural agent. On the contrary, the agent reported he had taken dinner at the postmaster's table and talked with him for hours and would have been able to talk further with him had the postmaster not been in hiding from the law because of his violation of the game laws. Furthermore, the postmaster had obtained his petition for the continuance of the route by misleading the people into believing that the post office itself was "to be suspended, the railway station abandoned, and railroad trains to cease stopping to take on passengers and freight, and that the town was to be abandoned."[26]

A supplementary report on all the trouble at Owaneco, Illinois, was equally tart. In great detail Agent Nevins explained the situation. Owaneco lay within seven miles of Taylorville and Pana, towns with a population of over 4,000 and within 21 miles of Millersville. The old routes, laid out without reference to existing service, crisscrossed and duplicated one another and left large gaps through which no service was given. Route 2 from Pana did cut into Owaneco territory, and he remedied this by moving it away from Owaneco as far as he could. But in drawing in the outgoing and incoming lines of the routes to make them more compact and to eliminate gaps and duplications, it had been necessary to reduce the length of Owaneco's two routes and give part of Route 1 to Millersville. While he had been disposed to help the postmaster at Owaneco who had vigorously asked for more territory, he had been unable to do so without injuring other post offices and patrons.

The routes as he had arranged them, Nevins reported, were all compact and omitted no one. In his opinion he had "never done a more skillful and thorough piece of work. . . ." The objections did not come, he declared, from the patrons who were being served by the rural routes, but "from the Butcher, the Baker, and the Candlestick-maker who live in the villiage [*sic*] of Owaneco, and who never receive a letter from the hands of the rural carrier." He wrote that the petition sent to the Department spoke for itself. "The only complaint here lodged is that of 'injustice' to Owanico [*sic*] and the 'business interest of the villiage [*sic*].' " Like most rural agents he did not believe that rural free delivery was established for "the aggrandisement of Postmasters of fourth-class postoffices, or to satisfy the cupidity of shopkeepers who wish to compel the farmers and their families to come to their villiage [*sic*] so that they may get a few dollars out of them."[27]

To test the reliability of their own plans the rural agents sometimes conducted polls among the rural route patrons themselves to find out where they wanted the routes to begin. When the businessmen of Davenport, Oklahoma, complained in 1909 that their territory had been taken away from them by the county rural delivery service, the rural agent who looked into the trouble found that routes from Avery, Stroud, and Chandler ran within three miles of Davenport. He visited these offices but was dissatisfied with what he had learned and decided to poll all those rural route patrons who lived in the territory claimed by Davenport. He marked out the area on a map four miles east and south and two and one-half miles west of Davenport and wrote each patron living in the area asking him to indicate the post office from which he wished to receive his mail.

Out of 136 replies he found 98 in favor of the service as it had been laid out; the rest were in favor of Davenport. "I returned to Davenport, Oklahoma," reported the agent, "and informed the gentlemen . . . of the fact that the people whom they claimed desired service from Davenport had expressed themselves to the contrary and while they expressed astonishment they did not seem wholly satisfied."[28]

A supplementary report from a rural agent explaining the situation in a county and his reasons for the recommendations he made, did not always end the matter. Agent W. J. Munro, when called upon to defend his handiwork in Mower County, Minnesota, seemingly justified his arrangement of the routes. Route 1 from Grand Meadow, as he saw it when he laid out the county system there, was much too long, its lines spread so wide that many farmers were either inconveniently served or left out altogether. More than that, it invaded territory properly belonging to Racine, and left many families unserved between itself and the Spring Valley route from the adjoining county. He had therefore reduced the Grand Meadow route in order to even up the territory and give service to those who had not had it before. Even if practical—which, in his opinion, it was not—Munro felt "it would have been neither fair or just to have made . . . Grand Meadow the point of installation of four routes and Racine one. . . ."

Just or not, the businessmen of Grand Meadow and some of the influential patrons living on the route would accept no changes in Route 1. Munro had noted that between "the little villages of Grand Meadow and Racine," there was "an intense competitive rivalry, which" verged on the ridiculous, and he might have foreseen that to cut off a part of the Grand Meadow route and give the territory to Racine would bring trouble. But even if he had expected trouble, he was probably not prepared for what happened.

Congressman James A. Tawney, a conservative Republican on whose behalf President Taft would one day make a famous speech at Winona and who had been trying since 1902 to have the county system installed there, began hearing from important constituents as soon as word of the new routes was out. Near the first of April, 1904, came a letter from M. O. Wilsie, President of the Grand Meadow Business Men's Association, informing him that the Association had passed a resolution of protest against the proposed changes in the rural routes leading from the town. "The contemplated changes . . . fail in almost every particular," wrote Wilsie, "to meet with the approval of the members of this association . . . ," and he asked for a readjustment of the service. State Representative W. A. Nolan was more emphatic. "The rural inspector . . . has simply raised the devil," he wrote Tawney. No one was satisfied; Route 1 out of Grand Meadow was chopped to pieces. A route was to start from Racine, come within three miles of Grand Meadow, and take in all the town's best territory; "Now, Tawney, for God's sake, see if you can't get another inspector to come here and look the situation over. . . ." Rather ominously, considering the year, Nolan added: "State politics looks pretty well mixed up at the present time, but up to the present . . . I have not heard of any candidates mentioned against Tawney [for the primaries], and *I do not believe there will be unless this dissatisfaction over the mail routes stirs up something.*"

But this was not the end of it. From the president of the First National Bank in Grand Meadow came a letter saying that he had been the first to petition for Route 1 out of Grand Meadow. He remembered that at the time he had circulated the petition people from Racine had mapped out a rival route that would have destroyed his own work. Now he learned to his "sorrow and amazement" that the route inspector had changed the route so as to give Racine *"the best part of the route No. 1."* which included himself and his friends. "You will perhaps better understand the situation," he wrote Tawney, "when I state that among those cut off from Grand Meadow by this proposed change are the president of the First National Bank of Grand Meadow and another director and heavy stockholder in said bank and town treasurer. Another is a member of the firm of Schmidt and Gammel stock buyers and meat men."

Protests from such powerful quarters often forced the Department to order another investigation of the county by a different rural agent, and this was done in Mower County. Within the month, a new inspection had been completed and a readjustment made. Matters were so arranged that by the use of a storage box at a crossroads, the president of the First National Bank and his friends were able to receive their mail from the Grand Meadow post office.[29]

Such situations illustrate the individual demands for special consideration which, along with the demands of postmasters and businessmen, were omnipresent problems to be considered in laying out the routes. Always there were people in rural communities who because of their position felt their mail should be brought directly to their gates rather than to a nest of boxes at a crossroads some quarter of a mile distant. Or they would insist that the carrier's direction of travel be such as to insure them an early delivery of the mail. Then there were those who tried to use the planning of the rural routes to increase their own prestige in the community. Lust for special privileges of this nature cost the Department and the rural agents dearly in time and trouble. County service in McLean County, Illinois, for example, was delayed nearly two years largely because of the efforts of one man, State Senator George W. Stubblefield, to lay out the service in accordance with his whims.

Rural Agent C. P. Johnson, a friend of Stubblefield's was sent to investigate McLean County in the fall of 1902. Unfortunately he was so pliant in Stubblefield's hands that the people in the county were soon being told that, if they wanted anything, "Stubblefield must be seen." Plans had already been drawn by February 1903 to give rural routes to small post offices throughout the county in an apparent effort to "take care of all" Stubblefield's "personal friends" when the Department felt compelled to replace Johnson with two other rural agents.

Stubblefield was miffed at this turn of events. He himself asked and had his good friend, Senator Shelby Cullom, ask the Department to return Johnson to the county. But the Department waited for the report of the new inspection while Stubblefield, according to the new agents, went about stirring up opposition to their work. In October 1903 the newly planned service went into operation, but it proved unsatisfactory and still another investigation had to be made. This time a compromise was reached. Johnson was recalled to work in the county but only on the condition that Rural Agent George A. Bennett be in charge. In 1904, almost two years after the original inspection had been made, rural delivery in McLean County was put on a workable basis.[30]

The planning of the mail service in McLean County had been checked in time to prevent a more serious miscarriage of route organizing than was finally adopted. But this was not always the case, and many individual mail routes winding through the countryside were shaped to comply with the brazen demands of prominent citizens.

In Maury County, Tennessee, in the early 1900's a local politician had secured an entire route for which there was no better reason than that it supplied his friends with house-to-house service. For himself he had obtained a backtrack of the rural route of three-eighths of a mile to bring his mail to his door. According to one rural agent the man had used the backtrack to show his influence in the establishment of rural routes and to "elevate his political prestige." He openly boasted about his achievements until the backtrack had become "the cause of dissatisfaction through the entire section."

How important this little token of his prestige was to him can be seen in the trouble he took to secure it. A backtrack of this kind could only be justified if a number of families were to be served by it, and, knowing this, he had claimed that six families would be served by bringing the mail over the backtrack to his farm. Then, in order to make good his claim he bought six boxes and had them placed in order: one apiece for his cook, his hostler, his laborer, and his tenant. One man who lived within a short distance of another rural route also had his box there, and rumor had it that he did this because he was in debt to the politician.[31]

In this clash of economic and personal interests, everyone else's claims seemed paramount to those of the farmers, and it was amazing that the farmers were able to get their mail as quickly and conveniently as they did. Preparing to lay out a county rural service, the rural agent would go into a county weighed down with a varied assortment of requests. In Fayette County, Iowa, in 1906, for example, the agent planning the new service there was advised that Congressman Gilbert N. Haugen had asked that the interests of Dr. R. F. Berry of Clermont, be taken care of. He had also a letter from the postmistress at Randalia and a petition from businessmen there, both demanding special consideration for their town. Only one person, a patron, A. J. Schmidt of Minkler, seemed to have no indirect axe to grind. All he wanted was better service when the routes were readjusted.[32]

In truth, the real farmers did far less complaining about their routes when they were being organized than anyone else. For the most part they accepted the routes as they were laid out without undue complaint even when it meant going some little distance to a crossroad for their mail. At times, however, when their interests in the mail service did not coincide with those of the businessmen and postmasters or when their interests were threatened by a rural agent's change of routes, the farmers could fight the change as vehemently as the townspeople.

When the farmers objected to the way their routes were laid out, they could petition their congressmen to intercede for them at the Post Office Department, or they could simply refuse to patronize their routes until they were changed—a weapon often more effective than petitions. What happened in Kosciusko County, Indiana, was a case in point. Congressman Brick had been promised county service there shortly before the election of 1902. In five years two investigations had been made in the county but neither had led to the establishment of a county service. In 1908 came a third. This time the Department put the agent's plans into operation in the face of opposition. The troublesome area south of Warsaw, which had too many patrons left unserved to ignore yet not enough to make up a new rural route, was finally added to what had been Route 1 from Atwood, while the route itself was transferred to Warsaw to become Route 7 from that post office. The farmers whose addresses had formerly been Atwood, were outraged, and took direct action. On the day the changes went into effect the Warsaw newspaper had a story. "Ninety angry patrons of rural route No. 7 tore down their boxes last night," it said, "and when carrier Frank Welch made his initial trip today he found only one box in place. . . . The former patrons declared they will get their mail from the general delivery window at Atwood."

The Department saved the situation only by instructing the carrier for the new route to stop at the Atwood post office on his way through the town, pick up the mail of those farmers who still wanted to receive mail from that office, and deliver it to them as he made his rounds.[33]

Out of this cauldron of conflicting rural interests, the pattern of the rural routes emerged very much as it remains today. The changes of some forty-odd years have left their marks of course, but there are still rural delivery patrons all over the nation who owe their post-office address to some conflict between the businessmen of rival rural towns or rival rural postmasters. And farmers who today still find peculiar twists and turns in their routes might discover if they cared to investigate that some of those twists and turns were the result of demands for special privilege by someone whose interests were not necessarily their own.

In 1906 a rural agent laying out the service in Jackson County, Illinois, had decided to begin a rural route from the little village of Raddle. Immediately the citizens of the rival village of Jacob, a little town to the south of Raddle, protested and demanded the route. Since the villages were on the same railroad and had equal rail service, the rural agent decided to let the district's Congressman, George W. Smith, and the county chairman of the Republican party, decide which of the two villages should have the route. Smith decided in favor of Jacob, and Jacob got the route. The Raddle post office lingered on until 1937 when even that was discontinued and Raddle had lost its identity. But Jacob, with its post office and rural route that in 1953 served 130 mailboxes, remains on the map. Who can say that the fate of these two small villages in Illinois, like the fate of others across the land, did not hinge upon a rural route and some such decision as Congressman Smith's in 1906?[34]

Mail wagons ready to start, Hillsboro, Texas

Rural mail carrier on his route near Crawfordsville, Indiana

Delivering mail in Carroll County, Maryland

Library of Congress
Like the post rider of pre-RFD days, a carrier delivers mail in the Kentucky mountains, 1940

Library of Congress
Post office and general store, Landsaw, Kentucky

Library of Congress
Post office in a general store, Lamoille, Iowa

6

THE RURAL MAILMAN IN THE HORSE-AND-BUGGY DAYS

The omniscience of an Arkansas rural mailman was tested by a patron's note. "I'm leaving for Texas," it read, "so please send my mail there."

Postal Service News, Mar. 1956

THE kingpin of the R F D was the rural mail carrier. Bearer of the news, friend and neighbor of his patrons, politician, handyman, and errand boy par excellence, he was rural America's most versatile public servant in the early 1900's and unlike any mail carrier the Post Office Department had hired before.

The rural postman was a traveling postmaster. Like Abraham Lincoln he took his post office with him, not in his hat but in his buggy, Model T, and, when progress at last caught up with him, in his V-8. Unlike the city mail carrier whose principal duties were to sort, collect, and deliver the mail, or the star route mail man who took the closed mail pouches from post office to post office across the nation's wide spaces, the rural carrier did all these things and the work of the postmaster too. His post office was his buggy and from its cramped interior he sold stamps, postcards, and envelopes. He receipted for registered letters and money orders as he went along, and in the earliest days of the service even canceled stamps. After parcel post began in 1913, the rural mailman delivered packages like an expressman. He also received them for mailing, weighed them by guess or with the little parcel-post scale he carried, and set the postage rate right at the farmer's gate. At one time he was permitted and even ordered to administer oaths to pensioners when they filled out their pay vouchers. In short, he did almost everything the fourth-class postmaster whom he replaced had done in addition to collecting and delivering the mail.[1]

But it was not enough for the rural mailman to be a mail carrier doubling as a fourth-class postmaster. Farmers were particular about the men who handled their mail, and some, like the old-timer who was afraid to leave a letter in an isolated rural mailbox for fear someone would take the stamp off it or the Maryland lady who wrote herself a letter to test the service, doubted that the R F D would ever work. And so the rural mailman had to be a kind of supersalesman, selling himself to his patrons and the R F D itself to skeptics. His success as a mail carrier and the success of the service itself depended on his ability to do just this; in turn his ability to sell himself depended very largely on his character and personality. So important was his personality in fact, that the Civil Service Commission, reporting on the R F D, once said in its best official language that there were "few branches of the public service the successful operation of which is so dependent on the personality of the employee."[2]

Obviously then, not everyone was equipped either with the character, the ability, or the temperament to be a rural mailman. For this particular job the Post Office Department had to find a special kind of man, and the man it found, or molded, to carry the mail to the farmers became as distinct an American type as the cowboy or the steamboat pilot of Mark Twain's day.

Since farmers were more likely to trust someone they knew or knew of with their mail than a stranger, the Department insisted that the rural mailman in each community be a man who lived in the area through which his route ran. This, the Department's first commandment, is still a basic rule. Second, he had to be "a man of character . . . ," an all-inclusive phrase used by the Postmaster General in 1901 and given substance in the reports and regulations that flowed like water from the Post Office Department in subsequent years. It meant, among other things, he must be absolutely honest with no criminal offense on his record. His morals, never specifically defined but always well enough understood in rural America, must be above reproach, and nothing brought a postal inspector running faster than a report that a mailman was dallying with one of his feminine patrons. Once a young carrier in Oklahoma came under suspicion for merely stopping to talk to "Young Ladies . . . all the way from a half to Three quarters of an Hour." And once when an Indiana rural mailman was charged with a violation of the moral code, not even a letter from his wife, tearfully supporting her husband, to Mrs. Woodrow Wilson could save his job for him.[3]

The rural carrier could drink no intoxicating beverages while on duty, nor could he drink to excess at any time. In fact, reading over the early postal regulations and reports, it is easy to get the impression the Post Office Department would have been very happy if all its rural mailmen had been teetotalers, and many of them were. So touchy was the Department on this matter that a Pennsylvania carrier who once asked permission to become a partner in an apple brandy distillery was flatly refused.

The Post Office Department was even concerned about the rural mailman's appearance. Not that he had to be handsome or even wear a uniform as city carriers did. But he must be neat and tidy, and whenever the occasion demanded, the Department never hesitated to remind him of this no matter how indelicate the subject might be. "It is reported to the Department that you are careless in regard to your attire and therefore present an untidy appearance," ran the admonition to the carrier. "Your attention is called to the fact that the Department expects carriers to be neat and tidy in their dress while officially employed in order that they bring no disgrace upon the service with which they are connected. It is expected that you will in the future endeavor to comply with this requirement."[4]

The rural mailman did not necessarily have to be a graduate of any school, but he did have to know how to read and write. His first civil service examination merely required him to be able to read the addresses on 25 envelopes and to fill in receipts for money orders and registered letters. But as the R F D matured so did the examinations, and by 1912 rural mail carriers were taking the same civil service examinations city carriers took. Even this examination, however, was not difficult to master, and the rural mailman could get by with little formal education.

Nevertheless, many rural carriers, like Fred White who wrote for the *Atlanta Constitution*, were literate enough to write R F D columns in their local newspapers, and the rural mailman's position in the community was such that most people thought him better educated than he was. They often compared him with the village schoolteacher—a comparison most rural carriers appreciated—and, in fact, many a rural mailman had been a country schoolteacher. But he was more likely to have been a farmer, a farmer's son or hired man, or even a displaced fourth-class postmaster. His roots were deep in agrarian America, and he was almost always cut from the same cloth as the people he served. At least this was so during the service's horse-and-buggy days. Between 1900 and 1930 he may well have been a veteran, since veterans of the Civil War, the Spanish-American War, or World War I were given preference. In 1920 his average age was forty-one.[5]

No saint but the next thing to it in the eyes of his friends along his mail route, the average rural mailman was a friendly, cooperative fellow, honest, moral, and reasonably intelligent, and just about what the Post Office Department had ordered insofar as this was possible. This was the way his supporters saw him. In 1911 young Congressman Kenneth McKellar from Tennessee, who knew many rural carriers in his own district and knew them well, called them "intelligent, honest, honorable, industrious, accommodating, and polite." They were, said he, "good citizens, good neighbors, and good friends." Seemingly, this view was shared by John O. Black, Chairman of the Civil Service Commission in 1910, who once declared that there was "no force of men with such a good record anywhere else on the face of God's green earth."[6]

If the farmers paid no such verbal tributes as these to their rural mailman, it was only because they were less articulate, not because they did not appreciate him. On the contrary, the man who brought them their mail was probably the most popular man in rural America in the early 1900's. No one was more eagerly awaited at farms all over the land than he. On almost any day, as he bounced along his route, he could look down the road and see his patrons standing by their mailboxes waiting for him. Men in faded blue overalls, women in long calico dresses, sunbonnets shading their eyes, and children in the nondescript outfits of farm children of two generations ago, all met the mailman when they could, and many an American who grew up on the farm before World War I can still remember the keen anticipation with which they waited for him and their excitement as they ran to the house shouting, "Here comes the mailman!"

Driving along in his mail wagon, with the big "U. S. Mail" sign painted on its side, the rural mailman was the only representative of the national government many of the farm folk ever saw, and he forged a kind of mystical bond between them and Washington. Time and time again it was pointed out that he was the first real assurance they had in that era so close to the hard times of the nineties that Uncle Sam had not forgotten them.[7]

All this may have added to his popularity and deepened the respect country people had for him, but it scarcely awed them. He was, after all, still their neighbor and friend, and oftentimes just the young man they had seen grow up in their neighborhood. Not even an official title and a postal wagon could make them forget they had known him for years. And so when they met him at their mailboxes, they joked and chatted with him and asked him to do all kinds of things for them and took liberties with him no other people in the nation's history had taken with Uncle Sam's mail carriers.

The farmers expected their mailman to know a good many things that were not in their mail, and to pass this information along to them. In the earliest years of the service, he was supposed to pick up the weather report before he left the post office, and weather was often a more meaningful topic of conversation at the mailbox than it is today. But he was also expected to know the vital statistics of the community—the deaths, the marriages, the births—and he usually did. Almost as soon as anyone in the community he knew when young couples along his route were expecting the stork, and nearly always knew, sometimes without being told, when a marriage was in the offing. Edward Snyder, a rural mailman in Maryland in the horse-and-buggy days, said he had seen more love affairs on his route than anything else, and could usually tell when they were about to culminate in marriage by the urgency of the correspondence that passed through his hands. One young man on his route, began writing a girl once a week, then twice a week, and finally every day. So well did Snyder read the signs that he took the young man completely by surprise one day by saying, "Ed, they tell me you're going to get married."[8]

Like the old fourth-class postmaster before him, the rural mailman knew virtually every important happening in his community, and much of it he shared with his patrons even if it sometimes bordered perilously close to gossip. Besides the vital statistics, he kept posted on the health of the families along his route, his patrons' visitors, the price of eggs in town, who was planting and who was reaping, who had a gobbler to lend, and a hundred and one little things that interested country people in those days. He even carried messages from one patron to another—outside the mail, of course—and if all the dispatches he carried had gone through the mails, postal revenues would have swelled impressively.[9]

It took time to spend a few minutes with everyone who wanted to hear the news at their mailboxes, and the Post Office Department instructed the farmers not to delay their mail carrier unduly. But these instructions were as much honored in the breach as in the observance. The mailman did try, and usually succeeded in maintaining a schedule as he was supposed to do, but it was a schedule that usually allowed for little chats with his patrons. A carrier at Norwich, Iowa, once checked his time and found it took forty minutes to walk his team two miles and serve seven boxes. Not an earth-shaking speed certainly, but one apparently synchronized with mailbox conversations.

Occasionally, however, the mailman would spend too long at one place or another, the mail would be delayed, and some patron, waiting impatiently at his mailbox, would be ready to explode when the carrier did arrive. But a patron who lost his temper ran the risk of losing the news too. There was a story of one angry patron who walked down to his neighbor's mailbox where his mailman was spending an unusually long time and demanded his mail. In silence his mail was given him, but it was not until the next day that he discovered, as the more patient farmers already had, that an elopement had taken place in the community.[10]

The farm folks were no more hesitant to ask favors of their rural mailman than they were to ask the news, and in truth, doing odd jobs and running errands for his patrons were almost as much a part of his job as carrying the mail. He was not obligated to do these extra duties, but he rarely bothered about whether he had to do this or that to hold his job. He simply did what he was asked insofar as it was possible because it was the neighborly thing to do and because he knew his patrons were not asking him to do anything for them they would not do for him if their positions had been reversed. A city mail carrier might never have understood this, but the rural mailman, steeped in the traditions of rural

America, thought nothing of being called upon to repair a patron's clothesline or run an errand for her when he reached town.

The rural mailman had no way of knowing, of course, what feats he might be asked to perform as he set out upon his route in the early morning, and each day was another adventure that might find him doing everything from feeding a patron's pigs to repairing a washing machine. A carrier at Red Oak, New York, once found a note from a young mother in the mailbox notifying him that she was dead and asking him to take care of her children. Rushing into the house, he found the woman still alive, and administered an antidote that saved her life. Another mailman at Hope, North Dakota, had to cut an old bachelor patron's hair with a butcher knife, and another in Massachusetts pulled his patron's molar with a pair of pliers.[11]

In general, the rural mailman shared in whatever fortunes or misfortunes occurred in the daily life of the farmers along his route, and to follow him for a day was to see all the many facets of rural life as it was fifty years ago. There were the heroics and the commonplace. One day he might untangle a cow from a tethering rope, and the next save a little girl from the bite of a mad dog. Indicative of what any carrier might expect was this note one of them found in a mailbox: "Dear Mail Carrier—Please feed our chickens and water the cows and the mule in the stable and if the bees have swarmed put them in a new hive. We have gone visiting."[12]

A rural mailman was often asked to address envelopes and postcards for those patrons who were more willing to trust their shaky penmanship inside an envelope than out. On at least one occasion, a carrier was not only asked to address an envelope but to supply the name of the addressee. "Please write the name on this letter of that fellow you saw me with yesterday," requested his young lady patron. "I guess you know him, don't you?" Sometimes the rural route patrons even asked their mail carrier to write their letters for them. Edward Snyder claimed to have written so many love letters for the Negro people on his route he worked out a kind of shorthand system to reduce the first paragraph which was always the same no matter who was dictating: "I take my pen in hand to write you a few lines to let you know that I am well and hope you are the same." After this came the heart of the letter with the setting of a date, sentimental tidbits, and crosses for some forty kisses at the end. Snyder estimated that all told he must have carried a million kisses over his route.[13]

Carrying mailable kisses was a rural mail man's duty, but playing Cupid was not. Yet whenever young love bloomed along his route, he was likely to have a hand in it. Probably the case of the young lady who asked her carrier to leave letters that came to her from a certain person in a neighbor's box was not unusual. In any event, it had happened to this carrier before, and he entered into the conspiracy remembering he had done the same thing for the girl's mother years before. An even greater contribution to the cause of young love was made by the rural mailman at Floris, Oklahoma. He was so interested in playing matchmaker he sent this jingle to a young lady on his route and signed someone else's initials to it:

My dearest ducky doodle,
If you will say the word;
I'll be your dear old noodle,
My darling little bird.

I have a nice 160 acres,
A little house and fence
We can raise ducks and potatoes,
And all for fifty cents.

The license costs but 50 cents,
The preacher needs no money;
Don't look at any other gent,
But please say yes my honey.[14]

There was a certain amount of danger in being the middleman in a rural love affair, however, particularly when it came to stamping letters. Sweethearts frequently left their letters in the mailbox to be stamped and mailed, and many an unsuspecting mailman, who accidentally placed stamps on such letters upside down, learned to his sorrow as he confronted some angry, weeping girl, that in love's language the turned-over stamp meant the sender wanted to terminate the correspondence.[15]

Busy as he was writing letters and watering his patrons' cows and doing all the little unexpected jobs that came his way, the rural mailman was even busier running errands for the people on his route. As often as not when he had finished his mail deliveries and was getting ready to go home, he suddenly remembered he still had a few chores to do. Perhaps he had three dozen eggs to deliver to one of his patrons' relatives who lived in town, and a ball of twine to pick up for Farmer Smith. Or he might have promised the maiden lady on his route he would pick up a light green spool of thread for her. So as soon as he had made out the report of his day's trip, posted the letters he had collected, checked his money, and taken care of his money orders, he hurried off to complete his errands.

Apparently rural route patrons in those slow-moving horse-and-buggy days, had unbounded confidence in their mailman's ability to do almost anything, for they sent him off on all kinds of errands. An Iowa carrier, for example, once had to buy a wreath for a little girl's hat so she could participate in a county church program, and a lady patron in Lloyd, Wisconsin, asked her mailman to pick out some dress material for her. He was so successful in this venture and the lady so pleased with his good taste that she continued to use him for this purpose from time to time.[16]

In the early years of the service, the farmers sometimes paid their mail carrier a small fee for bringing them goods from town. The nature of the payment was indicated in a note one carrier found in a box: "Mr. Carrier, please bring: Sugar, $1.00; Coffee, $1.00; prunes, 50¢; yeast foam, 10¢; cookies, 25¢; steak, 50¢; and bring sack (two if you can) flour, and here is 10¢ for your trouble." In spite of such paltry fees for the work involved, the Post Office Department at first encouraged this package business, because it did give the carriers a little something to supplement their low pay and do their patrons a favor at the same time. But the business, which was supposed to be purely local, soon began to get out of hand. Enterprising businessmen in the large cities—seeing a way to use the rural mailmen to their own advantage—began to ship their goods by express to the little towns from which rural routes emanated. There, by a prearranged agreement, the rural mailmen picked them up and carried them to their destination outside the mails and, of course, without postage.[17]

To entice the rural mailman into doing business for them, the large business firms advertised in the *R.F.D. News*, the weekly publication for members of the National Rural Letter Carriers' Association, and all of a sudden in the early 1900's the mail carrier found he could make money outside his regular job. "We Pay Big Money For Information," ran one advertisement from a Chicago store. "No soliciting, no work—just a little thinking and a few moments spent in writing us a letter." Other advertisements assured him he could make money by taking orders for household goods, distributing free samples of a certain product, selling insurance, and giving information on people moving West. One notice was an especially interesting sign of the times: "One postal card may earn any R.F.D. carrier a month's salary. If used to send us the names of persons contemplating building a farmers' telephone system. . . ."[18]

With moneymaking opportunities growing as fast as weeds along the roads many a rural mailman, good American that he was with his eye on the main chance, began to expand his package business into more profitable channels until, as someone noticed, his express business came first and the mail second. "They sell," said the *New York Sun* reporting on the activities of the rural mailman in 1904, "provisions, dry goods, furniture, horseshoes, farming implements, fertilizer, chocolate caramels, and tar roofing; take subscriptions for newspapers, magazines, and turf investment bureaus; insure lives and houses, erect lightning rods, and put down driven wells." One Iowa mail carrier's business was reported to be so immense he had three large wagons following him as he delivered the mail![19]

The mailman's practice of selling newspaper subscriptions was one of the easiest ways to get ahead in those days when the R F D was new. Driving along his route, he could, almost without effort, sell one subscription after another to news-hungry farmers who had never before taken a daily newspaper or a magazine, and for his good work, the newspapers rewarded him handsomely, either with money or a new buggy or some other cherished piece of equipment.

Because he was their best salesman in the countryside, rival newspapers sometimes vied for his services, and when they did, the rural mailman, probably for the first time in his life, found himself with the unaccustomed power to drive a hard bargain. This power he occasionally exercised, playing one newspaper off against another. When a newspaper in Mississippi, for example, failed to meet his terms, a rural mailman wrote the managers of the paper telling them he had been in a position to help them, but now he had taken up with a competitor. "Only today," he wrote, "I got three subscribers for them [the rival newspaper] and two people ordered me to stop [your newspaper] which I said I would do with pleasure. . . ."[20]

All this business activity on the part of the rural mailman worried the Post Office Department, partly because many nonlocal parcels that should have been mailed were being sent outside the mails and partly because home-town merchants, whose trade was falling off, were raising protests that could be heard all the way from Mount Ayr, Iowa, to Washington, D.C. The result was that in 1903 the Postmaster General recommended legislation to curb the mailman's business activities.

The difficulty with this recommendation was that many congressmen were reluctant to do anything to disturb the local errand service that had become so important to the farmers, and in the House of Representatives the matter was warmly debated. Only after a torrent of words had been unleashed did Congress solve this thorny problem. After 1904, it was decided, the rural mailman could no longer solicit business nor carry mail-order parcels outside the mails as he had. But his right to carry unmailable matter and parcels made up of strictly local goods weighing less than four pounds remained, and even today the rural mailman may still be used as the farmers' errand boy.[21]

The farmers made heavy demands on their mailman, it was true, and many rural carriers could hardly remember a day when they had not been asked to run an errand or "do a favor" for their patrons. Yet the relationship between a mailman and his patrons was not altogether a one-sided affair. Actually the farmers were as quick to grant favors as they were to expect them. On winter days after a new-fallen snow, while the carrier blazed a trail through drifted snow, the farmers were often ready to give him a hand when the need arose, to loan him a horse perhaps, to invite him in for lunch and warmth, or even to go ahead of him, if the drifts were very bad, to clear the road. A Connecticut carrier reported in 1902 that he had missed only one day during a spell of blizzard conditions because the farmers were out with cattle to break the roads for him. All day long, on one occasion, he had had eight yoke of cattle and one pair of horses ahead of him breaking trail.[22]

The rural mailman was the recipient of the farmers' openhanded generosity in a hundred ways. In the mailboxes he opened during the day he was as likely to find a piece of cake or a sandwich, or on a cool, frosty morning, a steaming cup of hot coffee, as a farmer's letter, and like the village preacher, he sometimes found his larder replenished as well. Everything from pigs' livers after butchering day to bags of onions came his way from grateful farmers who were anxious to help their mailman make ends meet. Even today the average rural carrier still finds his mailboxes stuffed with goodies from time to time and with as many presents at Christmas time as his predecessor along the route found in the earliest days of the service. But the modern carrier gets no help from his patrons in supplying fuel for his locomotive. In this, the rural mailman of two generations ago had an advantage over his automobile-enslaved successor.[23]

In the horse-and-buggy days, when the mail carrier's salary was small and the upkeep of his horses and equipment cost so much, the farmers rarely hesitated to help supply hay and grain for their carrier's horses when they knew there was need. An interested patron would simply jump in his wagon and tour the community, picking up first one thing from one farmer and something else from another until he returned after a few hours' work with a wagonload of feed for the mailman's horses. One group of farmers even went so far in 1903 as to sign an agreement pledging themselves to help their carrier: "We, the undersigned patrons on mail route No. 1, agree to donate the following amounts of grain to our esteemed friend and mail carrier, Jack Neal, responsive to the many kind and accommodating acts shown us."[24]

But not all the mailman's relationships with his patrons were so pleasant. Let the carrier misplace a letter or a magazine, be a little late at the mailbox, or fail to deliver the mail on a stormy day, and some of his patrons were ready to tar and feather him. Often they sent angry letters to the Post Office Department denouncing him. "I wish to inform you in regard to James Crilley mail carrier on Route No. 1 . . . ," began a typical patron's complaint. "He dont give satifachon he dont go all the way round his trip. . . . He dont carry supplies passes boxes with signals up goes in houses shows his mail delays time and misses the train almost every day. . . . Dont report to P.M. for she will try to shield him bot send A strange man Detective to meet him and look on him going the trip. . . . U.S. has lot of men to hunt things like this so dont throw this in the wast Basket but Investigate right away."[25]

Complaints like this were the most common, but the farmers'

charges against their mailman ran all the way from embezzlement to the less sophisticated transgressions of "mixing with bad women" and the use of profanity. Very often they arraigned him for drinking or drunkenness, and it was not unusual to find in the annual reports of the Civil Service Commission that carriers had been dismissed from the service because their patrons protested that they "drank to excess." Indeed, the mailman's jousts with John Barleycorn sometimes concerned not only the patrons on the route but the entire community. In the little community of Chestnut Bluff, Tennessee, in 1912, the village mayor and the Methodist minister took up the matter of the mailman's possession of liquor in a letter to the Fourth Assistant Postmaster General: "We the Undersigned do ask that you see to it the Rural Carrier on Rout No 2—*Chestnut Bluff Tenn* stops bringing whiskey on his Rout he has been doing this thing and can be proven. Wanting an eerly relief."[26]

Complaints against the rural mailmen were plentiful in the horse-and-buggy days, but unless the carrier was extraordinarily inept, charges did not come from the average farmer. Rather they originated with rural cranks or patrons with ulterior motives, and the nature of their attacks often told as much about the kind of neighborhood a mailman delivered the mail in as it did about the carrier himself.

Jealousy, old neighborhood quarrels, and imagined slights were all motives for condemning the rural mailman. When a carrier at Goodison, Michigan, failed to take some outgoing letters from a mailbox because of insufficient postage, an angry patron wrote the Department: "Now the carrier has it in for me . . . over some trouble in a secret meeting 'Ancient Order of the Gleaners' and did not take the letters just to be mean." This was as typical as the case of the Georgia carrier who was accused of drunkenness and of using profanity in the presence of a young woman apparently because his accuser wanted someone else to have the mail carrier's job. On one occasion, an Oklahoma carrier was attacked simply because a small group of people wanted to strike at his father who had been a witness in a bitter trial in the community.[27]

Among the most vindictive of all those who indulged in what the rural people called "spite work" against the carrier were those whom the mailman had excelled in the rural carrier civil service examination. With lies and distortions such men would stir up opposition to the rural mailman along the route and even threaten him with violence. On three separate occasions, the mail carrier at Luther, Iowa, had been subjected to a "good cussing" by a man he had beaten in the examination, but the day his old rival told him he could break every bone in his body "and several more things which would have been rather unpleasant," was too much. Before he had time to think it over, the mailman wrote out his resignation "to take effect the day of this letter."[28]

Twice a year, as a matter of course, a postal inspector rode the route with the mailman making a formal inspection, but since every complaint against him must be answered, the rural carrier might be inspected as often as charges were brought against him. Whenever the Department received a complaint against a carrier, both he and his postmaster were asked for an explanation. Occasionally a postmaster who harbored bitter feelings toward his mail carrier, for whatever reason, used this opportunity to undercut him. If this happened and if his own reply was unsatisfactory, a postal inspector was ordered to make an investigation. If the charges proved false the mailman came off with nothing worse than the embarrassment of an investigation. On the other hand, if the charges were true, the mail carrier might be reprimanded, suspended, or relieved of his job.[29]

This system had its unsavory aspects which were only relieved by the conscientious postal inspector's determination not to do the mailman an injustice. Yet it was the Department's only way of keeping its public servants in line; and if rural mailmen across the country tended to resemble one another and become a distinct American type, the patrons and their complaints and the inspectors and their investigations were largely responsible.

While the farmers had their grievances against their mail carrier, the mail carrier also had his against his patrons. He particularly disliked the farmers' habit of leaving loose change for stamps scattered about the bottom of the mailbox. On a cold winter morning he had to stick an ungloved hand into an icy box, feel around with numbed fingers until he had picked up all the change, and then try to transfer the money to his buggy without dropping any of it in a snowbank. If he failed, the money disappeared in the snow, and rather than search for it he often made it up out of his own pocket.

Another trait that annoyed the rural mail carrier was his patron's reluctance to buy more than one or two stamps at a time. Probably this was due to the farmer's thrifty nature. In any case he rarely left more than enough money to cover the cost of whatever postage he needed for that day, and if by chance he did leave more, he usually wanted change in return, not stamps. Edward Snyder once made the mistake of leaving stamps instead of change for one of his lady patrons. On the next day she met him at the mailbox and demanded the change instead of stamps. Yet according to Snyder, the day after that there was a quarter in the box and an unstamped letter!

But perhaps even this peculiarity was preferable to the custom practiced by some patrons of leaving eggs or butter or some other commodity in the mailbox to pay for a stamp. At least with the money for the stamps in hand, the carrier knew exactly where he stood financially. But the precise number of stamps a dozen eggs or a pound of butter would buy was always something of a problem and one probably rarely solved to the mailman's satisfaction.[30]

For the most part the mailman, unlike his patrons, had to bear his irritants in silence, since in the mail service, as in business, the customer was always right. But occasionally he would subtly try to induce his patrons to change their habits. To end the penny nuisance one carrier passed along this advice to his fellow carriers: "Never give back one cent after you get it. You will soon have all his [the patron's] pennies." Another carrier, hoping to shame a lady patron into stamping her letters, left in her mailbox the two cents she had placed there for postage but mailed her letter anyway. According to his report, he scored a major victory by this ruse, but unfortunately his technique required a certain faith in the perspicacity of rural route patrons, and there was no evidence that his solution was ever widely adopted.[31]

Actually the rural mailman could do very little to change his patrons' habits in the horse-and-buggy days, and he soon learned to accept with grace what he could not change. And if he could not accept the situation, he resigned as the rural mailman at Heilwood, Pennsylvania, did in 1910. When the Department asked this man to explain why he had refused to put mail in a patron's locked box even though he had a key to the box, the mailman, after explaining that there was no need for locked boxes along his route, was apparently overcome by the injustice of it all. "If it is necessary for me to carry a key to unlock Hill's box," he wrote, "you can consider this my resignation to take effect by Jan 1st 1910, as I positively will not bother with any locks on my route."[32]

But in spite of the number of times the rural mailman drove away from some crotchety farmer's mailbox muttering about the ungratefulness of mankind, he could be thankful that most of his patrons were decent, pleasant people, understanding when he was late, forgiving when he made a mistake. According to one South Carolina congressman the patrons on routes in his district in 1903 were confident they had the best mailmen in the service, and the carriers themselves, almost to a man, vowed they served the best people on earth. And this was generally the story of the mailman's relations with his patrons.[33]

Unique in the intimacy of his relations with his patrons, the rural mailman was also unique in the pride he took in his work and in his somewhat fierce determination to serve his route each day whatever the condition of road and weather. Indeed, no actor ever believed "the show must go on" with greater fervor than the rural mailman believed "the mails must go through," and he, more than any of the Post Office Department's mail carriers, added a new dimension to the paraphrase of Herodotus's famous lines that "neither snow, nor rain, nor heat, nor gloom of night stays these couriers from the swift completion of their appointed rounds."

Even Herodotus's Persian messengers could have battled no worse conditions of roads and weather than American winters brought to the rural mailman some fifty years ago. In many areas of the nation it was a common occurrence to see the mailman setting off in his sleigh or buggy or riding his horse to deliver the mail with the thermometer reading below zero and the wind whistling about his ears and the sky dark and threatening. Stoically accepting the worst the overcast sky could bring, the mailman would spend his day uncovering mailboxes and fighting snowdrifts that covered his road from fence to fence, and return at night to the post office to write terse, little reports of conditions along his route that gave only the barest inkling of his day's problems. Here is the log of one rural mail carrier in North Dakota for December 1910: "December 7—'Snowdrifts.' On December 16, '. . . severe snowstorm: too dangerous to go out.' On the 18th, 'snowdrifts.' On December 21, 'drifted roads'; on the 23rd, 'drifted roads'; on the 24th, 'roads drifted'; on the 25th, 'wind and snow'; on the 27th, 'blizzarding'; on the 28th, 'snow-clogged roads'; on the 29th, 'exhausted team'; on the 30th, 'drifted roads'; and on the 31st, 'soft-snow grade.' "

Sometimes the rural carrier never made it back to the post office at the end of the day. Instead darkness found him still miles from home, his team exhausted, his route unfinished. At such times he spent the night at the nearest farmhouse. A few carriers in the horse-and-buggy age never reached shelter at all. Caught in a blizzard at Appleton, Minnesota, in 1910, one rural mailman lost his way and had to spend eighteen hours cooped up in his postal wagon. When the storm broke he found one of his horses dead and the other nearly so. Ironically, he also found he had spent the night less than forty rods from a farmhouse.[34]

Admittedly, the rural mail carrier often fought the bitter storm less because of his pride in his job than for fear of losing his pay, or a part of it, if he failed to go. Although the local postmaster had the right to decide whether or not a rural mail carrier's pay should be cut for his failure to serve his route, it was generally understood that, regardless of weather, unless at least an attempt was made to deliver the mail, the carrier was in danger of losing his day's pay.

There is not much doubt that this consideration crossed Carrier L. W. Wilson's mind as he faced his job one stormy Minnesota morning. "I started down to the post office," he told a congressional investigating committee in 1912, "and in going five blocks I froze my face . . . the thermometer stood at 32 below zero. The air was filled with snow, so that it was impossible to see half a block facing the storm, and the wind was possibly 25 to 30 miles an hour. It was a very severe and violent storm. We reported at the office to put our mail up, and I started to take a part of my mail and go out and attempt to serve it on foot, and the postmaster told me it was foolish to make the attempt. . . . I told him . . . I could go out a mile and serve four boxes and conscientiously report that I had made the attempt. . . ."[35]

Carrier Wilson was obviously inspired by the profit motive in this case, as no doubt most rural carriers would have been under similar circumstances. On the other hand, nothing but devotion to duty compelled James A. Holt, rural carrier at Owensville, Missouri, to spend four hours in the floodwaters of a creek fishing out the mail that had spilled when his buggy overturned in the stream. He had been lucky to have saved himself, and no one would have blamed him or docked his pay if he had lost the mail. Yet he had returned to the water on the back of one of his horses and managed to save both the first-class and parcel-post mail.[36]

The conscientious rural letter carrier, knew the importance of delivering first-class mail as quickly as possible. He knew too that winter days were shut-in days on the farm and that then, when they had leisure to read more than at any other time, the farmers appreciated having their daily newspapers and magazines. The responsibility of delivering the daily to them, as well as of upholding the efficiency of the service, rested heavily on the conscience of most rural mailmen in the horse-and-buggy days, and probably a sense of duty as much as anything else drove them out in the face of a winter's blizzard to deliver the mail. A poem that went the rounds the year before World War I broke out, had it about right.

> A fierce and bitter storm's abroad
> It is a bleak mid-winter's day
> And slowly o'er the frozen sod
> The postman's pony picks its way.
> The postman and his horse are cold
> But fearlessly they face the gale:
> Though storms increase a hundredfold
> The farmer folk must have their mail.[37]

Pride, profit, or duty, whatever it was that motivated him, the rural mailman made heroic efforts through winter and spring to deliver the farmer's mail. "Go out into the country as I have done . . . ," said a Missouri congressman one day in 1911, "and you will see that there are certain seasons of the year when these men are almost entirely prevented from performing their duties on account of the conditions of roads and weather. . . . In my own district I know of cases where the roads have become well-nigh impassable in the spring of the year; times in fact when it is impossible for them to travel with a horse, much less with a horse and buggy—conditions under which the ordinary man would feel furnished a sufficient excuse to neglect his duty, but not so with many of these loyal, brave boys, for I have known some of them to put the mail upon their backs and attempt to walk over their routes, leaving the roads, which are impassable, and crossing the fences and through the field; traveling on foot as far as it was possible to go so to return within the schedule time to their office."[38]

To make doubly sure the mail would be delivered every day, rural mailmen were required to hire a substitute who would always be ready to take the mail when they could not. Many rural mailmen appointed their wives as their substitutes and so kept the salary in the family, and wives normally made good mail carriers. As a matter of fact, there were a number of regular women mail carriers in the service in the horse-and-buggy days, and many of them served their routes on blustery days with the same élan the men did. A woman carrier in Delaware once won a commendation from the Fourth Assistant Postmaster General for venturing out on her route in a severe snowstorm and serving all but four of her patrons at a time when none of her male colleagues at her post office dared set foot on their routes.

But the world of the rural mail service was basically a man's world, and the Department usually frowned on women carriers both because the work was sometimes heavy and because of nature's laws. For example, five years after the Delaware woman's heroic bout with the severe snowstorm, a postal inspector found it necessary to write the Department on her behalf. "Mrs. Donahue . . . ," he wrote, "is a married woman, and in the course of human events, has become pregnant. She is desirous of knowing if she would be allowed leave of absence without pay for a period of *nine months. . . .*" Such interruptions were naturally troublesome to the Department, and perhaps for this reason women were rarely taken into the service, if men were available, no matter what their score on the civil service examination. Nevertheless, those women who did become rural carriers seemed to take as much pride in their job as the men did.[39]

The pride the rural mailman had in his job was often reflected in his equipment as well as in the tribulations he endured. Like the cowboy who took delight in his fine boots and chaps and saddle, the rural carrier cherished good equipment. His horse and buggy were a part of his business and his way of life, and just as his trappings stamped the cowboy as a special kind of person, so did the rural mailman's equipment distinguish him from the farmers in the community and certainly from his fellow mail carriers in the city.

The city mail carrier needed only a pair of shoes, a uniform, two good feet, and two good legs to put him in business. But a rural mailman was unable to get by so cheaply. Although his needs varied from section to section, almost every rural mailman before World War I had to have at least one horse, harness, and a buggy of some sort. Most carriers thought they needed a minimum of two horses, and those who had long routes and had to keep two horses at some farm midway along their routes where they exchanged teams daily, needed as many as four. Where winters were severe and the snow deep, a sleigh was an unquestioned necessity.

Since the Post Office Department demanded only that a mail carrier's equipment be of creditable appearance, the R F D mail wagon did not have to be made from any one particular blueprint and the rural mailman was free to use almost any kind of vehicle. Nevertheless, there was a marked uniformity among those most commonly in use. Companies like the Delphi Wagon Works at Delphi, Indiana, and the Terre Haute Carriage and Buggy Company at Terre Haute, made a specialty of rural mail wagons, and the Terre Haute Company built one called "The Postman" which, according to the company, was found in every state. It had Sarven, non-malleable wheels, cushion springs, and a 1,000-mile long-distance axle. Like the wagon Sears, Roebuck and Company was offering in 1904, No. 11Y1033, for $47.25, "The Postman" was a one- or two-horse, four-wheeled vehicle that could be buttoned up in winter with sliding doors and windows and opened in summer. It had built-in drawers for money and postal supplies and pigeon-holes for the mail.

If the rural mailman was very progressive, as many of them were, and was keeping up with the advertisements in the *R.F.D. News*, the chances are he also had a little heater in his wagon in the wintertime. Judging from its advertisement, the Clark heater was just what the carrier needed. It used Clark's carbon briquettes for fuel, and the manufacturers boasted that it had "no flames, no smoke, no dirt," and it made "the closed vehicle as comfortable as a steam heated room in the coldest weather." Apparently the Clark heater was a great improvement over the oil heater that produced both dirt and smoke.

The color of his post wagon was again a matter for the carrier to decide, though for the sake of uniformity, the Fourth Assistant Postmaster General in 1909 urged them all to paint their wagons green and red. But blue, red, green or some color in between, like the rest of his equipment, it was apt to be neat and trim, and just as people sometimes believed they could tell a good farmer by the condition of his mailbox, so one could judge a mail carrier by his equipment.[40]

The cost of the mailman's equipment was never easy to determine precisely because costs varied in various parts of the nation. But harried congressmen, plowing through reams of statistics, tried earnestly to come to some conclusion on the matter. In 1902 Congressman Ebenezer Hill from Connecticut deduced that a carrier's equipment cost about $180. Five years later, an Illinois congressman placed the cost at about $330, and a survey of North Dakota carriers made in 1909 put the cost at $700. A joint congressional committee established in 1920 estimated after a prolonged investigation that on the standard horse-drawn route the average carrier's equipment had cost him $662.03.[41]

In view of the times, almost any of these figures suggest it was expensive to go into the rural delivery business, and indeed it was. But as far as the mailman himself was concerned, the original cost of his horses and equipment worried him no more than the continual expense of maintaining them. From 1902 on the cost of keeping a horse, like the cost of operating a car in recent times, rose constantly. The bushel of oats that cost 35 cents in 1904, was 59 cents in 1910, and 85 cents in the year of America's entry into World War I. Besides this, wagons and harness had to be repaired. Horses had to be shod, as often as every ten days in a Wisconsin winter, and their illnesses cared for.

Usually the rural mailman took especially good care of his horses. He exchanged information on their care and feeding with other carriers through the pages of the *R.F.D. News*, and he read religiously the veterinarian's column in the same paper. But all this did not prevent a horse from getting distemper or wearing out and forcing the carrier to pay either for a veterinarian's services or a new horse. And if in addition to all these expenses, the mailman had also been the victim of an accident along his route, his repair bill for harness and wagon could easily surpass his month's wages.[42]

Accidents were no novelty along the rural mail routes in the early 1900's. Stories of runaways, overturned wagons, broken equipment, and broken arms appeared often enough in the pages of the *R.F.D. News* to make them commonplace. A loud noise, a snapped tug, or an unfamiliar sight, such as a "horseless carriage," were enough to send horses, buggy, and mail carrier careening down the road until disaster overtook them. One day in 1903 a carrier at Salem, Oregon, was merely backing his team and buggy out of a shed after the noontime rest, when the tongue of the buggy dropped from the neck yoke and frightened the horses. Before he could check them, they had upset the buggy, leaving him with a broken shoulder and one of his horses with a broken leg.[43]

The cost of his equipment and the burden of his expenses, kept the rural mailman just one jump ahead of his creditors. If he fell behind in making his payments, his creditors wrote to the Post Office Department and the Department, though it stoutly maintained it was not a collection agency, wrote the carrier pointed little notes asking for an immediate explanation. With pressure being exerted at both ends and scarcely enough money to meet his obligations, it was no wonder the rural mail carrier was extraordinarily salary conscious throughout the service's horse-and-buggy days.[44]

The rural mailman's salary was a major problem in the days before the First World War, not only to him but to congressmen, senators, postal officials, and everyone else who had anything to do with it. He was such a maverick among his kind he could not even be paid on the same basis that other mail carriers were. In the city, postmen could be paid on a fairly equitable basis. They walked about the same number of miles each day, carried about the same amount of mail, and worked about the same number of hours. But in the rural service these things varied. One rural mail route might be twenty-eight miles long, and another only sixteen. One-hundred and twenty-five people might live along one route and only seventy-five on another. To complete his route one carrier might work ten hours, another only three. In spite of these variations, Congress could think of no other solution to the salary problem than to pay the rural mailman according to the length of his route. In 1904 a standard route was declared to be twenty-four miles long. If a carrier had such a route, he drew full pay. If his route was shorter his salary was reduced, but if it was longer, he received no extra pay for it.[45]

Few people who knew anything about it even pretended that this arrangement was fair. A route of sixteen miles over rough terrain and poor roads might take longer to complete than a standard twenty-four-mile route. A short route in a densely populated area running through a thicket of mailboxes, might entail more work than a longer route across the plains of western Kansas. But no allowance was made for this, and it was entirely possible for one carrier to work fewer hours than his neighboring colleague and yet draw more pay.

As perplexing as the problem of how to pay him was the more important question of how much to pay him. From the beginning of the service his salary had been scandalously low. The foremost argument against the R F D had been its anticipated price tag, and in the experimental days of the service neither the men in charge of it nor its friends in Congress dared advocate higher salaries for the mail carriers lest they add weight to their opponents' argument and eventually see the service chopped off.

Consequently, the rural mailman's pay of $300 a year in 1897 never rose above $500 while rural delivery remained an experiment, and only reached $600 a year in 1902 when the R F D became permanent. This was somewhat below the city carrier's maximum salary, and, unlike the city carrier who had few on-the-job expenses, the rural mailman had to buy and maintain his equipment from his $600. One carrier totaling up a month's bills in 1903 found that after he paid $3.00 to the blacksmith, $17.00 for feed for his horses, a $2.00 bill to the veterinarian, $1.75 for harness repair, and $1.25 for interest on his note at the bank, he had exactly $25.00 left. Of this he had to spend $8.00 for rent which left him $17.00 to spend for food, clothes, doctor bills, and the usual run of things.[46]

If the plight of this particular carrier was exaggerated, it was not greatly so. Hundreds of rural mailmen were in an almost identical predicament, and from time to time the Post Office Department was overrun with the resignations of those who believed they could do better back on the farm. Congressman Ebenezer Hill, for example, reported in 1902 that there had been eight resignations on one route alone in his district in Connecticut. The great majority of carriers, however, refused to give up, and instead lifted up their eyes unto Washington for help.[47]

To plead his cause in Washington the rural mailman had an organization called the National Rural Letter Carriers' Association. Founded in 1903, the Association never grew as rapidly before World War I as the city carriers' aggressive National Letter Carriers' Union, probably because the rural mailman with his agrarian roots and undimmed individuality mistrusted anything remotely resembling a labor union. Indeed, even today the National Rural Letter Carriers' Association, which has maintained its identity in spite of pressure to merge with the city carriers' union, bears more similarity to a fraternal lodge than a labor union, and the average rural mailman would probably hotly deny that his association was a union. Still, it played the union's role, and in the first thirteen years of its history, effectively substituting noise for numbers, rallied the rural carrier to his own defense and taught him how to get a hearing in Washington.[48]

Through the pages of the *R.F.D. News* and the editorials of H. H. Windsor and Wisdom D. Brown, two men who vigorously fought his battles for him in these years, the rural mailman kept abreast of the progress of rural delivery appropriation bills in Congress and the activities of his friends and enemies there. At the request of the editors of the *R.F.D. News* and the association's officers he gathered pages of statistics to show how his expenses were swallowing up his salary, and sent them to Washington where they were compiled and used by friendly congressmen to support arguments for increases in his pay. Through his association he also learned the value of having the farmers along his route write to their congressmen on his behalf when the debate on his salary bills reached a crucial stage, and so awesome did the possibilities of this technique appear to some members of Congress one of them warned his colleagues in 1902 that within three years "there will not be a man who can be elected to Congress or even to the United States Senate, unless he shall accede to the demands these people make."[49]

The effectiveness of this appeal to Congress was revealed in the rapid rise of the rural carrier's salary. In just twelve years from the time the RFD became permanent, the mailman's wages were revised upward five times while city carriers and postal clerks received but one raise in the same period. It was interesting too that the Post Office Department had not heartily recommended all these salary increases. In fact, in at least one case the Department had actually opposed the raise, and after an increase had been voted, tried by dubious administrative procedures, to withhold some of the increases from the carriers. But, again exhibiting that friendly disposition toward rural mail carriers it had usually shown, Congress forced the Department to disgorge that part of their pay it had withheld, so that the rural mailmen would receive all that Congress had originally intended.[50]

Even allowing for the fact that the rural mailman was a "Johnny-come-lately" in the salary race, that his pay did not match the city carrier's until 1914 when he received $1,200 a year for a standard route, and that he had equipment expenses the city carrier did not, still the speed with which Congress came to his aid was remarkable. It suggested not only the strength of his association but inspired the belief that this friendly, many-sided mailman, besides being a traveling postmaster, handyman, and errand boy, was also a politician of sorts with an almost legendary power in Congress.

Though the rural mailman's political power, like other ghosts that sometimes rise to haunt American politicians, was somewhat exaggerated, it did exist nonetheless, and there was no doubt that the man who carried the mail to the farmers often disclosed a strong political bent. The civil service statistics leave no doubt of that. Before the First World War and even into the 1920's and 1930's the Civil Service Commission reports show that he was the most politically prone of all Uncle Sam's civil servants. In 1915, to take but one year, the commission reported 157 violations of the political rules, and 68 of these were committed by rural carriers. Two years later, out of a total of 97 political activity violations,

52 were charged to rural mailmen. These were exceptional years to be sure, but from 1910 to 1925, the rural mailman led the parade of those punished for breaking political rules.[51]

Not every rural mailman was a politician, of course, and perhaps not even a majority were; but in the horse-and-buggy days it was hard for him to avoid some kind of political activity. This was partly due to the nature of the man himself. Friendly and gregarious and sometimes garrulous, the good rural mailman was a natural-born politician. Sometimes he had been involved in local politics before he became a mail carrier, and if so, then politicking to him was a mere matter of changing the locality of his activities from the general store to his mail wagon. But even if he had no political experience, he was often a man of strong partisan feelings who could take to talking politics as easily as he took to sorting mail. Thanks perhaps to the fact that he carried the news about with him all day and absorbed a good part of it as he rode along, he had a lively, if biased, interest in the affairs of the day, and to forbid such a man to discuss political issues with his public scattered along country roads was only to invite disobedience.

In fairness to him, however, it must be said that he did not initiate all the political talks in which he engaged. Since he was a representative of the United States government and better educated than many of his patrons, they often asked him for his political views and even, on occasion, how to vote. In such cases, it was asking too much of human nature to expect the politically minded rural mailman not to supply the correct information although it may have been against the rules.

If the rural mailman broke the regulations against political activity more often than other civil servants, the rural delivery system itself was partly to blame. Like the old rural mail service it replaced, the R F D was never completely free from politics in the early 1900's, and the rural mail carrier was caught in the political web it spun. For years the fourth-class postmaster, who had been the mainspring of the old rural mail service, had been a politician as well, and a vital part of his congressman's political machine in rural areas. Now, with his displacement by the rural mail carrier, the machine needed repair, and shortsighted indeed would have been that congressman who could not see that a good rural mailman whom he had helped to appoint would be, in many respects, more valuable to him in a political capacity than the fourth-class postmaster had ever been. And, with the administration in Washington also eager to see its own men carrying the mail to thousands of rural voters every day, it often happened that a man's political affiliation in addition to his character and intelligence would have something to do with his appointment as a rural mailman.

The first rural mail carriers were purely political appointees, appointed by their congressman and subject only to the approval of the patrons. When the R F D became permanent in 1902 and came under civil service, the rural agent who gave and graded the written examination was permitted to score the applicant on such intangible factors as their standing in the community and the patrons' reaction to them as well as on his answers to the questions. This arrangement was considered necessary to make certain the man hired for the job would be agreeable to the farmers. But in effect it permitted the rural agent, who was himself a political appointee, to select the rural carrier and thousands of carriers were appointed in this fashion.[52]

For obvious reasons the Civil Service Commission disapproved of this method of hiring mail carriers; in 1904 the rural agent's evaluation was discontinued, and the man who stood highest in the written examination was to be given first chance at the job. If as many as five families along the route disapproved of him, however, the post went to the next highest man.[53]

It is doubtful that the new system completely eliminated politics in the selection of rural mail carriers, and by putting so much emphasis on the examination, it may have inspired applicants to try to get the job by underhanded methods. In any event, cheating, and even bribery, were frequently reported in connection with the writing of the civil service examination. The letter of a candidate in Minnesota to the rural carrier examining board was illustrative of the lengths some men were willing to go to become one of Uncle Sam's rural mail carriers. "I will make you a present," he wrote the board, "of $25.00 if you give me the route. There is not anybody that knows what my standing is, for I never told what it was. That is all I can afford to give, but if I get the route and haul the mail for a month I will give you $25.00 more."[54]

Nevertheless, the appointment of the rural carrier was now as free from political jobbery as it was ever to be. Indeed, for a time this method of hiring was a shining example of civil service at its best, for no other civil servants were chosen on such a basis. Every other branch of the government chose its employees from the three applicants who ranked highest on any given examination, and this left room for a certain amount of political juggling. The Civil Service Commission praised the new method, and once said there was less friction in employing rural mail carriers than any other civil employees.[55]

The Civil Service Commission's high regard for this method of hiring rural letter carriers, however, did not prevent President Taft from changing it. In December 1911 he gave orders that a rural mailman's appointment be made from among the three who stood highest in any given examination just as all other civil servants were.

The *R.F.D. News* suggested that President Taft made the change because he knew the rural carriers were opposed to him, and he wanted to select men friendly to his administration, and this may have been his reason. Officially it was explained that the order was given so that the personality of the applicant, always of paramount importance in the rural service, might be considered in employing the rural carrier. Naturally the President's order forbade playing politics with the appointments, but in practice the rural carrier's appointment again became political, if indeed it had ever been anything else. And this change, coming as it did shortly before the Democrats were to take charge of the government in Washington for the first time since 1897, made possible a great number of political selections among the rural mailmen.[56]

Of all the political offenses with which the rural carrier was charged, none drew more unfavorable comment or caused more commotion than his efforts to pressure Congress into raising his pay. A particularly notorious example of this occurred in 1904, when, in spite of President Roosevelt's famous "gag order" forbidding civil servants from importuning their congressmen for salary increases, the rural mailmen all but overwhelmed their congressmen with letters and telegrams imploring Congress to raise their pay and continue their privileges such as selling newspapers and carrying parcels outside the mails. They had been inspired to act by Frank Cunningham, president of the National Rural Letter Carriers' Assocation, who had directed them to "get at least one influential patron or politician," and, if possible, someone who was acquainted with their member of Congress, to sign a telegram pleading the rural mailman's cause. So brazen was this disregard of the President's order that Cunningham was dismissed from the service.[57]

This political activity, however, was not the kind he usually engaged in, nor was it really the kind for which he was often punished. Hauling voters to the polls, displaying campaign material, and soliciting votes for some friend running for office were among his more common sins. Probably most of these violations never came to light, but they could be disastrous for the rural carrier when they did. After the election of 1904, Congressman Jame T. McLeary from Minnesota brought charges against a rural carrier for opposing him in the election. McLeary claimed the mailman had engaged in conversations hostile to him, delayed the mails, and distributed campaign circulars harmful to his interests. Some of the charges appeared to be true, and the carrier was dismissed from the service. But in his own defense, the rural mail carrier made the interesting observation that though he had passed out campaign circulars unfriendly to McLeary, he had passed out the same kind of circulars for McLeary in 1902 and nothing had been said about it.[58]

Sometimes the rural mailman became so absorbed in political affairs he ignored the civil service regulations altogether and tried to hold some minor political office or bombard his patrons with political propaganda. One man in Kirkland, Texas, held the chairmanship of the local Socialist party in 1911 and boasted openly that he had converted the people on his route to Socialism. And a year later, another carrier in Michigan was accused of distributing a pair of radical newspapers, *The Appeal To Reason* and *The Menace* to his patrons at his own expense and of denouncing the government as "being a bunch of grafters." Perhaps it was symbolic of the tolerance of the age and the supreme confidence of the American people in their system of government that both these men were only reprimanded for their heresies. In its own way the Post Office Department was putting to the test Jefferson's dictum that if there were any who wished to change the American form of government they should "stand undisturbed as monuments to the safety with which error of opinion may be tolerated where reason is left free to combat it."[59]

Much of the rural mailman's political troubles, however, stemmed from the vagueness of the civil service regulations governing political activity. These regulations assured him of his right to vote and to express political opinions privately, but he could not discuss politics publicly. Consequently, when he met his patrons at their mailboxes and drifted into talking politics, he may not always have known whether his conversation was private or public. At any rate, he could persuade himself he was speaking privately, and so when elections rolled around and politics filled the air, the politically bent mailman "loitered on the route," as the Civil Service Commission put it, discussing with his patrons the relative merits of this or that candidate for office and arguing the fine points of some political issue.

Occasionally as he loitered on his route talking politics, he crossed swords with a patron of the opposite political faith, and it was then, after the mail had been delivered along with a sharp exchange of words, that the irate farmer made a complaint against him, and the mail carrier was likely to find his name listed in the annual report of the Civil Service Commission opposite the notation: "Loitered on the route talking politics." On the other hand, as long as there were no complaints, the rural mail carrier went on loitering and talking, and no one will ever know how many votes he changed in those days before radio and television grabbed the rural air waves. His political opinions, like the extra services he performed, were free to the farmers, and short of muzzling him there was little the Post Office Department could do to keep him from giving them away.[60]

Even if they disagreed with their mailman's politics, many farmers were reluctant to lodge complaints against him for politicking or for anything short of drunkenness, embezzlement, or immorality. If he had been on the route for any length of time, the average rural carrier had built up such a reservoir of good will among his patrons they hesitated to hurt him. For he not only brought their mail, sold them stamps, and ran their errands, but being a public-spirited man, he was very likely to be a teacher in the local Sunday school, master of the local Grange, or president of the local school board.

Financially, the rural mailman's rewards were modest enough, though in hard times his job was coveted. But year in and year out, he took a part of his pay in the satisfaction he found in the chats with his patrons, in the friends he made along the route, and above all in the belief, nutured by the farmers waiting for him at their mailboxes, that what he was doing was important. And, there were other attractions in his job. Except in certain seasons his hours of work were not long, and the work itself was not often arduous. Normally there was still time out of each of his days to think, to read if he would, or to give a talk to a boosters club on the need for good roads.

No wonder then if the dedicated rural mailman believed he had the best of all possible jobs, and to many of them it was not a job but a calling. Neither overly ambitious nor overly mercenary, he was content with his station in life, and a Kansas congressmen depicted the kind of man he was with fair accuracy in the recommendation he wrote for his constituent who wanted to be a rural mail carrier: "He seeks not to serve among the pillared and domed and columned-edifices of Washington. He is used to being summoned to work by the clarion notes of the barnyard cock, and would be out of place among the 9 o'clock risers of the national capital. He neither drinks whiskey nor plays pennyante. He has never worn a dress suit or an opera hat. He is a plain homespun man, who loves the fresh air and the green fields, and the sunshine and the flowers, and the lady he loves is the goddess of simple rural contentment. He wants to carry the mail over a rural route."[61]

7

THE RURAL MAILMAN IN THE AUTO AGE

"I am in receipt of numerous complaints from the patrons on rural routes of this, and adjoining offices regarding the speed of the carriers who drive automobiles. The patrons claim they rush up to the mail box, deposit the mail and are off in such a hurry that it is only on rare occasions that they are able to purchase stamps or obtain official information."

John F. Ryan, postmaster, Batavia, New York, to the Fourth Assistant Postmaster General, Oct. 4, 1918. County Rural Delivery Records, Genesee County, New York, National Archives

BY 1914 the nation was moving rapidly from the horse-and-buggy era into the auto age. That year there were 1,711,339 cars registered in the United States, and already there was a car to fit nearly everyone's pocketbook. Large, full-page automobile advertisements in the leading magazines of the day leaped out at their readers proclaiming the good news and beckoning seductively to a susceptible public. Across the pages of *Collier's Magazine* for January 10, 1914, for example, were pictures of the Packard "38," three Cartercars with "gearless transmissions," three models of Abbotts, a Lyon-Knight—"the car of silence," the National that had gone "305.03 miles without a tire change," and the Oldsmobile Phaeton, advertised as the "Survival of the Fittest." True, most of these cars were priced somewhat above the average man's means. The Oldsmobile limousine ran a stiff $4,300, and the Lyon-Knight at $2,900 was also quite expensive for the day even though its manufacturers guaranteed "its performance to surpass that of any four cylinder poppet-valve of equal size. . . ."

Yet in the same issue of *Collier's* the man of modest income could drool over pictures of the Jeffrey Four priced at $1,550, Jackson's "Olympic Forty" for $1,385, the Mitchell Four at $1,595, the King at $1,095, and the Empire at just $900, and each of these had an almost irresistible appeal. For the "Olympic Forty" there was "no hill too steep, no sand too deep." The Empire was billed as the "Little Aristocrat," completely equipped with "demountable rims, rain vision windshield, gas head lights, side and tail lamps, and double tire irons," while the King was "The Car of No Regrets" with "more Service, Economy, Power, Comfort, Style, and Equipment than can be had in any other car near the King's price."[1]

Strangely, Henry Ford's famous car was not advertised in *Collier's*. But the Model T needed no advertising, for it was already the best-known car in America. A rural mailman in Illinois was using one in 1912 and speeding along his route as fast as 25 miles an hour at a cost of only 35 cents for his 24-mile trip. In 1914 there were a half-million Model T's on the road and they were selling for as little as $500. In fact, they had sold so well Henry Ford had announced in that very year that he would hereafter pay his employees the magnificent sum of $5.00 a day.

Called everything from a "rattling good car" to a "tin Lizzie," and the subject of thousands of jokes, the Model T was the surest sign that the automobile age had arrived and that the motor car was no longer the plaything of the rich. Looking at that little black Ford of 1914, one could hardly imagine that just eight years before, Woodrow Wilson had said that "nothing has spread socialistic feeling in this country more than the automobile; to the countryman they are a picture of arrogance of wealth, with all its independence and carelessness."[2]

Of all those who watched the intrusion of the automobile upon a peaceful countryside, no one was more excited about it than the rural mailman. He could almost believe the motor car had been invented especially for him so suitable to his purposes did it seem, and he was one of the first in the farmland to invest in an automobile.

For the rural mailman the auto age had really begun late in 1902 when the Bond Steel Company, makers of steel posts and rural mailboxes, inaugurated an experiment in delivering the mail by auto along the rural routes out of Adrian, Michigan. This test, which demonstrated among other things that the mail could be delivered twice as fast by auto as by horse and wagon, ran from November 28 to January 3, 1903. It ended with an optimistic report on the future of delivering the mail by auto and one major finding. "We have discovered," wrote a company official, "that heavy trace chains wrapped spirally around the drivers will enable the car to make regular time when the whole country is covered with . . . ice, with dry snow on top."[3]

The need for wrapping chains "spirally around the drivers" indicated the test had not been without its little problems, and indeed the editor of the *R.F.D. News* remained so unconvinced of the automobile's future as a result of the test he refused to recommend its use to the rural carrier. Still an era had been born, and in 1905 both an automobile department and automobile advertisements showed up in the columns of the *R.F.D. News.* The next year, the Post Office Department went so far as to give carriers permission to use their machines on their routes if they wished, and at the national convention of the Rural Letter Carrier's Association that year, the talk was all about automobiles.[4]

Passing up the Harrington postal wagons and motorcycles on display at the convention, curious rural mail carriers watched with rapt attention as a representative of the Oldsmobile Company skillfully maneuvered his Oldsmobile up the steps of the convention hotel. Even more exciting was the appearance of the Orient

Friction Drive Buckboard, an automobile built by the Waltham Manufacturing Company and used by the Post Office Department during the year to conduct its own experiment in delivering the farmers' mail by auto. Clustered about this automobile, the rural mailmen questioned its driver endlessly and marveled at its new friction drive which made it possible to stop at a mailbox without having to shut off the motor. They learned that simply by pushing pedals they could stop the Buckboard at a mailbox, keep the motor running, and then move on again without ever leaving the driver's seat.[5]

Such innovations as friction drive made the automobile all the more irresistible to the rural mailman, and as the cars improved the number of rural carriers who were bold enough to try them increased. One man was even rash enough to buy a Pope Toledo Steamer in 1908. Unfortunately, he was able to drive it only 100 miles in nine months because of "Steamer trouble," but, nevertheless, it was this kind of experimenting that helped winnow the workable from the unworkable in the burgeoning auto industry, and many an automobile, like the Saxon roadster, whose name has long since been forgotten, got their first real tests over the nation's rural routes. However, by 1914, the machines, as they were called, were so commonly used by the rural mail carriers, at least part of the year, that the Postmaster General's report for that year mentioned them in connection with the R F D for the first time and suggested a plan for making greater use of them.[6]

With all his boyish enthusiasm for the automobile and his eagerness to get on with the new age, the rural mail carrier found the transition from horse to Hupmobile filled with trials and tribulations he never bargained for. In the first place, he had to get used to his horseless carriage. He had to remember that it would respond neither to his "giddup" nor to his "whoa," but only to the movement of complicated levers and pedals. And unlike old Queen, the horse that drew the mail wagon along the rural route at Elliotsburg, Pennsylvania, before World War I, turning in at every mailbox automatically and starting up again as quickly as she heard the mailbox door slam shut, his automobile was not automatic. It could not be trusted to stay between the fenceposts without a firm hand at the wheel as his horse had done, and it had no more sense than the mail carrier who drove it.[7]

Second, his automobile was prone to develop what came to be called for want of a more specific description "car trouble," and there was probably not a rural mailman in all the land who struggled through this transition period who had not been stranded at one time or another by the infuriating idiosyncrasies of his gasoline buggy. As early as 1905 an experienced driver had warned the rural mail man that he must have some knowledge of his machine or else be stalled. "He must know how to wire his machine so as to get full benefit of his batteries," he had said, "and he must above all things have the patience of 'Job,' for you may be running a 25 or 30 miles clip for one minute and may be the next you will be 'dead' with a 'short' circuit, or not the right 'mixer' in the gasoline."[8]

Car trouble was bad enough in itself, but it was compounded by the absence of garages and mechanics along the way. And even when these signposts of a new age were within reach, they were not always helpful. The one-cylinder Brush a carrier bought in 1912 was continually stalling, and, as he recalled years later, there was no one around who could repair it. In time the rural mailman would be helped by the friendly advice given him in the "Good Automobile Suggestion" column in the *R.F.D. News* which was full of helpful hints on operating and maintaining his machine. Here he would learn that graphite was an excellent lubricant, that an unpleasant whistling noise might be a hole in the muffler, and a dry squeaking noise meant loose rims. This column also advised him to check loose spokes if his wheels wobbled, keep his foot off the clutch when driving, and fasten a tow rope when needed, to the "front portions of the frame" of his auto, not to the axle. Later, he would also learn that a raw egg in a radiator would stop leaks and that baling wire was a useful addition to his spare-parts kit, but in 1914 most rural mail carriers had yet to make their acquaintance with these useful bits of information.[9]

Greatest of all his problems in the new age, however, was not his automobile but the condition of the country roads he traveled over. For though the automobile enthusiast might parody the Rubaiyat with

> A roadster builded just for two—
> Bright sunshine, pretty road and pretty you
> Beside me riding fast and far
> Oh! this is Paradise, tis true,

the truth was that automobiling in rural America was still a seasonal matter and the pretty road most likely a dream. In summer the dry, dirt roads made driving possible and even pleasant provided there was not too much dust. But in winter and spring when the ruts in the roads were so deep a coon dog had to run five miles to find a place to get out, as the saying went, driving an automobile was not only unpleasant, it was impossible. Not even those high-wheeled cars of yesteryear with their running boards uplifted like a Gibson girl's skirts on a rain-soaked street, could navigate the oceans of mud that neutralized rural America during certain seasons of the year.[10]

The rural mailman knew this as well as any farmer, and knowing what he could and could not do with his machine, he rarely pressed his luck by using it on soft roads. As far as he was concerned his automobile was for the safe, sunny days of summer. Come the autumn rains, the winter snows, and the spring thaws, and he went back to his horse and wagon. A survey made in one congressional district in Iowa in 1915 showed that the rural carriers there who owned cars had been able to use them on an average of only 124 days in the year.[11]

Nevertheless, the rural mailman was steadily making the change from one era to the next and, left to proceed at his own pace, would have made the transition with very little commotion. But rather than permit him to move ahead gradually as the roads and automobiles improved, the Post Office Department began in 1915 to shove him into the auto age ready or not.

The two men responsible for this headlong rush into the new era were Albert Burleson, President Wilson's Postmaster General, and the man in direct charge of the RFD, James I. Blakslee, Fourth Assistant Postmaster General. Burleson was a Texan, the first from his state to sit in a President's cabinet, and Blakslee came from Pennsylvania. Geography notwithstanding the two men were very much alike. Both were stubborn, hard-working men who apparently agreed on the way to run the Post Office Department. Like many of his predecessors, Burleson believed the postal service was a business and should pay its way. Since this policy could only be achieved by economizing, economy had become the order of the day by 1915, and what happened to the R F D as it approached the morrow of the auto age was the result of this urge to save money.

An appraisal of the R F D had convinced Burleson and Blakslee that there were too many rural mailmen, too many routes, and too much money being spent on the service. Their remedy for this condition was to motorize the R F D where possible and to reorganize it along other lines where complete motorization was impossible.[12]

So it happened that the quietness that lay upon rural America in that autumn of 1915 was shattered by what seemed to some a cataclysmic revision of the farmers' mail service. Where road conditions appeared to make it feasible, old rural routes were converted to motorized routes of 50 miles or more in length. Elsewhere, but particularly in the Midwest, the old horse-drawn routes were lengthened and altered. Miles were added to one route here and another there, and those believed no longer necessary were completely wiped out. Routes that seemed to overlap were revamped, and those that retraced themselves for any length were rearranged to eliminate retraces. To give the service to more families, old routes were run over different roads, forcing older patrons to move their mailboxes and even to change their mailing addresses when the altered routes emanated from different post offices than those they had formerly used.

Wherever it went into effect, the revision was complete and devastating. In Buchanan County, Iowa, for instance, no routes were motorized, but almost all the horse-drawn routes were changed and lengthened, presumably on the assumption that the rural mailmen had already so shortened their hours of work by using automobiles when weather permitted they could well afford to spend longer hours on their routes in winter when they had to go back to their horses and wagons. Before the revision there were 33 rural mail routes in the county averaging a little more than 24 miles apiece. The reorganization as announced by the Post Office Department in 1915 called for only 25 routes, each to average over 28 miles in length. Thirty-two additional families were given free delivery service, but some 70 miles of mail routes had been eliminated, and 135 families forced to move their mailboxes all the way from one-eighth to over three-fourths of a mile to be on the line of the new routes. Significantly eight mail carriers were to lose their jobs by this reorganization, but the Department would save $8,482.[13]

So drastic was this revision here and elsewhere throughout the country that the rural mailman who was able to hold on to the job, which he had understood would be his for life if his work were satisfactory, considered himself lucky. Many were not so fortunate. Between 1915 and 1916, 939 routes were wiped out and with them went most of their rural carriers—martyrs, in a sense, to mechanization and the motor age.[14]

In an apparent effort to sift the best carriers for retention in the service, the local postmasters whose routes were being revised were asked to report to the Department on the efficiency and physical fitness of their carriers and to describe each carrier's equipment. But the reports seemed to have little bearing on whether a carrier was retained in the service. The postmaster at Galesburg, Michigan, had three rural carriers at his office in 1915. Of one of these, Arch D. Smith, he wrote: "Physical condition good. Prompt and efficient in his work and well adapted for the position. Equipment, Automobile in summer, two horses, a light wagon or bob in winter." He also paid tribute to the efficiency of all his carriers, declaring they were always on the job. He had never received any complaint against any of them, he wrote, neither had they missed any trips because of bad roads or illness. But a note at the bottom of the postmaster's report told their fate: "General Blakslee says drop these three carriers."[15]

Of course, it was far simpler for Blakslee to strike rural mailmen from the rolls than for the mailmen to adjust to the new situation, and many of them wrote anguished letters to the Department describing their plight and asking for reinstatement on some other route. Arch D. Smith, for example, asked for a job at Kalamazoo, Michigan, and in his letter disclosed his own predicament and that of many another mailman caught in the onrush of the transportation revolution. "I have all my equipment including [a] new Ford car," he wrote, "and will have to sell at a great sacrifice if some transfer cannot be arranged. Possibly you will think this is too much for me to ask but I feel that almost twelve years of service ought to stand for something with the Department."

But Blakslee was unmoved. He replied to this as he did to nearly all such pleas, telling Smith that if he heard of a vacancy at Kalamazoo within one year, he should apply for it. His application would be considered but no assurance could be given that he would receive the appointment.[16]

Meanwhile the rural mailmen who remained in the service had little time to lament the plight of their vanished comrades. They were too busy trying to cope with the changes in their routes to ponder the misfortune of others. In some cases simply locating their routes was a problem. Because postal inspectors who usually made route changes were costly and few in number and time was dear, many of the route revisions had been made in Washington by men poring over county maps that had been used when the routes were laid out some ten to twelve years before. True, the local postmasters had been asked to bring the maps up to date, but this was a poor substitute for sending inspectors to make on-the-spot changes.

Consequently, rural routes had been lengthened and altered with no real knowledge of the condition of the country roads, and the rural mailman whose route formerly followed the better roads, was likely to find his new route running over roads the farmers never used in winter and even across fields where there were no roads at all. As one congressman put it, "new routes were established where there were no roads, over creeks where there were no bridges, over roads that are impassable," and the carrier's route in Nebraska that had been redirected across a swamp and over an embankment forty feet high was ample proof of the congressman's contention.[17]

But the rural mailman's biggest problem was the length of his new routes. In the reorganization his horse-drawn route had been lengthened as much as six or seven miles beyond the standard 24 and doubled if it happened to be one of the motorized routes. As long as he could use his machine the extra miles he served on the old horse-drawn route made little difference. Barring car trouble, a flat tire, or an accident, he could finish his work in three to four hours on a thirty-mile route. But as soon as bad weather set in, he had to go back to his horse and wagon, and the additional miles that had been added to his route, and for which he received no extra pay since his route was not considered to be motorized, began to tell on him as the hours he spent on his route stretched into eight and ten and sometimes longer.

Gustave Roode was a rural carrier on Route 2 out of Botkins, Ohio, in 1917. His route was only twenty-six and a half miles long, but his trip report for the month of January of that year was representative of what happened to most of the rural mailmen at the dawn of the motor age. On January 2, he checked in at his post office at 6:45 A.M. He set up his mail and left to serve his route with his machine at 8:00. Three hours and twenty minutes later he was back at his post office, his route completed. At 11:50, a half hour after he had returned to the post office, he had finished his day's work. On the fourth day of the month he had a heavy mail and tire trouble, and he did not finish for the day until 1:26 P.M. That night there must have been a storm or perhaps a thaw. In any case, Roode had to go back to his horse and wagon on the fifth because of muddy roads. On the sixth, still using his horse and wagon, he was on the route from 8:27 A.M. until 3:36 P.M., and he did not complete his work until 4:20. And so it went. Out of the 26 working days in January, Roode had to use his horse and wagon twelve of them.[18]

The revision of the horse-drawn routes, however, did hurry the mailman's entrance into the auto age. Many of those who had remained faithful to horsepower in the flesh began to transfer their allegiance to horsepower beneath the hood when they saw their old routes lengthened. The postmaster at Centerville, Iowa, reported three of the carriers at his office bought automobiles because of the reorganization of their routes. But like Gustave Roode they could only use them part of the year. From the middle of December to mid-March they had to go back to horses and wagons, and, according to the postmaster, the roads were so bad part of that time the carriers literally wore their horses out trying to complete their elongated routes and did not return to the post office until after dark.[19]

It came as no surprise to those who knew about country roads in winter to find that conditions on some of the motorized routes of fifty miles or more in length were far worse that winter of 1915 and 1916 than they were on the lengthened horse-drawn routes. Wayne County, Indiana, was completely motorized January 3, 1916, when twelve motor routes, each averaging more than sixty miles in length, replaced 28 horse-drawn routes. Hardly had the motorized routes begun, however, than the bottom fell out of the roads. Rather than face the problem of carrying the mail by auto over such roads, two carriers at Richmond resigned, and the postmaster had to scour the countryside to find replacements. The mails piled up, and one man complained on January 20 that bank dividends mailed near the first of the year had not yet reached their destinations.

In desperation the Department sent inspectors to the county with a free hand to rearrange matters as they saw fit. Routes were changed, and horse-drawn routes were put back into operation in several places. Elsewhere, substitutes were hired to help the regular carriers, and it was only because they carried half the regular carriers' loads that the mail got through at all. Automobiles on such roads were out of the question, and both carriers and substitutes had to rely on horses to make their rounds.[20]

Disturbed as they were by the reorganization of the R F D, the rural carriers were scarcely more upset than the farmers, and a flying saucer landing in Belle Center, Ohio, in the year 1916, could hardly have created a greater ruckus than the rural route revision. To hear Congressman James Good of Iowa tell it, the rural delivery reorganization in 1915 was worse than the hog cholera epidemic of 1913 or the hoof-and-mouth disease the year following.[21]

If Burleson and Blakslee had ever believed the farmers were not concerned with the kind of mail service they received, they had only to turn to the *Congressional Record* for 1916 to correct their impressions. There, in the middle of debates on preparedness for war, memorials for the prohibition of alcoholic beverages, and discussions of pensions for old soldiers, they could find pages filled with petitions and letters and Grange resolutions that angry farmers had sent their congressmen protesting against the disruption of their mail service and demanding their old routes back.

With all the fire of the old Populists they complained that their mail, once so promptly delivered in the morning, now came only in the afternoons and sometimes during the winter it had not come at all. Those who had been forced to move their mailboxes recalled the good old days of Republican rule when their mail came directly to their front gates instead of a quarter of a mile or so down the road; and some of those who had lost their old mailing addresses when their routes had been switched to another post office simply refused to patronize their new routes at all, preferring to get their mail at their local post office as they had done before there was an R F D.[22]

Perhaps when he had proposed the revision, Blakslee had not understood country life enough to know that a post office was not an impersonal thing to a farmer as it may have been to an urbanite. A farmer's address like his name was so much a part of him that he was often identified around the county as Smith of the Stanley post office, or Brown of Arlington. In this way, he was known as his father, grandfather, and perhaps even his great-grandfather, who had all lived on the same farm, had been known, and to change such old addresses, many of which went back beyond the Civil War, was to create a minor revolution.

Yet there was more than sentiment in this. The farmers wanted to be identified with their community, the place where they traded and went to church and sent their children to school. When they needed medicine, they wanted to telephone their doctor in the village and have him send it out with the rural mailman. When the mailman started from a different town than that in which their doctor lived, this kind of service was impossible.

The inconvenience of the situation was illustrated by the case of one farmer who lived a mile and a half from the little town of Stanley, Iowa, where he had always done business and always received his mail. In the revision, he had been placed on a route emanating from Aurora, some five or six miles away, so that a letter from him to his banker in Stanley had to go by rural route to Aurora and then by train back to Stanley with the result that he could have communicated as easily with Chicago as with his own banker a mile and a half away.[23]

If this situation was unpleasant for the farmers, it was scarcely less so for the town's bankers and other businessmen who lost customers when their towns lost a rural route, and the R F D files in the National Archives are filled with their letters matching the farmers' protests against the new service complaint for complaint. The local newspapers too took up the fight against the revision, some because the circulation of their papers had been disrupted by the changes in the routes, and others simply because it made a good political issue to lay at the door of the Democratic party in the upcoming national election.[24]

With the farmers in an uproar over the revision of their routes, the small town merchants demanding "justice," and the rural mailmen, those staunch friends of the congressmen, being thrown off their jobs, the members of Congress sprang into action. Some delivered speeches in Congress, and some wrote letters to the Postmaster General and the Fourth Assistant Postmaster General. But others went directly to the Post Office Department in person and demanded either that the old system be restored or that the revisions be held up pending a bona fide investigation of the rural mail service in their districts.

Their reception there was something less than gratifying. Blakslee, passing polite, promised speedy inspections of counties that had not been inspected before the revisions went into effect, and occasionally he was willing to make satisfactory changes. But he was an obstinate man, the kind who had once dared imply during a Senate hearing that the senators lied, and on the whole congressmen found him in the early part of 1916 grimly determined to continue the revision of the R F D even if it meant his job. "The politicians may . . . get me," he once said, "but I have set a pace that will not be cut out by the politician. . . ."[25]

In some ways the Burleson-Blakslee stand was courageous and even meritorious. Unquestionably there was a need for a revision of the rural service. There were too many routes in some areas, and, as Blakslee tried to point out to hard-pressed congressmen,

4,300 rural mail carriers were working less than four hours a day at a time when Postmaster General Burleson was demanding a "full day's work for a full day's pay." This could not always be avoided, because the two- or three-hour route in summer might be a ten-hour route in winter when the roads were bad. Still there was merit in the revision, and if the two men had approached the matter more tactfully the arrival of the motor age along the rural routes would have been less like a breech birth than it was.[26]

But it was Blakslee's way, as it was the Postmaster General's, to plunge ahead, refusing to delay his reorganization and charging everyone who opposed him, particularly rural carriers, with ulterior motives. Since neither he nor Burleson would relent, Congress intervened. In an unprecedented move in the history of the R F D, Congress in 1916 took away the Postmaster General's power to reorganize rural routes as he saw fit and gave its answer to the auto age by classifying the rural routes as horse-drawn and motorized. The length of the standard horse-drawn route was to be 24 miles, the motorized 50 miles. Both routes could be extended by one-half their length by the Postmaster General, but new motorized routes could be established only upon a petition signed by a majority of the heads of families along the route asking that it be done.[27]

This legislation eased the rural mailman's entrance into the auto age. It slowed the establishment of motorized routes and forestalled what might have been a mass exodus of older carriers from the service. But the rural carrier's troubles were not over; at least not for the Republican rural mailman. Freed from the prospect of losing his job through the elimination of his route, he still had to confront the possibility of being dismissed from the service for political reasons. For the postal service in the Burleson years, as it had in the past, teemed with politics, and the active Republican rural mailman was among the first to feel the effects of the new regime.

When the Democrats came to power in 1913, sixteen years

separated them from their last administration in Washington. Hungry for the spoils of office they looked to Postmaster General Burleson, their wily dispenser of patronage, to find jobs for them. A long-time congressman himself, Burleson understood the congressman's need for jobs, and though it took more finesse in 1914 than in former years to find ways to reward the party faithful because of the growth of civil service, he was equal to the task. Fortunately for him, his problem of finding jobs in the R F D had been made simpler by President Taft, whose ruling that a vacancy in the rural carrier corps might be filled with any one of the three who stood highest in the civil service examination made possible political appointments.[28]

Postmaster General Burleson announced, of course, that he would fill every vacancy in the rural service with the man who made the highest grade in the rural delivery examination in any given county unless—and this was an important exception—"good and valid reasons" were submitted to the Department "showing that such action would not be in the best interests of the service."

This loophole was intended to provide flexibility in the hiring of rural mail carriers, so that the men employed would be certain to be acceptable to the patrons along their routes. But in practice it often meant that if the man with the highest rating in the examination was not politically desirable, "good and valid reasons" why he should not be appointed could be found, and the job could go to the eligible whose political views coincided with the administration's. Since Burleson had openly stated he would appoint no rural carrier without consulting the congressman in whose district a vacancy existed, he obviously intended to use this means to separate the politically sound from the unsound.[29]

The fruits of this policy were to be observed in Indiana, always the dark and bloody ground of political strife between Republicans and Democrats. At Frankfort in 1914, one applicant for the rural carrier's job had a score of 89.10 on his examination, but the second high man received the appointment with a grade of 86.55.

That same year the lowest of the three eligibles at Evansville with a score of only 83.15 filled a vacancy though he was a full three points below the top man; and at Zionsville, the lowest eligible, more than five points below the top man, was taken on as the rural mailman. Out of the 20 rural carrier appointments in the state from January through March, eleven of them did not have the highest scores, and Blakslee's answer to a critic in Congress who wanted to know what "good and valid" reasons kept so many of the highest ranking men from being appointed in Indiana, was that the information was confidential.[30]

But Postmaster General Burleson did not really try very hard to conceal what he was doing. In 1916, when the Civil Service Commission protested the appointment of two rural carriers at McPherson, Kansas, because they had received their jobs through political considerations, the Postmaster General simply replied that the men were well qualified for the job and it would be unjust to remove them. And Democrats in Congress, as unabashed as Burleson at what was going on, made only a token effort to deny that politics was playing a part in the selection of rural carriers. For sixteen years they had stood by watching the Republicans dominate the rural carrier force and felt, perhaps justifiably, their time had come. Addressing his Republican hecklers in the House one day, Congressman Lincoln Dixon, Democrat from Indiana, declared that 184 of the 205 rural mail carriers in his district were Republican, and his only regret concerning Burleson's policy was that there were so few vacancies that could be filled with Democrats.[31]

Burleson was doing his best to correct this situation too. For if he did not deliberately wage war on Republican rural mailmen, neither did he lose many opportunities to dismiss them from the service whenever an infraction of the rules made it possible. He was, of course, absolutely ruthless with the mail carrier who continued to share his Republican philosophy and prejudices with the farmers along his route, and woe to him who was caught at this little game, for dismissal from the service was commonly his lot. In six of Burleson's eight years in office for which the records on this matter are available, almost 2,500 rural mailmen were dismissed from the service for causes other than the elimination of their routes. This was over 600 more than the Republican administration had removed for cause in the previous nine years.[32]

The case of Arthur E. Willis of Waltonville, Illinois, offers a good example of what happened to the rural mailman who continued to preach Republicanism under a Democratic regime. During the 1916 campaign Willis had bet on the outcome of the election, argued vehemently on political questions, and in a private conversation criticized President Wilson. Had the Republicans won, all this would surely have gone unnoticed, or at the most Willis would have been reprimanded. Indeed, a reprimand was recommended by the Civil Service Commission. But, alas, the Republicans did not win, and Willis not only lost his bet but his job; Burleson refused to reinstate him even when the Civil Service Commission protested that his punishment was too severe.[33]

This disregard of the Civil Service Commission's recommendations was not at all unusual in Burleson's day. If the Commission recommended a more lenient punishment for a rural mailman who had stepped across the political rules than Burleson desired, he either ignored the commission's recommendation or added to the political infraction a string of violations of postal regulations he claimed the carrier had also committed and dismissed him on the sum total of the charges. Once in 1914 the commission suggested a rural carrier at Little York, Indiana, be reprimanded for loitering on the route to talk politics. But Burleson removed him from the service for being untidy, disrespectful to a patron, and for conspiring to conceal the truth as well as for talking politics. The next year he dismissed a mailman at Bryant, Indiana, because he had mixed up the mail and dropped it in the road. When the carrier charged that he was really being dismissed for political reasons, the Civil Service Commission, after making two investigations, declared he had been no more careless than ordinary circumstances permitted and ordered him reinstated. But Burleson would not budge even when a petition from 107 families on the carrier's route asked that he be given his job back.[34]

The inability of rural route patrons to influence the Department in these matters during Burleson's administration was most unusual. From the very beginning of the R F D, the Post Office Department had bent over backward to give the farmers as much control over their mail routes as possible, and their wishes had always been an important factor in the selection and retention of their mailman. But once Burleson decided a carrier must go, the farmers along his route were powerless to help him. A patrons' petition six feet long plus the support of Senators Knute Nelson and Moses Clapp failed to save John Lindbergh's job at Canon Falls, Minnesota, when he was dismissed, allegedly for failing to send a misdirected newspaper on to its rightful owner. And a mailman at Lucasville, Ohio, accused of immorality, was dismissed though he had a petition signed by 95 patrons asking that he be retained. He had asked to see the charges against him, so he could prepare his defense, but these were never given him, and, in effect, he was never really able to present a defense. His situation was much the same as that of the carrier in Morgantown, Indiana, who was separated from the service and told by a postal inspector that a petition reaching from "here to New York would do him no good."[35]

And yet the fact that it was possible in those years for a rural mailman to break the rules and still remain in the service suggested an unevenness in Postmaster General Burleson's administration of justice. In 1915 a rural carrier at Texico, New Mexico, and one at Chili, New York, were charged with holding local political offices in violation of political regulations. The New Mexico carrier was dismissed for his offense, but the New York carrier was only suspended. And while Burleson was laying a heavy hand on the mailmen in the Midwest, a rural carrier at Hazelhurst, Georgia, who had solicited votes, falsified his time record, refused to serve a patron, and was even drunk on duty, suffered only a reduction of pay. In Oklahoma, to take but one more example, the Civil Service Commission recommended a thirty-day suspension for the rural mailman who had unwittingly entered his name in a primary election. But the Post Office Department, in a sudden burst of generosity, merely suspended him for ten days.[36]

Managing the R F D, Postmaster General Burleson was like a juggler trying to keep three balls in the air at the same time. While he was busily reorganizing the service and weeding out undesirable carriers, he was sowing more seeds of uncertainty in the ranks of the mailmen by trying to convert rural delivery to the star route system. Driven by his passion to make the postal service pay, he saw in his proposal to let the rural routes out to contract, the prospect of saving fifteen to twenty million dollars a year. The low bidder would get the contract to carry the mail over a given route, and the day of the high-salaried rural mailman and postal deficits would be over.

Burleson proposed this change as early as 1914 and pursued it tenaciously through most of his administration. But to no avail. The shadows of Populism were long, congressmen had not forgotten how the battle for R F D had been drawn on the proposition of equalizing the mail service between town and country, and they would not undo what had been done. Once in 1914 a bill authorizing the contract scheme for rural delivery did come before Congress. But even though it was tagged as an administration measure, the heavily Democratic House would still not pass it. The chairman of the House Committee on Post Office and Post Roads was so angry at the congressmen who had refused to go along with the measure he called them "craven cowards" and said they had repudiated the "Democratic President, The Democratic Postmaster General . . . and the Democratic Post Office Committee of the House."[37]

What Burleson said privately about the defeat of his bill was not recorded, and perhaps it was as well. It could hardly have been pleasant, for he was always stubbing his toe on the R F D, and it must have been the most exasperating branch of the service to him. Filled with Republican mail carriers and very expensive, the R F D could only have been a cross to one who wanted to save money as badly as Burleson did and who was as much a spoilsman as he. Yet each time he tried to reform it Congress put him off.

For his troubles with the R F D Burleson blamed the rural mail carriers, the *R.F.D. News*, and the National Rural Letter Carriers' Association, and, in truth, this triumvirate did do much to foil his plans. The *R.F.D. News* had been critical of the Postmaster General's policies since the autumn of 1914, and Fred White, President of the National Rural Letter Carriers' Association had used the paper to warn rural carriers of policies that might be harmful to their interests. The carriers in turn helped protect themselves by writing to their good friends, the congressmen from their districts. Understandably, this infuriated Burleson, and he lashed out repeatedly at the rural carriers' organization and particularly at the *R.F.D. News*. Since the *News* was privately owned, he could do nothing about it, but President White was another matter. A rural carrier as well as president of the association, he could be removed from the service and he was, in May 1917, on the ground that he had circulated unreliable and inaccurate information among the rural carriers.[38]

Perhaps White found some solace in the fact that he was only one of a number of key officials from various postal employees' organizations whom Burleson had cast into the outer darkness. The President of the Railway Mail Association, the Secretary-Treasurer of the National Federation of Postal Employees, the President of the National Association of Letter Carriers, and then the President of the National Rural Letter Carriers' Association, Burleson had picked them off one by one as they opposed his policies, and if his goal was to break these organizations, he was reasonably successful. Particularly was this true of the National

Rural Letter Carriers' Association whose membership dwindled from 68 per cent of the total rural carrier force in 1914 to 15 per cent in 1917.[39]

Albert Burleson's administration of the postal service was an amazing performance. Even more amazing was his ability to remain in office. A rock-ribbed conservative, he could be blamed for much that was reactionary in the Wilson administration. True, he had waged war on such special interests as the railroads, the express companies, and telephone and telegraph interests as a progressive might have done. At the same time he had disrupted the mail service throughout the country, defied the Civil Service Commission, demoralized the postal employees, and virtually disbanded their organizations. Nearly every organized group in the nation having anything to do with the postal service was after him. Samuel Gompers, head of the American Federation of Labor, was saying in 1919 that Burleson would have "to walk the plank sooner or later," and that same year Senator Norris, talking about impeachment, submitted a resolution in the Senate asking an investigation of the Postmaster General. Friends of the administration begged Wilson to cast him overboard lest he sink the Democratic ship while the Republicans thought he was their best argument for returning their party to the White House. Yet Burleson, disliked and reviled, as perhaps no other member of Wilson's cabinet had been, stayed on to the end of the administration in 1921.[40]

For many a rural mailman Burleson's administration had been a harrowing experience, and the turnover in the rural carrier force had been enormous. In 1919 alone 8,615 mailmen resigned, and during Burleson's eight years in office something more than half the total force left the service, some to be inducted into military service, many to take higher paying jobs elsewhere, but also many because of Burleson's policies.[41]

Still a large number of old-timers remained on their routes and looked forward to a better day under the Republicans who had condemned the Democratic administration for its "destruction of the efficiency of the postal service" in their political platform for 1920 and who seemed to promise something better. After November they had not long to wait. The Republicans won the election and Burleson left office on March 4, 1921. With considerable exaggeration the *R.F.D. News* called it a memorable day "because it marked the welcome end of the grossest mismanagement and most notorious inefficiency in the history of the service."[42]

The change in administrations was almost immediately felt in the postal service. With Burleson's policies obviously in mind, Will H. Hays, President Harding's first Postmaster General, began his administration proposing to "humanize the service," saying that it was both wicked and poor business to treat postal employees as a mere commodity in the labor market.[43]

For the rural mailman humanizing the service meant receiving his pay twice a month instead of once, a more liberal attitude on making deductions from his pay for inadequately performing his duties, and a general relaxation of the tension that had built up during the Burleson years. Symbolic of the new policy was the reinstatement of Fred White, former President of the National Rural Letter Carrier's Association, whom Burleson had dismissed. It did not mean, however, that the service was free from politics. In this respect the Republicans followed Burleson's worst practices. New rural carriers still were not appointed in any district until the congressman from that district had been consulted, and carriers continued to be removed from the service against the Civil Service Commission's recommendations as they had been under Burleson. Every one of the rural mailmen at one post office in Indiana was removed in 1924, for example, and all of them just happened to be of the same political party. The Civil Service Commission's investigation showed these carriers were serving their routes in the same way their predecessors had, but in so doing they were violating postal regulations, and the Civil Service Commission could not save their jobs for them.[44]

But, on the whole, the rural mailman's lot was easier in the 1920's than it had been under Burleson, and the way in which the automobile problem was solved was indicative of a more humane approach to the motor age.

It was obvious by 1920, if it had not been before, that neither assorted car troubles nor bad roads would keep the rural mailman from using his machine on his mail route. A survey made of some 26,000 rural mail carriers that year revealed that over 18,000 of them were using their automobiles about eight months of the year. Like Burleson and Blakslee, the Republican Postmaster General Harry New, who followed Will Hays when he became president of the Motion Picture Producers and Distributors Association, was well aware that this phenomenon was revolutionizing rural delivery as it was so much of American life, and he was anxious to make the most of it. But because of the horse-and-buggy regulation passed by Congress in Burleson's day, he could not extend a standard horse-drawn route beyond 36 miles, nor could he establish a motorized route of 50 miles or more, without the consent of the patrons along the route.[45]

This zone between 36 and 50 miles, symbolic of the difference between the horse-and-buggy era and the auto age, had to be eliminated before the R F D could be effectively motorized, but congressmen, perhaps remembering the turmoil this had caused in 1915, were not ready to move in that direction until 1925. By then, there was virtually no opposition to a bill Congress passed wiping out the distinction between horse-drawn and automobile routes. By this bill the rural mailman's salary on a standard twenty-four-mile route was set at $1,800 a year with an additional $30.00 for each mile his route extended beyond the standard. Moreover, he was given four cents a mile for equipment. The Postmaster General could now extend and consolidate the rural routes as he wished, but he could not remove a mail carrier from the service in the course of consolidation. If he wished to consolidate routes, he must wait until a mailman had died, retired, or resigned, and then instead of hiring a new carrier to work the old route, he might combine it with another providing this would not impair the service.[46]

So passed an era. As the roads improved and carriers retired, the rural routes were hastily consolidated after 1925. Each year their numbers decreased until in 1960 only 31,379 remained of the 45,315 there once had been. Many of them had been absorbed into the city delivery service as areas that had once been rural became urban. Others were so changed in the process of consolidation that their original patterns remain only in their descriptions in the National Archives or perhaps in some old-timer's memory. As routes were erased year after year, those that remained became longer and longer until their average length in 1960 was a little more than 56 miles apiece.[47]

In a way the length of the rural routes marked the progress of the auto age, and the fact that the average route in 1930 was only 30.84 miles long was partly explained by the rural mailman's inability to go much farther the year round in his gasoline buggy in this period. For while Congress was in effect legislating the horse and wagon out of existence in 1925, the rural carrier was still having troubles with temperamental automobiles and poor country roads, and as late as 1931 buggy and automobile ads were still running side by side in the National Rural Letter Carriers' Association's paper.[48]

In this afterglow of the horse-and-buggy era, driving a car was no simple matter. Watching a rural mailman preparing his car for the day's trip on a cold winter morning, one might wonder if, after all, feeding and harnessing a horse might not have been easier. Taking hot water from the kitchen range, he would hurry out to his Model T and pour the water over the carburetor to help vaporize the gas. Then he would jack up a rear wheel to make cranking easier. Finally, with the spark lever up and the gas lever down, he began to crank, all the while pulling on the choke wire that protruded through the front of the radiator. Sometimes, he would perspire freely even in the cold before the motor would catch; and sometimes there would be trips for more hot water. But with luck, his engine would spring to life after the first few turns of the crank and the rural mailman would be on his way.

But once on the road, almost as many things went wrong with his automobile in this period as his automobile had parts. Beneath the strain of washboard roads, extremes of heat and cold, and constant stops and starts, axles and springs broke, clutches gave way, radiators froze as the alcohol antifreeze evaporated or boiled away, and brakes, particularly those on the Model T, were so often in need of repair that the resourceful mailman sometimes had to resort to pushing the reverse pedal in the floorboard to bring his automobile to a stop. Nuts, bolts, and even gas tanks fell out along the road. As late as 1940 one carrier lost a battery from his Model A. These losses might have been worse if the mailman had not discovered that baling wire could be used to hold his car together in emergencies. A mail carrier at Delta, Colorado, once ran into a snowbank and broke the front tie rod on his car. He was ten miles from a garage and the temperature was ten degrees below zero, but with his omnipresent baling wire he was able to wire the rod to the wheel and drive on to his post office.[49]

Running into snowbanks and mudholes along his route was everyday fare for the rural mailman in the winter and spring of each year, and the carrier who went a year in the 1920's and 1930's without having to be towed back to terra firma was fortunate indeed. Besides chuckholes and pools of water that could stall a motor instantly unless crossed with care he had to be especially careful of the turnouts leading to the mailboxes. These were often deceptive, and he might drive over one in complete confidence, deposit the mail, and learn only when he tried to start off again that the ground had been softer than it seemed and he was stuck.

Whenever this happened, he tried rocking his car back and forth hoping to spin his way out. Because the Model T could be sent forward and backward quickly and easily by manipulating the pedals in the floorboard, it was particularly good for this kind of business, and if any car could get the mailman out of a hole, it could. One of the standard Ford jokes concerned the farmer who asked to be buried with his Model T because it had gotten him out of so many holes.

Very often, however, the constant lunging back and forth only drove his car deeper into the mud until at last, axle deep, there was nothing to do but wait until the farmer came with his team of horses to pull him out. It was probably some such situation as this that inspired the poem John E. Sheppard, one-time Texas Attorney General, recited at the convention of the National Rural Letter Carriers' Association in 1955:

Lord, a-livin' in the country's altogether kinda sad;
You cain't do nothin' very good, you cain't be very bad;
And all the fun you ever had is settin' by the gate—
A-watchin' for the mailman, and hopin' he ain't late.
So I'm askin' that you treat him good—don't never let him down;
And when it's rainin' cats and dogs, don't let his engine drown—
And if you ketch him cussin', Lord,
Don't mark it up again him
It's many miles of dirty roads that put them cusswords in him.[50]

There was humor, if one was not involved, and irony too in the picture of a rural mailman being towed from a ditch by a team of horses his automobile was supposed to replace. But this vignette of rural life, so familiar in the 1920's and even in the 1930's, was passing in the 1940's, not because the rural mailman was never stuck in the mud in these years, but because when he was, the farmer's tractor instead of horses was more likely to pull him out. When this happened the horse-and-buggy age was gone indeed.

With its passing, there were more changes along the old mail routes. The traffic problem became important, and the Post Office Department ordered all mailboxes to be put on the carrier's right-hand line of travel, so he would not have to cross and recross the traffic lanes with his automobile to deliver the mail. There were complaints, of course, as there always were when changes occurred in the farmland. "You are informed," one independently minded farmer wrote the Department, "that said mailbox and post are my property, that I resent your meddling and defy your order. It is up to you to see that I obey you. . . . Your department has heretofore issued idiotic orders changing mail boxes to the gee side of mud roads so the carrier can poke mail into the box with his right hand. . . . 'For the good of the service!' Like h—l! Next I am expecting the Department to issue orders that the farmer must, in case of rain, get out and spread alpaca carpets for mail carriers to travel on while the road is muddy."[51]

But the farmer was fighting a losing battle. Efficiency and the safety of the mailman demanded that the mailboxes be moved to the "gee" side of the road, and in time they were. And as the auto age advanced there were more and more mailboxes on some routes and fewer and fewer on others. Where rural routes hugged the outskirts of the cities and the urban population spilled beyond the city limits to find living room, the mailman was likely to find thirty or forty boxes at one stop where a few years before there had been but one or two. This change not only increased the size of his mail, but made it almost impossible for him to keep up with the names and faces of his mobile patrons. This was a new problem for the rural mail carrier and one that served to weaken the close ties between himself and his patrons that had been so characteristic of the service.

But even on routes where the population was not so transient, the old intimacy between carrier and patron was disappearing as the years moved on. Life moved at a faster pace in the auto age, and the farmers seemed to have more places to go and were in more of a hurry to get there. Except for the distinct minority among them, they had less time for those chats with their mailman at the mailbox than they had had in the old days. Now that they could go to town almost as easily as they had formerly gone to their barns, their need to talk to their mailman diminished. Indeed, as one old carrier noticed, the automobile had made the biggest change in rural life of anything he had seen along his route in 47 years. Cars took the farmers to town, and buses took their children to consolidated schools, and, as he saw it, there were hardly any "country folks" left. "I could read the difference in the faces of the people," he said.[52]

Probably the mailman too was less anxious to talk with his patrons than he had been. Conversing with a patron meant burning extra gasoline and interrupted his schedule which for some reason seemed more important to a man with a steering wheel in his hands than a pair of reins. Then, too, there was something impatient about an idling motor that discouraged easy conversation. It was as if the motor's hum was constantly reminding the carrier and his patrons that the mailman must be on his way.

In the new age the rural mailman was very likely to live in the town from which his rural route emanated rather than in the country as a neighbor of the people to whom he carried the mail, and this may have sapped the old bonds between himself and the farmers. Furthermore, as the years passed, the Post Office Department quite often replaced a retiring carrier with an outsider, a transfer from another route or even from another civil service job, rather than hire a local man through competitive examinations. When this happened, obviously the old intimacy between the carrier and his patrons was at least temporarily and sometimes permanently lost.[53]

It was another sign of the new age that the farmers no longer depended so heavily upon their rural mailman to run errands for them as they had in the past. Town was now only a few minutes from a farmer and where he once would have asked the mailman to bring from town a set of sections for his mowing machine sickle, he was, after the 1920's, more likely to jump in his car and go for them himself.

Probably very few rural carriers lamented the loss of this errand business even though it too tended to change their traditional relationship with their patrons. In the new era they could scarcely have undertaken all the errands they had in the past because of the increased size of the farmers' mail. The *Saturday Evening Post* alone, to say nothing of the many other magazines farmers subscribed to, plus the inevitable third-class matter and the semi-yearly bouts with the Montgomery Ward and Sears, Roebuck catalogs, noticeably increased their working time as the years passed. Add to this the parcel-post business which began in 1913 and increased steadily thereafter, and the rural mailman's relief at not having to run additional errands for his patrons becomes understandable. "When I started carrying the mail," wrote a rural carrier in 1940, "a horse could easily carry a man and what mail I had. However, the mail has increased in volume to the extent that a pick-up truck is as much overloaded as a horse was at any time in the early days."[54]

The 1930's and 1940's were a kind of watershed for the rural mail carrier corps. On the one side were the men who had known only the modern R F D; on the other, ever decreasing in numbers, were the carriers who had grown old with the service and had made the transition from horse and wagon to an automobile. In 1920 Congress established a retirement system for the rural carriers making it possible for them to retire on a pension any time between 15 and 30 years of service, and in the 1930's new statistics began to appear in the Postmaster General reports noting the number of retirements each year.

From time to time, as under Postmaster General Burleson and later during the depression, the rural mailman was compelled to retire at the age of 65 if he had at least fifteen years of service, but at various times between 1920 and the present this requirement was not always in force, and some rural carriers spent half a century and more on their routes. One old carrier who retired in 1949 had spent fifty years, counting five years on star routes, carrying the mail. He had used twenty horses and fifteen buggies on his route by 1927. After that he had worn out three Model T's, one V-8, two Chevrolets, and one Plymouth.[55]

Most rural mailmen, however, never attempted to stay that long in the service. Many who had begun their careers about the time Theodore Roosevelt became President in 1901 reached their 30 years of service in the early 1930's and began to drop out. In 1933 alone 992 men retired and within the next seven years over 3,500 more had done the same.[56]

Death, too, was taking its toll of rural mail carriers, and one man who had bridged the horse-and-buggy and motorcar eras was led to wonder,

> What will happen over yonder in the land of perfect day,
> If we don't find any chuckholes in the road along the way;
> There won't be any washouts, and wind will never blow,
> And we'll never freeze our fingers digging pennies from
> the snow.
> I wonder if old Dobbin will be tied along the street
> Just waiting till the 8:15 comes sliding through the sleet.
> Or will we find "Old Lizzie" in that land of perfect bliss?
> When so often we had wished her in a hotter place than this.[57]

By 1930 the rural carrier death statistics appearing in the annual Postmaster General reports indicated that the old-timers among the rural mailmen did not have long to speculate on what they would find in that land of perfect bliss. Throughout the 1930's the number dying in the service averaged over 200 every year. Most of these men must have been among those whose years of service stretched back at least to the twilight period of the horse and wagon, and when their number is added to the list of retirements, it is plain how rapidly the cast of players in the drama of the R F D was changing in the second and third decades of the century.[58]

The men who became rural carriers in the auto age and are now delivering the mail to the farmers have changed with the times. They seem more businesslike and efficient than their predecessors were. Heavier mails and lengthened routes almost demand this. Many of them now live in towns, and it is likely that a rather large number of them were not even reared on farms. Many are veterans of World War II, and all are products of the new age when town and country are joined by the automobile. Their experiences have been broader and probably their intellectual horizons are wider than were those of the men who carried the mail with horse and wagon. Perhaps for this reason, they are greater joiners than the first carriers were, and membership in the National Rural Letter Carriers' Association, reduced to 15 per cent of the total number of carriers in 1915, was virtually 100 per cent in 1960.

Aside from its increased membership, the other changes time brought to the rural carriers' association were amazing. For the little organization that emerged from the horse-and-buggy days bruised and limping, blossomed during the motor age into a powerful body fully capable of defending and promoting the rural mailman's interests. Now it has a business large enough to require the use of an entire floor of office space in a large building in Washington, D.C., and influence sufficient to have had President Eisenhower speak to its members when they gathered in Washington for the association's national convention in 1959.[59]

From the early 1900's, the association had been dominated by Wisdom D. Brown, editor and owner of the *R.F.D. News*. So great had been his power in the organization, according to one account, that "he could go to a national convention, take a suite of rooms at a leading hotel, take a bath, dress, flash a diamond or two, pick up his cane and go to the convention hall and point out the men whom he would elect to office in the Association." Few mail carriers who had known the service's horse-and-buggy days would ever forget his great contribution to their cause in these years; but as the composition of the rural carrier corps changed, the attitude of many of the carriers toward Brown changed too. They came to resent his control over their organization and began, first, to reject his advice and then to oppose him. Hard feelings followed, and Brown began to use the pages of the *R.F.D. News* to attack the officers of the association.

Realizing that as long as the ownership and editorship of the *News* remained in Brown's hands, his power in the association would remain, a group of carriers tried to wrest the control of the paper from him, even going so far at one time as to establish a rival paper of their own. Faced by this open revolt, Brown sold the *R.F.D. News* to Cleland C. McDevitt in 1927, and though the rural carriers still did not own the paper, they were promised a greater voice in its affairs. In December 1927, then, the carriers discontinued the paper they had started, made friends with the new owner of the *R.F.D. News*, and had the paper rechristened *The National Rural Letter Carrier*. Whether by accident or design, the issue of the paper announcing this change carried as its weekly Bible verse: "Blessed are the pure in heart: for they shall see God." Finally, in 1943, the rural carriers' association bought the paper outright from McDevitt and so at last came into its own.[60]

With all these changes in the rural carrier personnel and in the carriers' own organization, it might have been expected that the rural carrier force as a whole would have thrown off the rural traditions and attitudes that characterized those carriers of a bygone day. And in many respects they have. In the pages of *The National Rural Letter Carrier* a rural mailman is seldom referred to as "brother" as they once were when agrarian ways were more pronounced. And at death, they are no longer recorded as "passing into the great beyond" or entering upon "their last long route." Notification of their deaths is efficiently noted now in the paper's rural carrier deceased column.[61]

Yet it is remarkable how much of the agrarian spirit still clings to the rural mailman. No one, for example, could mistake his organization, the National Rural Letter Carriers' Association, for that of the city carriers. For the city carriers have a union; but the rural carriers' association, which fairly reflects the spirit of the rural mailman himself, remains, in spite of its growth, a kind of rural fraternal order much as it was in the horse-and-buggy days.

Somewhat like the Grange, it has county, state, and national bodies, and its national officers are picked from the ranks of the carriers. National presidents of the organization serve only two years in that capacity, then leave their position of power along Pennsylvania Avenue to return to their rural mail routes. And like almost all good rural organizations, the association has a women's auxiliary, an active organization composed of the wives of rural carriers who share, as rural women have always shared since the foundation of the Grange, in the activities and interests of their husbands' organization.[62]

This is not to say that the Rural Letter Carriers' Association does not use pressure to promote its members' interest. Indeed it does and appears to have more influence on Capitol Hill than its membership alone would merit. This is not only because the rural mailman still possesses political influence along his route, but because there remains among the older congressmen a sympathetic interest in the rural mailman, an interest that goes back to their own boyhood when they ran to get the mail from the rural carrier. Perhaps it was the memory of seeing the rural mailman riding along in his buggy as he went out to the Smoky Hills to fish that led President Dwight D. Eisenhower, possibly the last President to remember such things, to speak to the rural carriers in 1959. And perhaps it was this too that led Speaker Sam Rayburn to say: "The rural carrier has always been one of the most popular men or women that came to the farm home. He always takes them something they want and never asks them for anything. So, he is popular. . . . I've seen rural carriers go and come for 40 years, they are a grand group of people and I want to say another thing about them. That when you do something for them they appreciate it. They are not like some other groups that say, 'Well, he should have done it sooner.' "[63]

The agrarian spirit still manifest in the rural mailman's association is also reflected in his weekly paper. *The National Rural*

Letter Carrier was tidied up once McDevitt and the rural carriers took over the *R.F.D. News* in 1927. No longer could one find those advertisements, apparently so embarrassing to rural carriers, on the treatment of piles from the inside or on rejuvenation by the use of Korex Compound that Brown had printed when he owned the paper. Instead, the advertisements ran increasingly through the years to automobiles and their parts and to new devices that could be used to make delivering the mail easier. Even so, the flavor of the old *Capper's Weekly* or perhaps the county newspaper, still permeates the rural mailman's weekly. Each issue has its Bible verses, and the homey reports from the women's auxiliary that appear so regularly in its pages, read almost exactly like the reports of Grange committees written some seventy years ago. And sprinkled through the speeches and reports and news items that appear in the paper, are the poems, original and borrowed, with which rural people have always emphasized, humorized, and emotionalized their writings and their speeches.

And yet, in spite of the traces of rural America that still cling to him and his organization, the rural mailman, like those other distinctive types who colored the American past, has lost the uniqueness that characterized him in the horse-and-buggy days. The rural carriers whose pictures graced the pages of the early *R.F.D. News* could hardly be mistaken for the ministers, businessmen, congressmen, or college professors of the day. Even when attending their association's national convention, dressed up in their Sunday best, there was a rustic, independent air about them. But the men who head the National Rural Letter Carriers' Association today look as much like urbanites as any prosperous, middle-class, professional group in the nation. The dominance of urban culture, which has become the nation's great common denominator, has so infused his life that neither the rules of the Post Office Department nor the singular aspects of his job, have been enough to preserve the essential distinctiveness that set him apart from his fellow man in a bygone day.

Cover of the 1894 Sears, Roebuck catalogue

University of Chicago Press

THIS BOOK
WILL BE SENT TO ANY ADDRESS
FREE
BY MAIL POSTPAID
ON
APPLICATION

SEND ME YOUR
BIG CATALOGUE

SIMPLE RULES FOR ORDERING.

ENKLA REGLER ATT IAKTTAGA VID BESTÄLLNING.

Einfache Regeln zum Bestellen.

DO NOT FAIL TO GIVE SIZE, COLOR, WEIGHT, ETC., IF REQUIRED WHEN WRITING YOUR O

Simple rules for ordering in the Spring 1906 catalogue

Rural delivery in winter near Concord, New Hampshire, 1900

Country road

The King Road Dra

Bureau of Public Roads

8

GOOD ROADS

Good road enthusiasts loved to tell about the man who reached to pick up a man's hat from the middle of a farmer's mud-soaked road and was surprised to find a head of hair beneath it. "Hold on, boss," said a voice, "don't take my hat; I've got a powerful fine mule down here somewhere if I can ever find him."

Archer Butler Hulbert, et al., *The Future of Road-Making in America* (*Historical Highways of America*, XV [Cleveland, 1905]), 97

THE average American farmer in 1900 had few material possessions more valuable to him than the road that ran past his farm and on into his marketplace. Over this road flowed the commerce of the countryside. The cotton that would one day clothe the shopgirl in London began the first leg of its journey along this road; so did the livestock, corn, and wheat destined to feed the American nation and a large part of the world as well. Here passed the farmer's children on their way to school, the farmer and his wife to Grange, and the entire family on its way to church. And finally over this road came the rural mailman bouncing along in his buggy to bring the daily mail to the farmer and keep him in touch with the world beyond his neighborhood.

As important as this road was to the American farmer, one might have expected to find it reasonably smooth, possibly graveled, and certainly passable all year round. But the average farmer's road was almost none of these things, and a stranger visiting rural America at the century's beginning could never have accurately judged the road's importance from its appearance. As late as 1904 only 151,664 of the nation's 2,151,000 miles of roadways had been improved with gravel, shell, oil, or some other substance. The rest, nearly 2,000,000 miles of them, were dirt; rough, rutted, often impassable, these were the farmers' farm-to-market roads.[1]

Country roads at the turn of the century were largely products of expediency. Born of necessity, they had been established with a minimum of effort and with no more planning than it took to figure the quickest route from farm to town. Skirting the banks of rivers and streams, following the floors of valleys, and going directly over mountain barriers in accordance with the rule that a straight line is the shortest distance between two points, their course had often been determined by prominent topographical features. Or else they had been built over old Indian trails which in turn had followed paths first made by animals.[2]

Even where the government had surveyed the land and laid it out in neat square blocks, the roads were not immediately strung straight along section lines as they were later to be throughout much of the nation. Herbert Quick, that sharp observer of the scenes of his childhood in Iowa, told how the change came about. "In the beginning," he wrote, "the landscape was a glorious undulating sea of waving prairie grass, on which floated here and there a quadrangular raft of tillage. The roads were wagon tracks running diagonally from the village to the farms, and in main roads from town to town; but these were gradually crowded by tillage from their antigodlin courses to their present places on the section lines, all running north and south or east and west."[3]

Established haphazardly, the farmers' roads were maintained in the same fashion. In nineteenth-century America their upkeep was the sole responsibility of the local government, which meant in practice that the farmers were almost entirely responsible for their own roads. True, the counties usually levied a road tax, but very little money was ever accumulated by this tax. Traditionally farmers paid the tax by working on their roads so many days a year. They might work at this as many as ten days each year, but however long they worked, it was never long enough for them, with their antiquated methods of road repair, to do much more than rearrange the dirt.

How the system worked was once described by a man with practical experience. "The first time I ever worked on the road I was the overseer," he wrote in 1902, "and my section was some 3¼ miles in length. After beating about in the usual fashion among the hills and mountains for two or three days 'warning out' my hands, the hour set for beginning work came, but the hands did not. By and by, however, they began straggling in, evidently expecting to make a short job of it. . . . The road had been 'scratched' once in the previous eighteen months, not worked at all, and was of course in desperate condition. By 11 o'clock most of the hands had come, each bringing some tool (so-called). What a conglomeration it was! Old dull axes, worn out shovels, hoes and mattocks—nothing fit to work with."[4]

But even had they brought better tools, it would probably have made little difference, for the farmers in 1900 were nearly as innocent of good road-building techniques as their grandfathers had been. Their usual practice was to scrape the dirt in the center of the road, smooth it over with a drag or rake and let it go at that. If they knew how to grade and crown a road so that water would drain off instead of in, they rarely did so. Nor had they in many places even developed the idea of drainage ditches at the sides of the road. Culverts to carry off the water from low places were a novelty, of course, and so too were bridges in some localities. Even such a simple task as removing the weeds and brush along the roadside in the autumn to prevent snowdrifts in winter was neglected. And to change a road, to abandon part of it and build another to make it straighter or the grade smoother was unthinkable. The road had always been where it was, and there it must remain.[5]

The net effect of the farmers' road-building efforts by 1900 had been to produce roads that served the farmers poorly in summer and left them stranded in winter. It was once estimated that in some areas as many as 27 tons of water fell each year on one mile of an ordinary road three rods wide, and when this happened to country roads improperly graded and unequipped with drainage ditches, rural America was absolutely mud-bound. As one rural postal agent surveying Macoupin County, Illinois, in the early 1900's put it, the roads at such times were "entirely out of the power of the road commissioners to remedy and only an appeal to the Almighty can ameliorate their condition."[6]

With no place to go, the rain and melting snow stood in puddles in the roads or saturated the soil creating marshes of mud that seemed utterly bottomless. Wagon wheels rolling over the roads at such times cut deep into the mud trying to reach bottom. Huge ruts were formed, sometimes deeper on one side than the other, so that a wagon moving through leaned heavily to one side. After a time the narrow ruts could be followed in comparative safety, but a head-on meeting with another wagon meant trouble. One wagon must leave the well-worn tracks and cut new ones. This was done only at the risk of overturning or becoming so deeply mired it was more than one team of horses could do to move the wagon.

The cost of poor country roads to the farmers was enormous. Farm spokesmen used to say in the days before World War I that a bushel of wheat could be hauled from New York to Liverpool for 1.6 cents less than it cost to haul it over 9.4 miles of a dirt road. In 1912, according to one estimate, it cost the American farmer 23 cents a ton mile to transport his harvest to market while in England it cost only 11 cents a ton mile, 10 cents in Germany, and in France 7 cents. Besides this, farmers were compelled to take their crops to market shortly after harvest when markets were glutted and prices lowest. If they waited for prices to rise, bad weather was likely to have made their roads barriers instead of boulevards. "The Iowa farmer," ran a little jingle, "cannot haul to market when the market is high; he must haul to market when the roads are dry."[7]

But poor country roads meant poor country schools, poor churches, poor community relationships, and isolated farmers as well as financial losses. The one-room schoolhouse so common to rural America could never become a larger consolidated school as long as roads made it impossible for farm children to travel greater distances to school. Nor could farmers participate in community affairs when the roads were so bad they could scarcely leave their farms except by foot or horseback. Rather than risk their horses, buggies, and tempers on their soggy winter roads, farm families stayed away from church, neglected their neighbors, and attended but few of their community's social functions. Grandmother Brown, recalling her experiences in pioneer Iowa, remembered that though her family lived only five miles from Denmark, they could go to church there only once in a great while because the task of pulling a wagon through the muddy roads was too much for the horses who needed their rest on Sunday just as the farm family did. It was exactly this situation Grangers had in mind in 1906 when they said "Bad roads spell ISOLATION for the American farmer in giant letters which reach across the continent from ocean to ocean."[8]

In spite of all this, the American farmers had not been nearly so concerned about their poor country roads through the years as they had been about the nation's railroads. If they were able to get their harvest to market before bad weather set in, this was all they asked. They were resigned to being isolated on their farms through the winter and spring, partly because this was the way things had always been but more because when they looked at those ten-mile strips of mud and water separating them from their marketplace and euphemistically called "roads," no salvation from their plight seemed possible.

Other people, however, besides the farmers were interested in good roads, and in 1892 a group of men, spurred on perhaps by the complaints of the bicyclists who were just then discovering the nation's poor roads and by railroad officials concerned with the high cost of moving the harvest from the farm to the railroad, organized the National League for Good Roads. The next year they prevailed upon Congress to establish the Office of Public Road Inquiry within the Department of Agriculture and endow it with an appropriation of $10,000. This was the beginning of the modern good roads movement.[9]

The work of the Office of Public Road Inquiry was largely educational. It published a number of circulars and bulletins on good road-building techniques, and in conjunction with a private organization, the National Good Roads Association, it sponsored the good road trains that toured the nation from Buffalo to Birmingham in the early 1900's and took the latest road-building procedures directly to the farmers and other interested road-builders.[10]

But circulars, bulletins, and good road trains built no roads. To get the farmers to work on their roads took something more than road-building demonstrations and speeches, and in the end it was not so much the work of the Office of Public Road Inquiry that induced farmers to repair their roads and mend their bridges in the early days of the new century as it was rural free delivery of mail.

The first indication that rural delivery would beget good roads came in 1899 when the Post Office Department declared that no rural routes would be established where roads were not usable the year around. True, this regulation was leniently interpreted when the R F D was young, and many a route was laid across roads fit only for mud turtles, but the regulation was still no idle threat. Literally hundreds of rural route petitions were rejected because of poor roads, and when they were, disappointed farmers came face to face with a practical, concrete illustration of the cost of poor roads for the first time in their lives.[11]

Many of them, particularly in the South, objected indignantly against being denied rural delivery because of poor roads, and so did their congressmen. But it was so obviously impossible to have good service over roads sometimes impassable, that even hard-headed farmers could see the point. And when they realized the Department meant business, they began working their roads as they never had been worked before.

The rural agents, laying out rural routes in those years when Theodore Roosevelt was in the White House and progress was a byword, noticed the phenomenon and mentioned it in their reports to the Department. Roads that had received no more attention in the past than some farmer's hearty curse, were now being drained, dragged, and crowned in a manner virtually unheard of a short time before. Bridges were built and culverts laid. Even the weeds and trash were removed from the roadsides.[12]

In the Midwest the farmers were helped immeasurably by the timely appearance of the King road drag. This simple device, popularized by a Missouri farmer named D. Ward King, was nothing more than a split log, one half fastened solidly about three feet ahead of the other. But if it were pulled over a muddy road especially after a rain, it smoothed the road and rounded it toward the center in such a way as to cause it to drain more easily. When the road dried it became quite hard, and farmers learned that a fairly decent road could be made if the dragging process were repeated several times. Besides, it was so cheap every farmer could have one, and so simple almost any farm boy could operate it. In 1906 King showed his drag to a group of farmers at Wellesville, Kansas, and within a week as many as 100 drags were reported within a radius of eight miles of the town and all but two miles of a twenty-five-mile rural mail route out of the town had been dragged.[13]

But the farmers could not do everything alone. Money as well as manpower was needed to build bridges and culverts. So great was the pressure to get the roads in shape for rural delivery that money for road repair was found here and there, and the Post Office Department estimated in 1908 that about $72,000,000 had been spent on rural delivery roads since the beginning of R F D.[14]

As often as not the goad that set the farmers to patching up their roads was the Post Office Department's rural agent who laid out the routes. He would enter a rural community with all his maps and paraphernalia and begin checking roads almost immediately. If he were establishing a single route, he could tell at a glance whether the roads to be traversed by the route were satisfactory, remediable, or simply impossible. But if he were establishing a county rural delivery system, eliminating old fourth-class post offices and dovetailing the rural routes into one another so the entire system virtually depended on the successful operation of each separate route, he had to worry about roads all over the county, and the job of putting them all in reasonable repair was sometimes comparable to cleaning the Augean stables.

Nevertheless, the conscientious rural agent was a determined man, and the means by which he could bring about improved county roads were illustrated in Jefferson County, Kansas, in 1905. Situated in the eastern part of the state, the county was heavily wooded, hilly, and cut by streams, and the roads, according to the rural agent, were the worst of any county in Kansas he had seen except Leavenworth County.[15]

Realizing that a good county service was impossible unless the roads were repaired, he placed an editorial in the leading county newspapers, informing the farmers that if they wanted a successful mail service they would have to put the roads touching on their farms in good order. And they must do this, he warned, before he had completed his report so he could inspect the work they had done. After this, he laid out the routes he wanted to recommend, carefully noting the exact location, by township, of the roads most in need of mending. He published this information in all the county newspapers and sent word to the township trustees to get busy on their roads if they wanted a good rural delivery service. In the meantime, he interviewed a number of people who wanted to donate their labor in the cause and sent them off to different areas to work.[16]

By mid-summer of that year Jefferson County fairly swarmed with road workers. No one had ever seen anything quite like it. By August 9, hills had been pulled down, rocks removed, grades improved, drainage ditches plowed at the roadsides, and culverts built, and almost all the worst roads had been put in good shape.[17]

If as sometimes happened, the farmers were less cooperative in repairing their roads than they were in Jefferson County, the zealous rural agent could use extreme pressure to bring about improvements. While work was progressing in Jefferson County, a rural agent had laid out a service in DeKalb County, Missouri, which depended for its success on the building of a bridge on Route 2 out of Maysville. One of the county judges had given the agent a written pledge that the bridge would be built, but shortly after the routes had been established, plans to build the bridge ran into opposition.

The trouble sprang from nothing more than the outbreak of an old neighborhood quarrel, but it was so intense one man told the rural agent he would rather have rural delivery driven from the county than see that bridge built. Consequently, the county's two other judges backed away from signing the bridge-building agreement. Whereupon the rural agent recommended that there be no county service in DeKalb County until the postmaster at Maysville certified that the bridge was in place.

This was always the rural agent's ace in the hole, and if threatening the farmers and their road commissioners with the loss of R F D could not force them to mend their bridges and roads, nothing could. Usually it brought the desired results as it did in DeKalb County. Bridge-building promises were renewed there, and three farmers living near the bridge site on Maysville Route 2 signed an agreement promising to keep the area "open and in good condition for crossing" until the bridge was built.[18]

Pledges like this, both written and unwritten, were commonly made by the farmers while their rural routes were being built. Eager to have their mail delivered, the farmers often met the rural agent as he came by their farms and enthusiastically agreed to improve their roads for the rural mailman. "It is impossible for me to name the number of individual pledges to put the roads in better condition and clear the snowdrifts in winter," wrote a rural agent from Iowa in 1900. "Road officers and county supervisors by the score have voluntarily pledged themselves to expend the road revenues for the improvement of rural free-delivery routes." Within the next year they had made over a hundred written agreements to improve their roads to make sure their people would have a rural delivery.[19]

Burning with enthusiasm to obtain a rural mail route, farmers and their road commissioners made promises they might later have wished to forget, and sometimes did, once their rural routes were in and the novelty of having their mail delivered wore away. But there were always reminders for short memories. Once the routes were operating, the Post Office Department, like an old-fashioned schoolmaster with his birch whip in hand, lectured the farmers on the necessity of keeping their roads in order and stood guard to see that they did. Twice a year its postal inspectors went over the rural routes checking road conditions, and if necessary, told the farmers that free delivery would be discontinued unless they repaired their roads. If farmers were willing to fix their roads but needed special help, the Department called upon the engineers from the Office of Public Roads for advice.

This cooperative road-repairing venture between the Post Office Department and the Office of Public Roads began in 1906. The procedure was simple. At the request of the Post Office Department, an engineer was sent to examine rural route roads needing special attention. Having made his investigation, the engineer suggested ways to improve the roads and exacted a promise from the road authorities that the road would be repaired. He then wrote a report of his findings, and those reports, now on file at the National Archives, are sharp reminders of the tremendous problems involved in digging the farmers out of the mud.[20]

First, last, and always, however, the rural mailman was the Post Office Department's mainstay in its continuing campaign for better roads. "If bad roads are continuously maintained," ran a postal inspector's letter in 1910, "the carriers are most responsible in not reporting to the postmaster; then the postmasters in not bringing the matter to the attention of patrons and road officers; and finally, in cases of continued neglect in failing to report to the Department."[21]

So the major responsibility for good rural post roads was the rural mailman's, and no one in rural America was a greater booster for better roads or knew more about the bad ones than he. Six days a week, month in and month out, he traveled the 26 miles or so over a route that varied little from year to year, until he knew his roads as well as he knew the wrinkles on his forehead. He knew the ruts and washouts along his route, his road's composition, where the rain would stand after a spring downpour, and where the snow was likely to drift in winter. He knew what bridge needed repair, where culverts should be, and where the weeds should be trimmed at the roadsides.

Because poor roads could double his work and might even cause him to forfeit a day's pay if because of them he could not deliver the mail, the rural mailman was only too happy to pass his knowledge of his roads to the county and state road officials who compiled a mass of information on roads that would make their repair easier. Theoretically, when his roads needed repairing, the rural carrier was supposed to tell the postmaster about it and let the postmaster pass the word along to the commissioners. But, in practice, many a rural mailman went himself, when his day was done, to tell the road commissioners about a stretch of road that needed working or a bridge that had to be mended. And since rural route roads nearly always took precedence over others, road commissioners were usually prompt to respond to his request.[22]

By their constant nagging rural mailmen could make themselves obnoxious to road commissioners, however, particularly when they called on the Post Office Department for help. In the summer of 1907 the Department wrote the road supervisor in Chesterfield County, South Carolina, several times warning him about the condition of his roads. At length the supervisor wrote a tart note to the Fourth Assistant Postmaster General saying he knew the roads in his county were bad but he had neither the money nor labor to do more than he was doing. "I am trying," he said, "to have the bad places patched up with what little money we have but this is a busy season of the year and farmers have to work now if they make any crop and the most of the people in Chesterfield County are farming." He did have one suggestion though: "The Department has a fixed salary to pay its carriers which is a very good salary too and if the present carriers are not willing to carry the mail at said price without any grumbling that other fellow will be glad to do so."[23]

The tone of his letter suggested that perhaps the road supervisor himself might have preferred to have the rural mailman's job rather than his own, and there must have been any number of harried men in his position in those years who felt the same way. Their responsibilities were so immense and their resources so small that they could hardly be blamed if they felt frustrated and resentful when the Post Office Department told them their roads were inadequate.

Even as the South Carolina road supervisor was writing his testy letter, the country road situation was rapidly improving. At long last, state governments across the land were beginning to recognize that the road problem was too big for local governments to handle, and from 1900 to 1910 state after state passed laws designed to help local governments improve their roads. There were laws creating commissions to develop state highway systems and laws appropriating state funds for local road improvement. Laws were enacted allowing local governments to issue bonds to finance road construction and even authorizing the use of convict labor for maintaining country roads, and to see, especially in the South, a chain gang shoveling dirt beside a rural mailbox in those pre-World War I days was commonplace.[24]

Many of these laws owed their existence in some measure to the agitation for good roads aroused by the R F D. Some legislatures, in fact, were so impressed by the connection between rural delivery and good roads, they enacted special legislation for rural route roads. In Giles County, Tennessee, for example, where rural carriers had been opening and closing gates along their routes for years, rural route roads were declared by the state in 1907 to be public roads and all obstructions ordered removed. An Indiana law, passed that same year, specified that all rural route roads must be properly maintained, and for every day such a road remained defective, the responsible county supervisor would be fined not less than $1.00 and not more than $25.00.[25]

Of course, the R F D was only one of the pressures inducing the states to write good road laws in this period, and whether it was more influential than the Office of Public Roads, the good road associations springing up like sunflowers on a Kansas prairie, or even the rise of the automobile no one can say. Its contribution was, at least, important. Nothing else brought the sense of urgency to the good roads movement that rural delivery did. When the Post Office Department withheld rural routes from farmers whose roads were poor, state legislatures were confronted, as President Cleveland would have said, with a fact not a theory, and compelled to write good road laws they might otherwise have preferred merely to discuss.

Anyone wise in the American way of doing things could have guessed that once the states had begun to help build roads, it would be but a matter of time before the national government would also be asked to help. Indeed, the good road advocates were already waging a campaign for national aid while the states were still in the process of writing their road laws. But here the good road movement floundered for more than a decade, blocked by the theory that such aid was unconstitutional.

This theory went back at least as far as 1817 when President James Madison vetoed John C. Calhoun's Bonus bill on the grounds that its provision to use national funds to build roads within the states was a power not delegated to Congress. Subsequently, Presidents James Monroe and Andrew Jackson both vetoed similar bills for nearly similar reasons; and with the Democrats in control of the government most of the time up to the Civil War and Southerners increasingly touchy about states' rights, the idea that the national government should not help states with their internal improvements, as roads were then spoken of, became firmly fixed. In fact, the Democratic party implanted this idea in their political platform in 1840 and kept it there right up to the Civil War.[26]

After the Civil War this question was almost forgotten—perhaps because people came to believe railroads would take care of the transportation problem—until 1893 when the government was asked to appropriate $10,000 for the Office of Public Road Inquiry. What followed this request in the House of Representatives revealed the deep-seated, pre-Civil War attitudes:

> Congressman C. B. Kilgore (Texas): "Is not the purpose of that proposition to open a way to Federal supervision over dirt roads?"

Congressman William Hatch (Missouri): "It is not; and there is not a member on the Committee who would entertain that proposition for a moment."[27]

That seemed to settle the matter, and for another seven years almost nothing was said about national aid for local roads beyond the piddling appropriations made each year for the Office of Public Road Inquiry.

Then, early in the new century, attitudes changed, and people began talking about national aid for local roads as if they had never been afraid to mention it before. Roy Stone, director of the Office of Public Road Inquiry, had noticed the change by 1903. In 1892 he declared, "we dared not whisper, 'National aid to road building' save in secret: now we can shout it on all the highways and byways."[28]

What had happened in those eleven years to produce this change? The answer was clear: in 1892 there had been no rural delivery; in 1903 there was. As early as 1901 good road zealots, seeing that the R F D provided an argument for circumventing the Constitution, had latched on to it and were playing it for all it was worth. The Constitution, said they, gave Congress the power to establish post offices and post roads; the government was already building and maintaining post offices, so obviously "establish" meant "build and maintain"; hence, the government had the right to build and maintain post roads as well as post offices, and since every country road used by the R F D was a post road, the government had the right to build and maintain country roads.[29] It was that easy to demolish, at least by argument, a precedent more than three quarters of a century old.

This was the beginning. And for fourteen years a steady stream of bills with national aid for state roads their object, poured through congressional hoppers. Some were bills to improve rural route roads only; and some, like the one Tennessee's Walter

Brownlow first proposed in 1902, were broader in scope. But always rural delivery remained the heart of the argument for national aid, and one wonders how federal support for roads would ever have been won had there been no R F D. Like Aladdin's lamp, the good road people found that the R F D could be rubbed again and again, and the genie would always produce some good reason why the national government should help finance local road improvement.[30]

The twentieth century had no more than reached its first birthday, when the nation heard that because of rural free delivery it was the national government's duty as well as its constitutional right to help the states with their roads, and this made so much sense that even a man like Alabama's Colonel J. M. Faulkner, who had fought for states' rights in the 1860's saw the light. "Though . . . I am a strict constructionist of the constitution of the United States," said he, "still wherever it is clear that a duty is of a public nature, I am strongly in favor of having that duty performed by the Government. Now, it is a fact . . . that good roads and rural mail delivery go hand in hand. We can not have rural mail delivery without having good roads, and, believing that we are entitled to both . . . , I believe that we should leave nothing undone to secure these as rights which belong to the people."[31]

Two years later the Colonel's argument was modified slightly to put justice as well as duty on the side of national aid. Justice demanded, ran the argument, that if the government would deliver the mail, it must deliver it to all farmers, and this could be done only if farm roads throughout the nation were improved. According to a good road supporter from Nebraska, justice in this matter could be served in but one of two ways: "Either . . . the whole scheme of rural free delivery must be abandoned because it cannot be carried out with equal justice to all people or . . . the National Government must help the less favored communities improve their roads, thus making universal free delivery possible."

Even the congressmen who were haunted by the specter of paternalism were silenced by the common-sense argument that if it was paternalism for the government to help states build roads, it was paternalism to deliver the mail to the farmers.[32]

These arguments were everything arguments should be. They were logical and they were appealing, and when they were linked with the idea that the government, by supporting rural route roads, would be helping the farmers, those trusty guardians of the Republic and makers of real wealth, they seemed nearly irresistible. But Congress did resist nonetheless, and for years the supporters of national aid had all the arguments in Congress but few of the votes.

Like federal aid to education in recent times, government support for state road building was too bold, too costly, too different, to be launched overnight, and congressmen needed time to ascertain what their constituents thought. Or maybe South Carolina's Senator Asbury Latimer had a better explanation for the delay when he told a good road audience that the reason there had been no road legislation for over 75 years was because the people sent "to Congress men who live in the cities." Whatever the reason, it was 1912 before a bill proposing national aid for state roads first appeared on the floor of the House of Representatives for debate.[33]

The bill was introduced by Congressman Dorsey W. Shackleford from Missouri, and, after all that had been said about the connection between good roads and rural free delivery it was no surprise that it was a bill to improve post roads. Every road in the country, according to this bill, over which the United States mails were carried, whether by star or free delivery carriers, was to be classified as A, B, or C, in accordance with its degree of improvement. A and B roads were macadamized and gravel; dirt roads were class C. For carrying the mail over these roads the United States government would pay an annual rental of $25 per mile for roads of the first class, $20 for the second, and $15 for the third.

The responsibility for classifying the roads was left to the Secretary of Agriculture, and no allotment would be made for any road that did not meet class C standard.[34]

Shackleford's bill was a masterpiece of compromise. First, it left the road completely under state supervision to please the states' righters; second, it offered an incentive to the states to build up their roads to class C standard at least; tied to the improvement of rural post roads, it answered the constitutional objection; and finally, it provided for the improvement of the farm-to-market roads, the very kind of roads most people had in mind in 1912 when they talked about roads. In fact, it was so appealing that 25 congressmen dropped their own good road bills to support it, and the House adopted it by the lopsided count of 240 to 86. Good road legislation seemed within grasp at last.[35]

But outside the halls of Congress trouble gathered. The automobile people did not like the Shackleford bill and set themselves to fight it with pen, ink, voice, and whatever other means seemed suitable.

Just how much influence automobile interests had had in the good roads movement up to this time is not easy to determine. Because the automobile and the good roads movement appeared on the American scene about the same time, it has been easy to assume the former inspired the latter. The trouble with this easy assumption is that it puts the horseless carriage before the horse, so to speak. The good roads movement had already begun by the time Charles Duryea drove the first American gasoline automobile on its maiden run in 1893, and people were already talking about national aid for roads in 1901 when there were only about 15,000 automobiles registered in the whole country.[36]

But in the beginning the good roads movement was essentially agrarian and had nothing to do with automobiles. The very fact that the Office of Public Road Inquiry, later called the Office of Public Roads, was attached to the Department of Agriculture, indictates the nature of the movement. True, the farmers had neglected their roads shamefully until the 1890's, but after the inauguration of the R F D they had become the heart and soul of the good roads movement. And why not? Good roads meant not only free delivery of their mail, but cheaper transportation of their crops from farm-to-market, better churches and schools, and an end to isolation, and it was only logical that they should have taken the lead in the fight to win government aid for road building. Their support of the Shackleford bill was also logical, for it provided for the upkeep of the very kind of roads the farmers were interested in.

The automobile people, however, who had up to this time played no conspicuous part in the campaign for national aid, now stepped in to wreck the farmers' bill. It developed that they had no particular interest in improving farm-to-market roads. If federal money was to be spent on roads, they wanted it spent on hard-surfaced, interstate, and transcontinental highways that stretched from coast to coast so that Americans might "see America first." They did not want the money wasted, as they said, on roads that began "nowhere and ended nowhere."[37]

Merciless in their attack, they dubbed the supporters of the Shackleford bill "Knights of the dirt roads," and the *Washington Times* fulminated against following "the rural mail carriers . . . to erect a road system without any plan nor purpose." And by the time the bill reached the Senate, the American Automobile Association had written senators urging them to vote against the bill.[38]

The Senate did reject the measure perhaps because of the American Automobile Association, as some of its members claimed. But the bill had no friend in the White House, and this must have been a factor in its defeat. As a matter of fact, President Taft was not only opposed to this bill, he was opposed to the principle of government aid for roads, and even the approaching election of 1912 was not enough to make him change his mind. Invited to attend a good road convention in the autumn of that year, Taft gave his answer to his private secretary. "I am not going to the Good Roads Convention," he wrote, "for the reason that I would make more enemies if I went than if I stayed away because I would have to tell the truth. I do not believe in involving the Federal treasury in a weight of obligation to build roads that the States ought to build."[39]

And that was that. The best Congress could do that year was to appropriate $500,000 to be used jointly by the Post Office Department and the Department of Agriculture to improve certain rural route roads and to study the economic effects of such improvement. Of course this was only a stopgap measure passed to relieve pressure and stall for time while the problem was studied, but it turned out to be important. It established the principle, later called dollar matching, of forcing the states to share with the national government the expense of road repair, and proved that cooperation between the national government and any unit of government below the state level would not work. Both these bits of experience proved valuable when Congress finally got around to working out its final road-building bill.[40]

In the meantime, Shackleford, undaunted by his defeat, was back in the House in 1914 with a revised version of his bill which he hoped would answer the objections to the original. But when the Senate rejected this too, he and his supporters saw they would have to meet the demands of the automobile people if they wanted national aid for roads. So two years later, they rewrote their bill once more. They eliminated the rental feature of the original bill, broadened the term "post roads" to include all roads over which the mails were carried or might be carried, and so made it possible for the national government to give assistance to rural route roads or to roads that might be linked with other interstate roads to form a transcontinental road. But the national government could pay no more than half the cost of any project, and it would deal only with state highway commissions.[41]

To these provisions the Senate added a few of its own. One was particularly important. It specified that the amount of money each state would receive for its roads would depend on the ratio that state bore to the other states in population, area, and mileage of rural route roads.

Late in June the bill had made its way from the conference committee back to the House and Senate for final action, and an anxious President Woodrow Wilson wrote Senator John Bankhead: "I am so deeply interested in the good roads bill," he wrote, "that I take the liberty of writing to ask you what you think the prospects are for an early consideration and action upon the conference report. I should like to help in any way it may occur to you."[42]

The President's interest had not always been so keen. Since 1913 supporters of federal aid for roads had found him reluctant to take a stand in spite of the promise in the Democratic platform of 1912. Behind the scenes he had opposed the rental feature of the Shackleford bill, and his public statements on the subject of good roads had been mere platitudes. As late as February 1916 he was still not openly committing himself to federal aid. But in the summer of that year, he was noticeably more progressive, and so he worried about the fate of this progressive measure.[43]

Even as he wrote, however, the bill was in the process of being approved, and in July, with a pen his cousin John Wilson, an ardent advocate of good roads, had asked to keep, the President signed it and ushered in a new era in the relationship between the state and national governments.[44]

After nearly sixteen years of tough campaigning, the fight was won. But was it a victory for the farmers? Some thought it was and said so. But less than a year later Fred White, president of the National Rural Letter Carriers' Association, was not so sure. "Powerful organizations formed and now being formed, and with big Capital behind them," he wrote in February 1917, "are seeking to capture this appropriation for good roads from the Rural People who were to be benefited by this Federal expenditure."[45]

He referred, of course, to those who had wanted to build transcontinental roads, and he was right. They were after the appropriation, and though they had to share the funds for a time with those who wanted to build rural post roads, in 1921 they were able to get what they wanted. That year the Federal Highway Act was amended so that federal appropriations for roads could no longer be spent on rural post roads generally, but only on roads that would eventually form transcontinental highways.[46]

Thus were the farmers and rural mailmen despoiled of their victory, and both of them had to continue the battle of dirt roads without federal aid for years. But the fruits of the farmers' long struggle were not permanently lost, only delayed. The Federal Highway Act had established the principle of state and federal cooperation, and years later, as the transcontinental highways were completed, the act was amended once more to give federal aid to secondary, farm-to-market, rural route roads. The first of these amendments came in 1936, and government aid for these roads has continued to the present.[47]

PARCEL POST

"He [the farmer] sees the rural mail carrier go by with a load of twenty-five pounds. Yet if he wishes to send a pound of butter to town he must pay sixteen cents for a four cent service. Then statesmen prate about the deficit caused by the rural free delivery, as if he were a pauper on the nation's bounty, while they deny him a parcels post for fear he will buy goods cheaper somewhere else and thus do less trading with his local merchants. Is it to be wondered at that he believes the merchant's welfare is deemed of more importance than his own?"

E. E. Miller, "Factors in the Remaking of Country Life," *The Forum*, 48 (Sept. 1912), 362

NO PERIOD in American history was more politically exciting than the early 1900's. Like a man taking a large dose of Dr. Roc's Liver, Rheumatism, and Neuralgia Cure to purge himself of half a dozen ills, the nation in those years drank deeply from a bottle labeled "Reform" to cure its maladies, and the effects were everywhere in evidence. There was a movement for everything, for pure food and drugs, for conservation, against the trusts, for women's rights, for prohibition, and so on until the person who could not find a crusade to his taste must have been abnormally well-adjusted.

The good roads movement found a home in this environment,

and so did the campaign for parcel post, and if good road advocates owed something to the RFD for their success, the parcel-post supporters were even more in its debt. For had it not been for rural delivery, it is likely there would have been no parcel post as we know it, and Americans would still be relying on private transportation companies to deliver their Christmas packages.

Parcel post is now so much a part of the American way of life it scarcely seems possible the nation had once been without it or that it had ever been a controversial subject. But there was a time, not more than two generations ago, when just to mention it in a crowd was enough to start a debate. Like so many controversies of that period, parcel post stirred up ageless arguments, and even now, fifty years later, those arguments once heard in country stores and one-room schoolhouses across the land bear a certain resemblance to those one hears over his television set when controversial matters are discussed.

When the century opened, the United States had no real parcel-post system. A person could send a package through the mail if it weighed no more than four pounds, but it would cost him 16 cents a pound to do so. If he wished to mail 12 pounds, he must send three separate packages, and since there was only one rate, the total cost of mailing his three packages would be $1.92 regardless of whether they were going 20 miles or 200. To these regulations there was one exception. After 1899, when the first of many parcel-post conventions with foreign countries had been signed, an American could send as much as an 11-pound package through the mails from the United States to a foreign country for 12 cents a pound, four cents a pound cheaper than he could mail his domestic four-pound package within the country.[1]

Such as it was, this was the nation's only parcel-post system, and because of its flat-rate provision and low-weight limit on each package, the Post Office Department had been losing money on it for more than a generation. For Americans had learned to send their small, long-distance packages by mail to take advantage of the flat rate. The rest, large and small, they usually sent by the express companies who gobbled up huge profits that might have been made by the Post Office Department under a different system.[2]

Since that day back in the 1830's when William F. Harnden began his one-man business, riding trains and carrying packages in his carpetbag for people who wanted his services, the express service had been a booming business. Discovering that people had packages to send and receive or errands to run in distant places for which they would willingly pay a fee was almost like striking gold. And like a gold strike, it was too good to keep secret. Shortly, other men followed Harnden's example, men like Henry Wells, William G. Fargo, and Alvin Adams, who rode the rails carrying their own carpetbags to get their businesses started and with so much success that they had organized the nation's major express companies before the Civil War.[3]

As the railroads blanketed the nation after the Civil War, so did the express companies, and by the turn of the century, they could be found in all sections of the country. Of the principal companies, the Adams Express, the American, and Wells, Fargo were the largest and best known. On any day, one could see their wagons in those years, the Adams green, the Wells, Fargo red, and the American dark-blue and red, clattering through the streets of the large cities, their visor-capped drivers pulling and straining at the leather reins in their hands as they maneuvered their horses and wagons through the busy streets. In winter, when the snow lay heavy and deep on the streets, wagons were exchanged for brightly painted sleighs drawn by matched teams that jogged over the snow to the jingle of silver bells attached to their collars, and long after the horse and buggy era had passed, people looked back nostalgically to the times they had heard the express sleigh in the streets and seen a Christmas package or perhaps even Grandmother's trunk being delivered to their door.[4]

The express companies carried everything from fresh oysters to jewels. Wells, Fargo and Company hauled mail, gold, and people all over the West for more than half a century, and a combination of express companies under the direction of John Butterfield once delivered ballots for the 1864 election to the New York troops scattered hither and yon across the battle fronts of the war. The United States Express Company after 1889, had a contract to carry all the government's currency from place to place about the country, a contract so ironclad that when the company's officials discovered a Treasury official trying to avoid the express fee by having his clerks carry $10,000,000 in gold certificates from Washington to Philadelphia at a cost of $100, they were able to collect $2,000 for this service their company had not even performed.[5]

Because they moved their trade so fast—more than twice as fast as regular freight—the express companies did an enormous business in transporting perishable goods as well as other merchandise. Farmers with poultry and milk products, berries and other garden crops to sell depended on the express companies to ship their goods to market no less than did the restaurant owner who expected them to bring him the fresh fish his menus called for.

Transportation was, of course, their main business, but it was not their only business. As they prospered they went into such sidelines as banking, writing money orders, and finally traveler's checks, and they became so omnipresent in the business world it was an isolated American indeed who had never done business with them.

But everything they did had a price, and a high one at that. Six companies controlled some 90 per cent of all the express business in the nation before World War I, and there was no better example of monopoly in the country even in an age of monopolies. After the Civil War they had carved the nation among themselves and maintained control of the trade of their respective areas through the exclusive contracts they had made with the railroads. Here, unregulated until 1906, they arrogantly served the public, rendered only mediocre service, made inordinate profits, and confused the public with some 600,000,000 rates. Indeed so perplexing was the rate structure that even express agents themselves could not always give the exact rate from point to point, and Franklin K. Lane, a member of the Interstate Commerce Commission in 1912, once had three rates quoted to him on the same package by the same express agent on the same day.[6]

How these 600,000,000 rates had been set in the first place was something of a mystery. The usual contract express companies made with the railroads specified that express rates should be at least one and a half times higher than freight rates. But normally they were much higher than that and obviously designed to take all the traffic would bear. That the express companies juggled their rates to suit themselves was suggested by a letter one company sent its agents at Christmas time in 1897. "The season is approaching," the letter read, "when zealous expressmen make a distinction between regular patrons and those who, as agents of Santa Claus, appear but once a year, which distinction is displayed by a forgetfulness of the classification and obtaining a little higher price than would be charged the regular shipper."[7]

On top of all this, express companies adequately served very few areas. There were only 35,000 express offices in the nation in 1912 compared to more than 58,000 post offices, and only at the big city offices did the express companies deliver packages directly to one's door. Everywhere else the service stopped at the depot, and people had to pick up their own packages.[8]

In all rural America in 1900 there was, of course, no direct express service from the railroads to the farms, and only those farmers who lived near a town with an express office and could bring and carry away their own parcels could make use of the system at all. At best it was a clumsy and expensive service, and though farmers used it as the rise of Montgomery Ward and Company after 1872 attests, they did so sparingly and grudgingly and out of dire necessity.

It was not because there had been no demands to change this

system that nothing had been done about it by 1900. Postmaster Generals had been recommending a parcel-post system capable of cutting in on the express trade since 1880, and in 1891 Postmaster General Wanamaker had begun a vigorous parcel-post crusade. Arguing that a parcel post would prevent the express companies from running off with all the profitable, short-haul trade, the irrepressible Wanamaker had pressed his parcel-post recommendations on President Harrison three years running. But as often as he urged it, the President ignored it. Not once did he even call Congress's attention to it. Perhaps he thought it was useless, but probably the best reason for his silence was summed up by Postmaster General Wanamaker himself in 1891. "In point of fact," he wrote in his report to the President that year, "there are but four strong objections to the parcel post, and they are the four great express companies." With some variation, this became the classic statement for two decades on the opposition to parcel post.[9]

After Wanamaker there was no one in a responsible government position for more than a decade who cared to do more than suggest a parcel post. Besides the nation was caught up in an economic panic, the exciting political campaign between Bryan and McKinley, and the Spanish-American War in those years, and only reformers like James I. Cowles had much time to think about parcel post.

Cowles was one of those crusading gadflies churned up by the troublous decades that closed out the nineteenth century. Born into a wealthy Connecticut family before the Civil War and educated at Yale, he, like so many of those turn-of-the-century hotheads, made a career of journalism and reform, and of all his enthusiasms parcel post was his greatest. A journalist once called him "The Fighting Father of the Parcel Post," and perhaps he was. At least no man worked harder or sacrificed more for the cause. For years he spent his talents and time and a good part of his fortune on the parcel-post movement. Some of his friends even suspected he sometimes went hungry to save money for the campaign, and the story goes that when his house burned his comment was that "it was insured," and now he "would have more money for parcel post."[10]

Cowles's parcel-post crusade began slowly. Such was the temper of the times it took a pariah, someone like the Populist Senator Marion Butler just to mention Cowles's work in the Senate before 1900, and it was not until that year that Cowles's own congressman introduced a parcel-post bill in Congress for him. But introducing such a bill in Congress in 1900 was like dropping a pebble in the sea. Even the congressman who introduced it seemed half afraid of it and had the record show it was introduced by request, and the Senate was so touchy on the matter that the next year it would not even permit a parcel-post article to be printed in the *Congressional Record!*[11]

One had only to look at the Senate roll that year to understand why. There, from the State of New York sat Thomas C. Platt, president even then of the United States Express Company. There, too, from the same state was Chauncey M. Depew, one of the largest stockholders of the American Express Company, former president of the New York Central Railroad, and still, as he sat in the Senate, a director of that railroad. And around these two men, led by shrewd Nelson W. Aldrich from Rhode Island, assembled as conservative a group of men as ever chilled the marrow in a reformer's bones.[12]

But Cowles was no man to be paralyzed by the strength of his opposition. In 1902 he organized a Postal Progress League to push the parcel post along and began bringing influential men into the organization to give it prestige and respectability. Within a year the National Grange had lined up in support of parcel post and the movement seemed to be gaining strength. But two years and a number of rejected parcel-post bills later, the campaign remained virtually where it had been four years before, and there it might have stayed had it not been for the growth of the R F D in these years.

From its beginning rural delivery had been, in a modest way, the farmers' own express service. No sooner had the rural mailmen started making their daily rounds, than the farmers began converting them into expressmen. Medicine, food, clothes, tools, harness, whatever they needed they asked their mailman to bring on his next trip from town. And if they wanted to send something into town, eggs, cheese, or perhaps a broken piece of machinery to repair, the rural mailman took these too. If by chance they had a parcel coming express, it was not even considered too much to ask him to stop by the depot and pick it up for them.

This package service was immensely popular among the farmers, and particularly so after the installation of rural telephones. In less time than it took to drive a team and buggy down the lane, through the gate, and onto the main-traveled road, a farmer could call his doctor or storekeeper and order everything from medicine to machinery to be sent out with the mailman. Such was the speed of the service that if the farmer's storekeeper or doctor could catch the carrier before he left the post office with the day's mail, a package could be delivered only two or three hours after it had been requested.

One drawback in the system was that it did not help the government's revenues, for almost every package the mailman carried, he carried outside the mails. Every time he stopped at the depot to pick up an express package for a farmer, the government lost the postage that would have been paid if that package had gone through the mails. Of course, most such packages weighed more than four pounds and could not have gone through the mails anyway, but even when the mailman had a mailable package for one of his patrons, a sack of crackers from the local store perhaps or a bottle of pills from the doctor, he carried it outside the mails because this was a part of the errand service he was permitted to perform. The doctor or the storekeeper or sometimes the farmer himself would pay him "a little something for his trouble," as the expression went, but the government got nothing. In effect, the

Post Office Department had created a wonderful express system in the R F D but was unable to reap a dime of income from it.

There was another problem too. Because the rural carriers were allowed to solicit business along their routes as well as deliver packages, their express business mushroomed, and the Post Office Department was confronted not only with the loss of postal revenues but with the outraged complaints of those who suffered from the new economic power suddenly wielded by the rural mail carriers.

John D. Rockefeller had learned that the control of transportation meant power, and the rural mailman's express service was a good illustration of the principle on a tiny scale. A rural carrier would solicit meat orders, for example, among his patrons for the local butcher. At the end of the day he would turn in his orders to the butcher and next day pick up and deliver the meat packages along his route to those who ordered them. The butcher then paid the mailman for his services and was only too glad to do so, for he had obtained a small monopoly in the meat business along that route.[13]

A case cited in Congress in 1904 illustrates the problem. A certain book publisher was selling a book to farmers for $1.18, absorbing as he did the 22 cents postage it took to mail the book to farmers along the rural routes. At the same time, the publisher sold the book in carload lots, and presumably much cheaper, to a mail-order house, which in turn sold the book to the farmers for $1.18, the same price the publisher had sold it for. But the mail-order house sent the books express to the rural mailmen who had taken orders for them in the first place, and they delivered them for five cents a copy. On each book sold in this way, the government lost 22 cents postage, the mail-order house was probably making more on each sale than the publisher, and the publisher was actually being penalized for sending the books through the mails.[14]

Naturally those who suffered by such procedures complained,

and it was up to Congress and the Post Office Department to solve the nearly unsolvable problem of how to stop this unfair discrimination and at the same time continue the express service the farmers had liked so much. Eventually Congress compromised and wrote a wordy law limiting the mailman's express. What the law meant when the Post Office got through interpreting it was this: a rural carrier could no longer solicit business, but he could carry unmailable matter—liquor and inflammable material excluded—and parcels weighing more than four pounds outside the mails; but whatever he carried could not go express part of the way but must go directly from the merchant to the farmer or vice versa, and the patron, not the middleman, must pay the mailman if any payment was made.[15]

This legislation was enough to destroy the rural mailman's brief taste of economic power and virtually ruin his express service. Unable to solicit business and forbidden to receive payment for his services from businessmen who had formerly paid him, his parcel business dwindled. Worse still, many of the items the farmers wanted to send to town or receive from their storekeepers from day to day were actually mailable and weighed less than four pounds and so had to go through the mails if the mailman took them, and this at the prohibitive rate of 16 cents a pound.

There were laments from the countryside over the loss of this service, but in the long run the collapse of the rural mailman's express was a boon to the parcel-post movement. For Congress had hardly put a crimp in the rural delivery parcel business when the Post Office Department awoke to the fact that with the average farm family sending and receiving less than 10 packages a year through the mails under the existing package regulations, the government was keeping a damper on business that might be profitable if the regulations were changed. So partly to appease the farmers but mainly to increase postal revenues, the Department recommended that Congress raise the weight limit and reduce the postage on all packages delivered along rural routes that had been mailed at the post offices from which those routes began.[16]

Without saying so, the Department was really calling for a rural parcel post, and almost any child could appreciate the logic behind its recommendation. In the first place it would give the farmers a workable express service. Secondly, it would help erase the eternal postal deficit. Every day except Sunday, thousands of rural mailmen were making their rounds with their wagons half empty, and there was no reason in the world why they could not carry more of the farmers' parcels as well as the mail. Since the plan was restricted to rural routes there would be no railroad transportation to pay for and no need to hire additional men, and every nickel made from carrying local packages would go to the Post Office Department. It was bound to increase postal revenues. One Postmaster General went so far as to estimate that if the weight limit on rural packages was raised from 4 to 11 pounds and the postage reduced from 16 cents a pound to 5 cents for the first pound and 2 cents for each additional pound, and if each of the nearly 40,000 rural carriers delivered only three 25-cent packages a day, it would more than wipe out the postal deficit![17]

First suggested in 1904, the rural parcel post was not really pushed until 1907 when George Meyer was appointed Postmaster General. In private life Meyer was a conservative banker from Boston's Beacon Hill and would not normally have been expected to get mixed up in the parcel-post controversy. But the Panic of 1907 had strained the government's finances and the Post Office Department was facing a $6,000,000 deficit. So Meyer began to crusade for a rural parcel post which he was certain would eliminate the postal deficit; and from then on until parcel post became a reality there were really two parcel-post movements—one rural, the other general.[18]

In retrospect, it is easy to see what effect the rural parcel post had on the general movement. When it was first suggested, the parcel-post campaign of Cowles's Postal Progress League was almost lifeless. Its arguments had been exhausted and its bills in Congress had been stalled. Up to that time hardly a congressman had made a speech on the floor of the House directly supporting the league's bills. The Post Office Department's proposal changed all that. True, it made a rural rather than a general parcel post the center of attention for nearly eight years, but it gave all parcel-post enthusiasts a rallying point. It provided them with a bookful of new arguments, and within a five-year period attracted a motley group of new friends, each with his own axe to grind to be sure, but friends nonetheless with something more than enthusiasm on their side.

In time two Presidents, Roosevelt and Taft, endorsed a rural parcel post, the first because it would, he said, "benefit the farmer and the country storekeeper," and the latter presumably for the same reason though probably both of them had in mind that it would increase postal revenues too. The National Rural Carriers' Association supported it because it would help wipe out the postal deficit. This in turn would keep city congressmen from trying to undercut the expensive R F D and might even mean a salary raise for rural mailmen. Speaking for a sizable body of the nation's farmers, the National Grange gave its approval of a rural parcel post, not because it necessarily wanted a limited package service but because it might lead to something better.

Much of the nation's press, particularly the periodicals, ran features on its behalf, inspired surely in part by disinterested motives and partly by the belief that the increase in postal revenues resulting from the service would eliminate the necessity for increased postage on their own magazines which was just then under consideration in Congress. Finally, senators and representatives from rural areas openly and frankly supported the rural parcel post because their constituents wanted it, and because, after all, it was reasonable and would cost the government not one extra red cent to operate. It was almost like getting something for nothing.[19]

But even a reasonable proposition had no immunity from the attacks of special interests, and rural parcel post had none. Indeed, its very reasonableness, which made it more likely to pass Congress, made it more dangerous to its enemies, and the torrent of opposition that met this seemingly innocuous proposal engulfed the nation in an angry debate that lasted five years.

Logically one would have expected to find the express companies in the foreground of the fight against a rural parcel post, since a parcel-post bill of any kind was a possible threat to them. But the express companies, already under suspicion, did not need to commit themselves openly. In the country storekeepers, the small-town businessmen, and the great wholesale merchants in the cities, they had as vocal an opposition to parcel post as ever buttonholed a congressman.

The business world the small-town merchants knew when rural parcel post was suggested was still the world of the general store and the cracker barrel; still the world of the smooth-talking, flashily dressed drummers who traveled from town to town and store to store, carrying bags packed with samples of their line. "My name and connection, sir," they would say as they presented their cards to the local storekeepers, and then they would begin to lay their samples on a counter. Sophisticated, by country standards, and pleasant, they talked and joked and told strange stories of the interesting world outside rural communities and, with a "gift of gab" and a bit of homespun psychology, sold the local merchants everything from caps to corsets. At night, settled in a room at the town's hotel, they wrote up their day's orders, mailed them next morning to their firms in the cities, and moved on to the next town. Some weeks later the merchants picked up the goods they had bought at the express office, sorted them, priced them, and put them on the shelves in their stores to gather fingerprints and dust until at length they were bought.[20]

This was the way business had been conducted in rural America since the Civil War. It was profitable to the drummer, the wholesaler, and the rural merchants, and they would almost literally move heaven and earth to defend it.

No one in rural America in the early 1900's guarded their interests more closely than the rural merchants. With one eye on their sales and the other on guard for trouble, they would ferret out threats to their security ordinary men would never dream existed. Wary and watchful, they seemed to live in a perpetual state of anxiety. One congressman, having grown up in a little Missouri town after the Civil War, recalled that the small-town merchants in his area had always been complaining. They complained when the railroad fares between their towns and the city were reduced, when an electric road was built between Independence and Kansas City, and when macadamized roads were being constructed, all because they feared these innovations would draw trade from their stores.[21]

In a rapidly changing world, they leaped from crisis to crisis. Many of them had been among the bitterest opponents of the R F D because they feared that farmers who no longer came to town for their mail would no longer come into their stores either. But when they could not defeat the system, they worked furiously to turn it to their own advantage. Now, just as they were making their peace with the system, came the possiblity of a rural parcel post, and they were thrown into new paroxysms of fear.

No one not a small-town merchant would have seen any real threat to the traditional pattern of rural business in a rural parcel post. On the contrary, the fact that only packages originating on a rural route or at the post office from which a rural route began could be handled at the cheap rate, suggested it would help more than hinder the local businessmen. They were the ones who could most easily and profitably put a package in the mail for their farm customers. There was the possibility, of course, that shipments from mail-order houses could be expressed to small towns, broken up by one of their agents, and mailed to the farmers through the local post office at the reduced rate. But this was so complicated and expensive few people regarded it as a serious threat.

No, what really worried the local merchants was the fear that a rural parcel post was only a stepping-stone to a general one, and the first congressman who ever spoke for the measure in the House of Representatives had no sooner broached the subject than he was asked if it was "not an opening wedge for a parcels post system."[22]

This was the heart of the matter and the real reason rural merchants fought it without quarter for so long. For if ever a rural parcel post became general, they were confident farmers would buy from mail-order stores, and their own stores would be as empty on Saturday afternoons as the village schoolhouse in summer. The way they saw it, either the parcel post would win and they would be destroyed or vice versa and they meant it to be vice versa.

The Iron Age, a magazine published by the American Hardware Manufacturers' Association, sounded the call to arms in 1909. Shrilly attacking the rural parcel-post measure, it advised all the enemies of parcel post "to lose no time and spare no effort in combating this insidious attempt to establish a parcel post even on a limited scale," and the small-town merchants flocked to the colors.[23]

They were no mean antagonists. Many of them were well-to-do. They had prestige in their communities and political power as well, and they knew how to make their influence felt in Washington as well as any pressure group in the nation. Working within their established organizations like the Illinois Retail Merchants' Association or the National Association of Retail Grocers, they sent their leaders to Congress to testify against a parcel post, mailed thousands of anti-parcel-post petitions to their congressmen, and even tried to get President Taft to oppose it. They wrote personal letters too, so many of them that one unhappy congressman, trying to explain to a visitor why Congress had not established a parcel post, pointed to two sacks of letters on his desk, one large, the other small. "As soon as we know Americans want parcels post," he said, "they can have it." Unfortunately, the large stack of letters on his desk came from the opposition to the measure. "Every man among them," he said, "thinks of No. 1—either he is in the express business or he is a country merchant afraid of losing trade if folks buy through the mails."[24]

Of course, the congressman was right. Like the farmers, the merchants were thinking of No. 1, but one would never have guessed this from reading through the reasons for their opposition. Instead one would have thought theirs was a lofty, idealistic movement designed to promote the nation's welfare. "In considering this matter," wrote a merchant to his congressman, "we have endeavored to eliminate any selfish business reasons we may have against the passage of a . . . parcel post and to look at it solely from the broad view as to what is best for the country."[25]

A rural parcel post, they said, would subvert rural delivery from its original purpose of educating the people, drain the rural communities of their population and capital, and create a mail-order trust, "the most oppressive that human ingenuity could devise." It would ruin country towns and with their destruction "the farmers' local market would be destroyed, educational, social, and religious privileges would be seriously deteriorated, and the country-town realty values so depreciated that a much heavier burden of taxation would be thrown upon the farmers' already overburdened shoulders, while no compensating advantage might be expected from the Mail Order Trust."[26]

Besides the increase in taxes a rural parcel post would lay upon the farmers, the merchants worried about things they had not worried much about before—about the farmer's mental health, which would be injured by reducing the number of his trips to town, and about the impossible burden the new system would impose on the rural mailman who was not equipped to handle the increased business a package service would bring.

Dangerous to the farmers' health, the country town, and the

rural mailman, a rural parcel post, in the eyes of its opponents, was also a grave threat to the American system itself. It was class legislation, socialistic, and paternalistic, three odious terms used by all standpatters of the period as their final line of defense against change. Serious men spoke gloomily of the threat. "Rest assured," said one congressman, "that if we begin by carrying the dairyman's milk to the creamery we will end by milking the cows and manufacturing the butter."[27]

Nor, as they saw it, would a parcel post be fair to them after all they had done for their local communities. They were the ones, they reminded the farmers, who had given them credit in bad years, paid taxes for the upkeep of the local schools, contributed to the local churches, and, in fact, helped build the community. A congressman who had once been a drummer and saw the merchant's point of view remembered that when Logan Valley in Nebraska had been settled, every settler in the valley had relied on the local storekeeper to keep him going until his crops matured. "These settlers," he said, "would have starved to death had they been compelled to depend on the mail-order houses." And who stood by the country merchant in those times? The traveling man and the jobber, of course. "The merchant had but small capital," the congressman continued, "the traveling man was the credit man, and on his representation the jobber and manufacturer stood with him. So, hand in hand, the pioneer farmer and the pioneer merchant, the pioneer traveling man and the pioneer jobber have built up the Middle West." Was it just, then, to undercut the local merchants with a parcel post?[28]

Pioneer merchants they may have been once, but in the early 1900's many of them were well established, and on their side in the fight they had two valuable assets—money and organization. By 1911 the nerve center of the opposition had moved to Chicago where, sometime between 1909 and 1910, the American League of Associations had been formed for the specific purpose of fighting a rural parcel post or any other kind for that matter. Built around seventeen Chicago firms, including Marshall Field and Company and the famous Butler Brothers Store, it spread across the nation to envelop nearly 300 member firms, and though the express companies were not listed among its membership, rumor had it they had made substantial contributions to the organization. One thing was certain: the organization had plenty of money. No one knows how much it spent, but it was able to afford a lobby in Washington and enough employees to prepare thousands of "canned" anti-parcel-post petitions.[29]

By comparison, the parcel-post supporters were a ragtag mob. Made up of a confederation of diverse groups, some wanting a general and some wanting a rural parcel post, they had neither the money nor the central organization their opponents had. About all they had were numbers and arguments and persistence, none of which helped too much in a Congress whose machinery was controlled by the opposition.

For more than five years, parcel-post supporters tried repeatedly to pass a parcel-post bill and failed. Bill after bill providing either for a rural or a general parcel post went to the Post Office Committees of both houses and never came out. At the same time, every effort, and there were many of them, to attach a parcel-post amendment to the Post Office appropriation bill was thrown out by parliamentary maneuvers. Everything was tried. New arguments were raised and bills were hopefully changed to make them more palatable. Once there was a serious proposal in both the House and Senate to conduct an experimental rural parcel post over the rural routes of only four counties of a state. But even this was never allowed to come to a vote.[30]

The plain facts were that the leadership in Congress, whether because of the express companies, as some said, or rural merchants, or for some other reason, did not want a parcel post, and what happened to this proposition was an object lesson in the ability of a handful of men in Congress to stall legislation.

The Speaker of the House from 1903 to 1910 was Joseph G.,

"Uncle Joe," Cannon, congressman from Illinois. He was chairman of the powerful, handpicked Rules Committee, and so tight was his grip on the House machinery that rarely if ever did a bill reach the floor for debate without his blessing. As one of the great standpatters of all time, so opposed to change, it was said, that "if he had attended the caucus on the creation he would have been loyal to chaos," Cannon was no supporter of parcel post, and parcel-post bills going to House committees without his blessing might as well have been inscribed, according to one disgusted congressman, like Dante's *Inferno*: "Abandon Hope, all ye who enter here."[31]

In the Senate where committees were appointed and dominated by Senator Nelson Aldrich, parcel post's prospects were even worse. At least the subject had often been discussed in the House, but only rarely was it even mentioned in the Senate.

So the fight raged on, in and out of Congress, and so important was it to the Americans of the day it became a favorite debate topic in schools and colleges across the country, and a brief handbook for debaters on the subject appeared, filled with all the arguments, pro and con. Supporters of parcel post settled down for a siege, and some observers saw in the mustering of the two forces a great battle between the commercial and agrarian interests of the nation. A farmer from Illinois writing to his congressman put it this way:

> At a farmers' meeting held here today,
> One hundred and twenty men had their say;
>
> . . . .
>
> They say that men of means, a mighty throng,
> Who have time to write petitions long,
> And whose wealth is mines, and bonds, and bills
> And notes, and gold in their money tills,
> Are now flooding Congress to their utmost
> With letters opposed to the parcel post.

> Now, the farmers, having no time to write you there,
> Or to draft petitions or send their prayer,
> Will depend upon you to demand their right
> To a parcel post, and will win their fight.[32]

On New Year's Day, 1910, it was still uncertain how long the embattled conservatives could hold the line. They were then still in control, and no break in the system had yet appeared. But only a few months later, their fortress was crumbling as one by one the stout old timbers that had held it up began to disappear. An old foe of parcel post, Thomas Platt, had already left the Senate the previous year, "broken in mind and body, almost friendless," so *The Nation* said, and his colleague Chauncey Depew was defeated for reelection in 1910. And when in that same year, Nelson Aldrich announced he would not run again for his Senate seat, the very heart of conservatism seemed to have stopped beating.[33]

Meanwhile, on the other side of the Capitol, "Uncle Joe" Cannon's rules had been changed by a dramatic revolt against his leadership in March, and as if to put the final touch to the conservative rout, the Democratic party captured the House of Representatives in the November elections for the first time in sixteen years.

It had been a big year for the progressives, and as the new Congress prepared to meet in December 1911, for its second session, parcel post seemed to have almost no enemies. Even the Congressman from Massachusetts, John Weeks, who had been chairman of the House Committee on Post Office and Post Roads and had been helping to keep the lid on parcel post for five years, had written the President's secretary in September saying that "while if I had my own [way] the government would never do any business, I am convinced that the extension of the Parcels Post is coming, and, therefore, I am anxious that it should come along *rational* lines."[34]

So at last it was no longer a question of whether there would be a parcel post—only a question of what kind. On this, there were almost as many ideas as congressmen, but it was reasonably clear the Congress was moving away from a simple rural parcel post to a general one. For one reason, much had been made of the fact that every civilized nation in the world had a general parcel-post system except the United States, and the nation's pride was touched. Also the absurdity of being able to mail an 11-pound package abroad for 12 cents a pound when there was no comparable system at home had begun to rankle in the breasts of progressive Americans. "We have no parcels post until you reach the ports," said Woodrow Wilson as he campaigned for the presidency in 1912, "and from the ports to the other side of the Atlantic you can have parcels-post rates, but you can't have them inside the United States. Because—may I conjecture the reason—because there are certain express companies which object."[35]

But these were not the principal reasons for the switch from a rural to a general parcel post. Nor did the main arguments any longer center around the possibility of wiping out the postal deficit or even on the mailing of packages from local stores to the farmers. Now there was a loftier vision; now parcel post was being pictured as a giant express service that would no longer stop at the local depot but would connect city and village and countryside in one vast transportation system.

The key to the structure, of course, was the R F D. Establish a general parcel post, men said, and the rural routes would carry goods from the cities all the way to the farms. Better still, back over these routes would flow the farmer's butter and eggs and produce, direct to the city consumer. By eliminating the middleman and the high cost of transportation, the farmer would receive more for his produce, yet the cost to the consumer would be less than it had been under the old marketing arrangement, and the high cost of living everyone was talking about would be substantially reduced.[36]

Here at last was the argument to end all arguments and to capture the imagination of farmers, urbanites, and politicians alike.

It was a package done up in a bright ribbon and fancy paper with something in it for everyone except the express companies and the middlemen whose protests were reaching fewer and fewer ears as men became enchanted with the possibilities of a new and revolutionary way of marketing goods.

Rural spokesmen were almost beside themselves over the prospects. For years farmers had tried one way and another to get around the middleman they regarded as a parasite. Yet for all their efforts, he was still taking a large portion of their profits. Someone in the Department of Agriculture had gathered statistics to show that in 1911 the farmers had received a total of $6,000,000,000 for crops for which consumers had paid more than $13,000,000,000. Seven billion dollars, these figures showed, had gone into the process of getting these goods into the hands of the consumers.[37]

Obviously, there was a leak in the pipe from farmers to consumers somewhere, and some congressmen thought they knew where. According to David Lewis, the House expert on the subject, the trouble was that the transportation of farm products had not been direct. "The conduit," he said, "is broken in three pieces and at the end of each piece a commission process takes place which at length doubles the final price." With a general parcel post this would not happen. Farm goods would flow all the way past villages and towns if need be, at one price and without interruption direct to the consumer in the city, and the effect on food prices would be revolutionary. In Washington D.C., for example, in 1912, consumers were paying 66 cents for two-dozen eggs. The wholesale price of those eggs was 52 cents and the farmer had received 44 cents for them. By using his proposed parcel-post system, however, Lewis showed that those eggs could be shipped directly to the consumer for 49 cents, bypassing the middleman and saving the consumer 17 cents. By the same process if a consumer bought 3½ pounds of dressed fowl, 3 pounds of butter, 3 pounds of country sausage, 10 pounds of country-cured ham, and a half bushel of apples, Lewis's figures showed he could save $2.31.[38]

Curiously, in the final stages of their fight for parcel post, the farmers and their friends were given left-handed support by the express companies themselves. One might have thought that, having been berated for more than fifteen years, the express companies would have tried to mend their ways and set their houses in order. But for some unaccountable reason, vested interests of the day seemed to have a compulsive urge to commit suicide. Under attack, they tended to become arrogant and to pile abuse on abuse until at last they were completely at odds with the general public. This had been the reaction of the liquor interests to the prohibition movement, and it was the story of the express companies who, like the Gadarene swine, seemed possessed of devils driving them on to their own destruction.

Many people had hoped that when the express companies had come under the jurisdiction of the Interstate Commerce Commission in 1906, their worst abuses would be checked. But this did not happen. At first, they simply flouted the commission's authority, giving inaccurate and incomplete reports of their business. In 1911, when the commission at last got around to making a detailed investigation of them, there was a widespread feeling that the express companies could never be properly controlled.

Nor would they regulate themselves in spite of their patrons' complaints. They made no effort to bring their profits more in line with their investments. They carried no package for less than 25 cents, and after 1909 they were charging on the average sixteen and a half times more for hauling a ton of freight than the railroads charged for regular freight.[39]

Still people patronized them simply because there was no comparable transportation system, and the money continued to flow into their coffers. By 1910, Wells, Fargo and Company had piled up huge reserves, and the disregard the directors of that company had for public opinion was nowhere better illustrated than the fact that they chose this inopportune time, when they were already being roundly condemned for their profits, to declare a 300 per cent dividend to their stockholders, 200 per cent in new stock and 100 per cent in actual cash.[40]

But they had at last overreached themselves. By 1912 the bitterness of people toward them was unmistakable, and the demand for a general parcel post was partly the result of that bitterness. "Twenty years ago," said the Master of the Washington State Grange, "we were willing to take any Parcel Post Congress would give us. . . . Now we do not propose to wait any longer, but intend to have the best Parcel Post service in the World. . . ." Furthermore, he predicted they would wipe the express companies "off the face of the earth, take over their equipment and working staff, and consolidate all the express companies into one perfect Postal Express system."[41]

And there was a chance this would happen as the congressional session moved into 1912. With progressivism running at flood tide, no man, not even an old friend, dared lift his voice in favor of the express companies. Two bills introduced in the House and one in the Senate, provided for the establishment of a general parcel post and the condemnation and government purchase of the express companies. Besides these, some eighteen more bills providing for parcel post in one form or another were dropped into congressional hoppers.[42]

Nine of these bills called for a rural parcel post. The rest were general parcel-post measures with a bewildering variety of postage rates and weight limitations on mailable packages. The House Committee on Post Office and Post Roads had offered a rural parcel-post bill, but supporters of tenacious old James Cowles, whose moment of glory was near at hand, demanded a flat-rate, general parcel post in which the postage on parcels would be determined by weight alone without regard to the distance they had to go. In the meantime, on the other side of the Capitol, Senator Jonathan Bourne of Oregon, introduced a parcel-post measure basing postage rates on the weight of the parcel and the distance it was to go.[43]

There was something in all these bills to suit the fancy of almost every parcel-post advocate. The problem was to get everything everyone wanted into one bill. The House solved this by compromising and writing an experimental rural parcel-post measure and setting up a commission to study the matter, so a permanent system based on the commission's findings could eventually be established. But the Senate, late in the summer, after the two major political parties had endorsed a parcel post at their nominating conventions in June, threw out the House bill and substituted the Bourne measure.[44]

Eleven months of study had gone into the senator's bill, and he was proud of his handiwork. Perhaps he had a right to be if for no other reason than that he and his advisers from the Post Office Department had worked out a pattern for establishing postal rates on mailable packages that was as novel as it was important.

Rates based on weight and distance could become as complicated as a Chinese puzzle as every express agent knew, and one of the most attractive features of the flat-rate proposal was its simplicity. Bourne knew this, and knew that his major problem was to find a simple way to determine postage rates based on weight and distance, so even the dullest of Uncle Sam's postmasters could quickly tell their patrons what it would cost to mail their packages.

At first, he had thought concentric circles could be drawn on a map around each of the nation's post offices in ever widening arcs, each circle representing a zone, and each zone representing a different postage rate for a package mailed from a post office in the center of the circles. But since the nation had nearly 59,000 post offices in 1912, this, to use his own words, would have been like "engraving the Lord's prayer on the head of a pin," even if he had had a map ten feet long and ten feet wide.[45]

Bourne thought next of making each state a postal zone but

discarded this idea because of the obvious inequality of sending a five-pound package through the states of Massachusetts and Texas for the same rate. Counties, he excluded for the same reason.

That left only the possibility of dividing the nation into zones based on lines of latitude and longitude. Zones formed by these lines would at least be approximately equal and always the same. But they too posed a problem. Suppose one person lived just inside and one just outside a degree line. Both men might send their packages approximately the same distance, over 80 miles across the degree, but the one inside would pay less than his neighbor who lived just outside the degree.

The solution to this was to divide each degree into quadrangles, 30 minutes east and west and 30 minutes north and south. Every post office within a certain quadrangle would be given the same index number, and every person within that quadrangle could send parcels anywhere through that and through any adjacent quadrangle at the same rate.

These quadrangles would never change, and regardless of how many new post offices were established they could easily be worked into the scheme by giving them the proper index number. Besides, all the post offices with their index numbers noted could be catalogued alphabetically, and when a local postmaster had to figure the postage on a package, he could quickly find the index number of any post office in the country, check its zone and rate on a chart specially prepared for his own office, and set the rate. Bourne thought any man with intelligence enough to be a postmaster could set a postage rate with his system in twenty seconds. The scheme seemed foolproof and so simple representatives from railroad and express companies to whom Bourne explained the plan had agreed "that no express company or railroad company anywhere in the world to their knowledge had ever evolved such a scientific and practical working plan for rate ascertainment on the distance traveled. . . ."[46]

President Taft endorsed Bourne's bill, and even the express

company officials, if their praises meant anything, seemed willing to accept it. But obviously any parcel-post measure the express companies might accept and the conservative President Taft endorse would be skeptically regarded by the farmers, and it was. A memorial from the National Farmers' League for Postal Reform, explained their objections.

In the first place, the postage rates set by Bourne's bill were so high in certain zones as to be virtually noncompetitive with the express companies. Secondly, it made no provision either for C.O.D. or parcel insurance. It limited the weight of mailable packages to 11 pounds when farmers had been talking about a maximum weight limit of no less than 100 pounds, and it did not permit the Postmaster General or the Interstate Commerce Commission to change rates or raise the weight limitation. Instead, if experience suggested that rates could be lowered or the weight limitation raised, Congress would have to do it through the slow process of legislation. Finally, and unforgivably, from the farmers' point of view, there was no provision in the bill for handling farm products in the mail. It was as if the senator, a mild progressive but no farmer, had not really understood that parcel post was a farm measure, designed primarily to fill the transportation gap between producers and consumers and to lower the cost of living.[47]

When the Bourne bill reached the House of Representatives, August 15, 1912, staunch old champions of parcel post wanted nothing to do with it. Congressman David Lewis called it a child born without "eyes, or hands, or ears, or toes, and feet," while the chairman of the House Committee on Post Office and Post Roads, apologizing for his frankness, said it was "not in the interests of the farming community of this country . . . ," but "in the interests of the mail-order house and express companies and the railroads. . . ."[48]

So the House sent the bill back to the Senate without accepting or changing so much as a comma, and set up a conference committee to work out its differences with the Senate.

Late in August, with the election some two months away and senators and representatives straining to end the stormy session that had been at work since December 1911, the conference committee hammered out the nation's parcel-post system. While the Bourne zone plan remained a part of the final bill, nearly all the major farm demands were also written into it. The Postmaster General in cooperation with the Interstate Commerce Commission, could make changes in postage rates and weight limitation on packages without going back to Congress. Parcel insurance and C.O.D. provisions were added to the bill, and a Congressional Commission was appointed to study ways to improve the system. But the most important addition to the bill was the provision permitting farm products to be handled in the mail. Once this was added, farmers could look forward hopefully to January 1913, when the new system would go into effect, marking what President Taft believed would be "a new era in the history of the development of the nation."[49]

The fight for parcel post had been long and very bitter, and if it seems strange that such a prosaic proposition had once stirred the passions of so many Americans, it must be remembered that the early 1900's were tempestuous times. People who could "stand at Armageddon" and "battle for the Lord," as they did in those days, were capable of summoning up a towering indignation at unrighteousness, real or imagined, and not a little of this spirit had manifested itself in the parcel-post fight. Besides, to the fighters in the ring, the stakes in the outcome of the fight were high. The farmers were sure parcel post meant increased prosperity for them, while country storekeepers, traveling men, and city wholesalers were just as certain it meant their ruin, and compromise between the two was impossible.

One must also remember that, as the people saw it in 1912, parcel post was no small undertaking. By entering the transportation business, the government was invading the sacred field of private enterprise, really for the first time in its history in a permanent fashion, and with what peril no man knew. This, in itself, was enough to excite Americans. Indeed, such was the boldness of the venture, only the pre-existence of the rural delivery system, that could connect with the rails and provide an express service direct to almost everyman's door, made Congress willing to undertake it. Had there been no R F D, neither the farmers nor their congressmen would have been interested in the movement, and without them, there would have been no parcel post. Perhaps all this was in the mind of a Virginia congressman in 1916 when he told his colleagues in the House of Representatives that "Rural delivery made possible parcel post."[50]

10

FROM FARM TO TABLE AND STORE TO FARM

"I suppose you wonder why we haven't ordered anything from you since the fall. Well, the cow kicked my arm and broke it, and besides my wife was sick, and there was the doctor bill. But now, thank God, that is paid, and we are all well again, and we have a fine new baby boy, and please send plush bonnet number 29d8077. . . ."

A farmer's letter to a mail-order store, "By Mail," *Scribner's Magazine*, 69 (Apr. 1921), 477

THE nation's brand new parcel-post system began January 1, 1913, and that day and the next a rash of stories about first packages appeared in the nation's press. Obligingly, the postmaster at Princeton, New Jersey, kept his post office open until after midnight on New Year's Eve so friends of President-elect Woodrow Wilson could mail him the first package from that office, while across the country at El Paso, Texas, the postmaster himself delivered the first package to arrive at his office to the city's mayor. But the first official package was the one Postmaster General Frank Hitchcock mailed from Washington, D.C., to the postmaster at New York City. It contained a loving cup, supposedly to be enshrined sometime in a national museum, and arrived at its destination in just seven hours.[1]

The Post Office Department had worked hard preparing for this day. Special parcel-post stamps had been engraved, and over 30,000 parcel-post scales had been purchased for the nation's larger post offices. Happily the Department had also continued the employment of the extra men and wagons it had hired to take care of the Christmas rush, and it was well that it had. For post offices around the country had no sooner opened their doors to the new service, than thousands of Americans rushed in with their packages, eager to be initiated into the mysteries of parcel post.[2]

Mailing a package in the early days of 1913 was almost like performing an occult rite of some kind. In some places postmasters had thoughtfully placed mirrors above the parcel post scales, so the more untrusting citizen could see from the counter, if he wished, just what his package weighed. He could also see the postmaster or clerk, as the case might be, going through a puzzling routine, consulting a parcel-post map, running a finger up and down a chart, hesitating a moment, and finally marking the postage due on the package. For the average person, it was too complicated to follow. He simply paid whatever the postmaster said he owed, confident that Uncle Sam, unlike the express companies, was not going to cheat him.

At first there had been those doubting Thomases who speculated that the new service with its clumsy zone system and special parcel-post stamps would not be used very much, but they had been put to shame within a week. In just four days some 200,000 packages were mailed in New York City alone, and before the month of January was out, the Bureau of Engraving had increased its daily output of parcel-post stamps from 5,000,000 to 10,000,000 a day.[3]

That month the Postmaster General called parcel post's success "the greatest and most immediate ever scored by any new venture in the country . . . ," and each succeeding month, dazzling new statistics supported his statement. In April, the Post Office Department discovered that parcels were flowing through the mails at the astronomical rate of 250,000,000 a year! Six months later, during the first two weeks in October, over 17,000,000 packages were mailed indicating that the yearly flow was at the rate of about 300,000,000.[4]

It was enough to have clogged the postal machinery to have all these packages pouring through its arteries, and it must have come as a surprise to those who thought the Post Office inefficient to see it not only handling so many packages but doing it with dispatch. To the surprise of some, parcel post was even better than the express service. Several newspapers sent packages to designated points by both express and parcel post to check on the service, and in almost every case parcel post was faster. The *Chicago-World*, for example, sent two packages to New York and found the one sent parcel post not only beat the express package to its destination but cost twenty-three cents less to send.[5]

Indeed, the government's first venture into private enterprise had been so successful that first year, one observer thought it would induce the Post Office Department in the Wilson administration to support such old Populist proposals as government ownership of telegraph and telephone lines, and might even lead the government to take over the railroads themselves. "The importance of parcel post, therefore," he wrote, "goes far beyond the service immediately rendered. Its demonstrated success through several years is likely to change fundamentally our conception of government."[6]

All in all it was an impressive showing, except for one thing. The eagerly awaited, much discussed, producer-to-consumer trade, contrary to all expectations, had failed to develop, and to a large number of Americans this was parcel post's great test. If it failed here, it "will have failed," said one newspaper, "in its chief mission."[7]

It had been no accident that President Woodrow Wilson had received eight pounds of New Jersey apples in his first parcel-post package, or that the mayor of El Paso had received a dozen eggs.

Parcel post had been established to transport just such items from farm to city, and it seemed reasonable to suppose this would be its principal use. "Let us imagine that the Gotham family," wrote one journalist, "immured in the city by the demands of Father Gotham's business, knew that twice a week during the summer they could get from Farmer Ruralis, forty miles out in the country, a hamper of fresh-killed poultry, green peas, string beans, asparagus, strawberries, lettuce, cherries, summer squash, and what not; that the 'sass' would be only a day from garden to table; that prices would be lower than market prices; that the cost of transportation would be only thirty-five cents in and, say, eleven cents for the empty hamper back again. Would the Gotham family be interested? If they would not they deserve wilted vegetables, mushy fruits, storage chickens, and soaring prices. Would Farmer Ruralis be interested in building up such a business. . . ? If not he deserves the last twist of the thumbscrews applied by wicked ogre middleman."[8]

Time, supermarkets, refrigerated foods, fast transportation, and apathy about the middleman's charges have long since deadened the appeal of this idea, but to many an urbanite in 1913 it was irresistible.

To be sure, it was a way to reduce the city man's cost of living which was high at the time and going higher; but it was more than that. American cities then were filled with men and women to whom the mere mention of "sass" from the farm not only brought back a mouth-watering remembrance of sweet, fresh foods spread out on a farm table at noonday, but cherished memories of their own days on the farm, when, somehow, things seemed better. Perhaps it was nostalgia; or perhaps, like the Greek wrestler, Antaeus, who lost his strength and security when he lost contact with Mother Earth, they too had lost a sense of security they hoped to regain by a kind of lifeline direct from themselves to the farmers. "A man gets something from living near the earth," wrote William Allen White, "from running barefoot on the earth over the open field, and the waters of the creeks, and the sunlight on the prairie—something real yet something indefinable, which gives him a life inheritance in physical reserve," and possibly it was this "indefinable something" city Americans hoped to renew by trading directly with the farmers.[9]

Whatever their reasons, a good many people had set their hopes on this farm-to-table trade, and when it failed to develop, parcel-post theorists went scurrying off to find out why.

At first, parcel-post regulations caught the blame. The postage rates were too high, the weight limit on packages too low, and the special parcel-post stamps an unnecessary nuisance. This, at least, was the view of the Wilson administration and Albert Burleson, who became Postmaster General in March 1913, began to change the system that summer. He put the C.O.D. provision, which had been temporarily withheld, into effect in July and got rid of the special parcel-post stamps at the same time. The next month he raised the weight limit on packages mailed in the first two zones to 20 pounds and reduced the postage in these same zones.

He might have raised the weight limit even higher, but those 30,000 parcel-post scales the Department had bought registered only up to 20 pounds. When this little oversight was corrected in the summer of 1914, Burleson raised the weight limit again, this time to 50 pounds in the first two zones and 20 pounds in all the others.[10]

But all these changes did not help the producer-to-consumer trade very much. About all they did was to make it possible for every isolated miner and mountaineer who happened to get his mail over a star route to forsake the old freight lines and begin to mail everything from ore to furniture by parcel post. Even bricks were sent this way under the new regulation, and a bank at Vernal, Utah, was constructed out of parcel-post bricks mailed in from Salt Lake City.[11]

So little attention had been paid to the star routes in the arguments for a package service that when the parcel-post bill was passed, they were not even mentioned, and only because President Taft interpreted the law very broadly was the service extended to them. As long as an 11-pound package was the most that could be mailed, this made little difference anyway. But as soon as the weight limit was raised to 50 pounds, the avalanche descended, and isolated postmasters began opening up their post offices in the morning to find 50-pound bags of beans, coal, flour, and sundry articles waiting to be mailed.[12]

What happened on the star route at Mogallon, New Mexico, was the best example of this new postal business. Nestled in the mountains some distance from Silver City, Mogallon was a little community of about 2,000 people. No railroad connected it with the outside world; only a mountain road over which a stage coach-freight line brought goods in at the princely price of $3.00 a hundredweight. Then in 1914 word came that 50-pound parcels were mailable to and from Silver City at the rate of $1.08 per hundredweight, and the star route contractor who had agreed to carry letters and papers over the mountain suddenly found such things as crude oil and casks of molasses in the mail. Not only the townspeople but the Mogallon storekeepers as well, used his services until, according to one account, almost 10,000 pounds of new matter entered the town every day. Of course, the Post Office Department had to adjust the pay of the contractor and lost money by doing it, but Mogallon, New Mexico, had become a parcel-post town. "It lives," wrote a reporter, "eats, dresses, and enjoys itself largely through mails."[13]

But the farm-to-city trade on the R F D routes was still in the doldrums after more than a year of parcel post. The trouble now seemed obvious: the farmers did not know where to sell their goods, nor the consumer where to buy. The middleman had always supplied the connection between the two, but in this business there was purposely no middleman, and it was plain enough that the trade would never develop unless some way could be found to get the consumers and producers together.

Ordinarily, it would not have been within the Post Office Department's province to solve this problem. But the times were not ordinary. Already, the Department was interloping in the field of private enterprise, and there seemed no good reason why it should not go a step further and play the role of middleman between producer and consumer. So beginning in the spring of 1914, before the garden season came, the Department announced its farm-to-table movement.

The plan was simple. Rural mailmen would collect the names of farmers along their routes who wanted to market their products by parcel post and turn them into their postmasters. Postmasters would make up lists of these farmers' names and addresses, and city mailmen would distribute them in the cities along with the mail. If everything went as planned, the city consumer could correspond with the farmer, order his own eggs or butter or "sass," and the farmer would put them in the mail and send them off.[14]

News of the farm-to-table movement spread rapidly. The press gave it an extraordinary amount of attention, the Agriculture Department published a spate of bulletins on the subject, and the *R.F.D. News* prodded the rural mailmen to write for farm-to-table lists and help form farm-to-table associations among the farmers. "Talk! Talk! Talk . . . ," ran an item in the *News*. "Call a meeting of farmers and gather in the most convenient schoolhouse or Sunday School room." And with a nod to the rumor that some rural mailmen had been dragging their feet on parcel post, the *News* gave this advice: "When a patron meets you with a parcel post package, grin; and the bigger the package, the broader the grin."[15]

For the farmers there were farm-to-table reminders everywhere. At night, by the light of his kerosene lamp, a farmer could read his farm bulletins, squint at the parcel-post rates printed there, and mull over advice on what prices to ask for his goods and how to contact consumers. And at his county fair, strolling with his wife through a pavilion filled with prize grain and jars of canned foods pinned with blue ribbons, he was almost bound to run into a parcel-post booth where he could see the latest in parcel-post containers and packaging techniques.[16]

The experiment had begun in eight major cities, and the results that first year seemed satisfying and even phenomenal. The postmaster at Washington, D.C., called it a "complete success" and said that thousands of the city's householders were purchasing "almost all their meats, vegetables, and dairy products through the mails at a saving of twenty per cent." Favorable reports came too from Atlanta, St. Louis, Boston, and San Francisco, and as the war clouds gathered over Europe that year, the experiment looked so good even some of the express companies began their own farm-to-table movements.[17]

The exact condition of the express companies one year after the beginning of parcel post was still uncertain, but there was no question but that the new package system had made deep inroads on their business. The United States Express Company was already closing its doors, and journalists were writing, a little previously, the obituaries of the others. But some companies were still very much alive and determined to prove that what the Post Office Department could do, private enterprise could do better. So they sent farm experts into the country to drum up the farmers' trade, fix prices, and get the best merchandise possible. They turned their express offices into clearinghouses where orders were taken and goods picked up. Organizers were placed among the large corporations to organize buyers' clubs. Over 200 such clubs were organized in New York City while in Chicago, one club, reported to have 700 members, was purchasing $5,000 worth of eggs, butter, ham, bacon, and fresh vegetables every month.[18]

All this had happened in just one year, and if favorable publicity from city journalists and enthusiastic postal officials made the farm-to-table service seem better than it really was, still there was reason enough to hope the movement was catching on. Optimistically, Postmaster General Burleson extended the experiment to 18 additional cities and finally by 1916 to 35.[19]

In those two years there were innovations in the experiment as imaginative postmasters tinkered with the system and found ways to improve it. The original farm-to-table lists, for instance, became more complicated. It was not enough for consumers to know only the farmers' names and addresses. They wanted to know what the farmers had to sell and what their prices were, and enterprising postmasters like Otto Praeger in Washington, D.C., began making lists including both these items. These new lists were really mail-order catalogues in miniature, where the poorest farmer in Virginia, if he were honest, could have his name and wares listed for nothing.

Here and there the experiment seemed to be working exceptionally well, and where it did, invariably an enthusiastic postmaster was behind it. This was the case at Kansas City where the postmaster had organized such a vigorous campaign in 1915, over 500 parcel-post turkeys went through his office that year, and early the next year his business was attracting some 75 letters a day. He was a man of ideas and initiative, and one of his widely publicized proposals was to urge those old enemies of parcel post, the traveling men, to buy farm products in the farm areas they traveled through and send them back to their families in the cities by the new package service.[20]

The Kansas City postmaster, however, was only an amateur compared to D. B. Traxler, postmaster at Greenville, South Carolina. By 1916, this man had literally turned his post office into a mail-order house. In the lobby of the post office was a parcel-post table filled with bulletins listing not only the names and addresses of farmers who had something to sell, but what they had, how much, and prices they wanted. For convenience' sake, Traxler had even arranged a bulletin for every important product, such as this one labeled "BUTTER":

Name and Address	*Quantity*	*Price*
Mrs. L. L. Thomason, Simpsonville	3lbs, Fresh, country, weekly	35¢ lb.
Miss Annie Kirksey, Pickens	3lbs, Fresh, country, weekly	35¢ lb.
Mrs. Ken Dowten, Troy	3lbs, Fresh, country, weekly	35¢ lb.
Mrs. E. W. Dobbes, Mayesville	3lbs, Fresh, country, weekly	35¢ lb.

Almost every farm woman in the vicinity of Greenville must have been spending hours at the butter churn, for butter provided most of Traxler's business. Nearly 150 pounds of it went through his post office every week in the spring of 1917, country fresh, as the bulletin said, and sold for 13 cents less than creamery butter.

But there was scarcely a farm product grown within a hundred miles of Greenville that could not be found for sale on Traxler's parcel-post table. Ten bushels of Nancy Hall potatoes could be bought from Mr. Hogan at Scranton, and H. B. Richardson on Route 2 out of Summerton had everything from Brabham peas to Coulliette cottonseed for sale. The women, however, spinsters and widows perhaps, dominated the egg and poultry business. Mrs. M. L. Crisp of Mountville had two young White Leghorns for $3.00 and selected white Guineas for $1.25 each. Three Barred Cocks were for sale by Miss Cora Brunson of Holly Hill, and Miss Mattie Arve of Battle Creek had a few eggs and dressed chickens to sell.

Then there were all kinds of prepared farm products for sale. One could buy 15 gallons of cane syrup from Frank Canaday, Route 3, St. George. Smoked hams, sides, jowls for 18 cents a pound, and smoked sausage were listed, and one man had a 48-pound can of lard, just two pounds under the parcel post weight limit, for sale for $9.50.

Traxler had "want" lists as well as for sale bulletins on his parcel-post table, and these were often as long as the others. On one list were the names of those who wanted collard seed, kittens, puppies, chickens, butter, peanuts, and Tom Watson watermelon seed: Mrs. J. E. Fulton of Georgetown wanted a "good young Jersey cow for butter," which, of course, could scarcely go through the mails, nor could the pair of Emden geese Mrs. R. B. Rowland of Spartanburg wanted, but Traxler's table was not exclusive, and presumably one could even have advertised for a wife through this parcel-post business.

For one medium-sized post office, this was a big operation. Traxler's enterprise had even brought orders for turkeys to Greenville from as far away as New York City, and he himself had once made arrangements to sell turkeys to the Waldorf-Astoria.[21]

But a parcel-post business like Traxler's was the exception not the rule. After experimenting for two years, the farm-to-table movement was still bogged down and theorists were as puzzled over its failure as they had ever been. Postmaster General Burleson accused the rural mailmen of sabotaging the service, and at least one postmaster thought the trouble lay in the "grasping spirit" of the farmers. There was some truth in both charges, but neither went to the bottom of the problem. Hard as it was for parcel-post enthusiasts to believe, the farmers were just not too interested in the movement. Those were good years for the farmers. The prices they received for their products were reasonably high, and undoubtedly this made them less anxious to sell by mail. Then, too, marketing by mail was not as simple as it sounded. It was easy enough to sit in an office and picture fresh foods from the farms flowing like a river in flood into city homes, but something else to package a dozen eggs or wrap a pound of butter for mailing and then try to find a customer to send them to. To make a deal by mail, as many as three or four letters often had to pass between consumer and producer, and by that time, besides all the trouble, the consumer's savings and the producer's profits had been eaten up in postage. Under the circumstances, even the consumer's enthusiasm for buying direct began to wane.[22]

Still, people kept thinking it would work if only they could solve the communications problem. Among those who thought so was a California merchant named David Lubin. He believed post offices should be converted into mail-order stores and forthrightly suggested just how it should be done. Every farmer who wanted to sell by parcel post, according to his plan, would go to the post office and pick up colored cards marked with his own special number—white for eggs, pink for chickens, and yellow for butter. Each week he would decide how much of each item he had to sell. If he had a dozen eggs, one chicken, and one pint of butter, he would mark his price on each card and send one white, one pink, and one yellow card to the post office.

At the post office his cards would be put in special white, pink, and yellow pigeonholes, and when Mrs. City Consumer came to the post office she could run through the cards, note the prices listed there, and select those representing the items she wanted at the prices she would pay. Suppose she picked out two egg cards, two butter cards, and one chicken card all numbered 33. This would mean she wanted to buy two dozen eggs, two pints of butter, and one chicken from farmer number 33. She would then write her name and address on the cards, take them to the postal clerk, and pay for them with coupons she had already bought at the post office. The clerk would find the name and address of farmer 33 in the post-office index, and mail him the cards. The farmer would then package and mail the commodities, and when the rural mailman picked them up, he could leave the lady's coupons with the farmer. Eventually, the farmer could cash them at the post office.[23]

No father was ever prouder of his child than Lubin was of his farm-to-table mail-order plan, or more enthusiastic either. He even thought cotton could be marketed this way! Early in 1916 a reporter from the *San Francisco Examiner* found him in his hotel room at the Fairmount, munching Swiss cheese sandwiches and talking about building up a greater farm-to-table business than was done by all the nation's mail-order stores combined. He had already twice carried his plans to Chicago to get the reaction of the nation's two largest mail-order stores, and the government's parcel-post committee had heard him out. Now he was on his way back to Washington to help push through an appropriation for his scheme.[24]

If faulty communication between the farmer and consumer had been the basic farm-to-table problem, and it seemed to be, the Lubin plan might have solved it. In the spring of 1916 some California Grangers around Sacramento tried it out, using 27 producers and 34 consumers and simulating actual postal conditions. So successful was the experiment the California State Grange recommended it and sent the details of the experiment to Congress. And Congress did appropriate $10,000 for some such plan as Lubin had in mind.[25]

But Americans never found out whether it would have worked or not because the Post Office Department never got around to trying it out. Lubin's biographer said it was because profiteers, afraid for their profits, so vilified Lubin and misrepresented the facts that support for the plan withered like a flower in the desert. Perhaps so, but America's entry into World War I was the official reason Postmaster General Burleson gave for not conducting the experiment.[26]

Yet the war that ruined the Lubin plan also kept the farm-to-table movement alive when it seemed about to collapse. For now the movement could be used not only to help keep down the cost of living but to conserve food, and in early 1918, with food growing scarcer in the cities and the Germans about to launch their great offensive along the Somme and no one knowing how long the war would last, saving the food that formerly went to waste in farmers' fields and cellars was absolutely imperative. "Food and fuel will win the war," cried a congressman, but they had to be transported to where they were most needed, and Congress was willing to risk $300,000 on another farm-to-table experiment to try to do the job.[27]

So the Post Office Department tried once more to unite farmers and urbanites by parcel post. But this time there was a difference. For this new experiment, special parcel-post trucks were to be used to fetch food from the farms instead of the regular rural mail service which, alas, after all the arguments made in its name, was now thought incapable of doing the job.

The brains behind the new experiment belonged to James I. Blakslee who, whatever his shortcomings as an administrator, knew the ins and outs of transportation about as well as any man in Washington. Whether because he was born and raised in an old railroad family in Pennsylvania or whether as Fourth Assistant Postmaster General he had learned so much about transportation trying to motorize the rural mail carriers, he was, in any case, one of the first to see the transportation revolution coming.

So far has the world come in the transportation field since 1918 that Blakslee's farsightedness hardly seems remarkable now. But then the United States was only at the doorway of the motor age. Horses and buggies were still as much a part of the American scene as long dresses, and most of the nation's roads were fit for no other kind of transportation. Only the year before Congress had passed the first Federal Highway Act, and registered cars and trucks combined numbered only a little more than 5,000,000 that year. Most of the country's goods and people too were still transported over steel rails and as far as most people could see, they always would be.[28]

But Blakslee saw beyond this. For him the future belonged to the gasoline motor, and he tried mightily, if prematurely, to spawn the new age with his parcel-post trucks; and always in the back of his mind, as he laid his plans, was the experience of the railroads, for him a kind of blueprint for the new age.

Blakslee's plans were grandiose and his talk was big. "Motor truck postal service," said he, "will ultimately be one of the biggest things in the history of the Post Office Department." Not for him a piddling experiment, but a nationwide system of motor truck transportation, modeled somewhat on the rural mail route system. Plans were announced to establish some 4,000 miles of truck routes, extending from Portland, Maine, to New Orleans along the eastern coast, and from San Francisco to Sacramento and Redlands to Los Angeles along the Pacific. More would run through the Midwest, through Ohio, Indiana, Illinois, and West Virginia. There would be a fleet of 1,500 trucks traveling like trains over national highways. They would pick up the produce gathered from farms, and deposited at designated spots along the main thoroughfare. Like the railroads too, all of these roads, even the feeder roads into the main highway, were to be maintained by parcel-post profits and by those who used them. It was in connection with this plan, Blakslee first advanced the idea of "financing highway construction by means of a general wheel tax." To the editor of *Motor* magazine he wrote: "I am . . . endeavoring to perfect the details of a plan whereby it would be possible to apply . . . the principle that the cost of construction and improvement of highways should be borne by those who use the highways, exactly as the cost of the construction and maintenance of a railway is defrayed. . . ."[29]

On March 20 a test run of the new service was made over a route from Lancaster, Pennsylvania, to New York City, a distance of 180 miles. Everything worked perfectly. The parcel-post truck carried 4,000 day-old chicks, 200 pounds of honey, 500 pounds of smoked sausage, 500 pounds of butter, and 18,000 eggs, and in transit only two chicks died and 9 eggs were broken. The truck burned 20 gallons of gasoline, used up 2 hours in stops, and made the run in just 12 hours. Postage from the trip amounted to $31.60, far more than enough to pay the driver his wages of $4.00 and the $6.00 gas bill. "It is," said New York's Secretary of State, "an epoch in the history of the United States and the world."[30]

Blakslee worked night and day to push the experiment along, and no task seemed too much for him. He gave speeches on the subject, wrote articles, and listened to advice from everywhere on how to improve the system. One man wrote to suggest that the parcel-post truck drivers stay in the country overnight, so they could begin picking up the produce earlier. Someone else wrote that the trucks were too big and too slow and the routes paralleled the railroads too closely. The manager of the Troy Trailer Company suggested that the experiment be expanded into traveling stores. An Autocar, he wrote, and two or possibly three trailers, hauling all the groceries a housewife would need, would travel up and down the streets, like a modern popsicle man, and use what he called "jumper boys," forerunners of the modern "carry-out" boys, to take orders and carry groceries.[31]

But in spite of Blakslee's colossal efforts, the parcel-post truck experiment was much like putting new wine in old bottles. The old problems were still there, and so were some new ones. Blakslee was rushing the age, and had to suffer the consequences of pioneering. Since neither motor trucks nor roads of the day were always reliable, trucks got stuck or missed schedules waiting for roads to dry up or broke down completely. In the spring of 1920 one of his route agents wrote him that the regular Harrisonburg truck had "been making a funny noise" for some time and had finally collapsed. Another truck had to be sent to pick up the cargo and a new rear end ordered for the disabled vehicle. Because of all this, the agent wrote, he had been too busy to take care of the rest of the business.[32]

Even when no such catastrophes occurred and the trucks moved smoothly along at their scheduled rate of 12 miles an hour, their cargoes were not always safe. Butter spoiled, potatoes froze, and eggs broke. Once a spare tire jarred loose and smashed a half gallon of oysters, for which Blakslee made the disgruntled driver pay. Another time a farmer wrote Blakslee that his last shipment of eggs had arrived in Washington scrambled. "Be there any way which you could suggest as a preventive of the above statement," he wrote, "then I would be glad to continue sending several dozen a week."[33]

Often there was a scarcity of farm products, and Blakslee would write desperately trying to find farmers who would sell by parcel post. Once, at least, even nature blocked his efforts when a farmer wrote him that he would have no extra eggs to sell until "molten [*sic*] season" was over. Then again it was a matter of getting good produce and full measure too. A shipment of 286 bushels of potatoes from McConnellsburg, Pennsylvania, for example, turned out to be 12 bushels short by weight. When this was adjusted, customers began complaining that the potatoes were "run of the field," and when Blakslee held up payment on them, the farmers pressured the Democratic postmaster at McConnellsburg to get them their money. Fearing a political catastrophe, the postmaster wrote hurriedly to Blakslee suggesting immediate payment for the potatoes before "the whole proposition had a black eye in the community."[34]

Potatoes and customers, they were the bête noire of Middleman Blakslee's life, particularly in the winter of 1919 and 1920. The Department had advertised potatoes for sale that winter, and hundreds of people sent in their orders and their money too. Potatoes, however, were scarce, and good ones even scarcer, and when Blakslee's men were able to buy them and attempted delivery, nothing but trouble followed. Some of the potatoes were spoiled to begin with; some froze in transit; prices varied, deliveries went astray, and customers complained loudly enough for Congress to hear. One harried official wrote Blakslee that he could "fill the mails with complaints from people who have ordered potatoes from October to December," and an item appeared in the paper, *Trades Union*, saying that "if the Post Office Department accounts for stamps as well as for money received for potatoes taxes will be huge." According to this story, some people had been waiting over four months, either to have the potatoes delivered or their money refunded. One irate customer, however, refused to wait. "Please settle this matter as soon as you can . . . ," he wrote Blakslee, "and if it can not be settled any other way I will join the movement to carry this with other matters in the hands of a number of complainants against the service, to the attention of Congress when it assembles next month."[35]

There had at least been the hope as the experiment moved along that the communications problem between producer and consumer would be solved by forming associations centered around the local schools at each end of the line. The farmers at the producing end would bring their products to their local schools where the parcel-post trucks would pick them up in the early morning. The foodstuffs would go from there directly to schools in the cities where members of consumer organizations would buy them just as they would at chain stores.

This innovation would eliminate the necessity of letters between farmer and urbanite, allow the farmer to mail in bulk and the buyer to select the goods he bought instead of being forced to accept whatever came in a parcel-post package. It was the nearest thing to the Lubin plan anyone had come up with, and Blakslee with his usual optimism had written a personal note to the Indianapolis postmaster saying "you can imagine how such a program would arouse the interest of 400,000 school masters throughout the country who might be pleased to act as the representatives of the producer-to-consumer distributor of food products. . . ."[36]

As usual, however, Blakslee's enthusiasm outran that of all the schoolmasters, consumers, and producers combined. In time, two such organizations did develop—the Mount Joy producers' group organized at the Two Tavern school near Gettysburg and the Park View consumers' group in the Park View school district in Washington—and if things had turned out differently, they might have been as historic as the first rural mail routes. One enthusiastic congressman did, in fact, sense their historical importance. He called the development "the first direct communication between rural and urban communities by means of motor transport service in American history," and obviously thought of it as a model for the rest of the nation.[37]

But it never worked out. The problems were great, and Blakslee was attempting too much. He was even using the parcel-post trucks to carry first-class mail as well as foodstuffs, and there was every indication he hoped eventually to supplant the railroads in carrying the mail just as Postmaster General Summerfield would do to some extent some thirty-odd years later in the Eisenhower administration.

Maybe if he had had more time and had attended strictly to the farm-to-table experiment, he could have made a go of it. But in 1919 a postal inspector's adverse report on the experiment disclosed that his favorable statistics on the experiment were not all they seemed to be, and Congress, with whom he had never gotten on anyway, began breathing down his neck. Senators and representatives called him visionary, said he was a dreamer, and blasted the experiment as socialistic.

Once two years before, Congress had been able to laugh at socialism when the truck experiment first came up. Senator Hiram Johnson had even said "let us go on with this essay into socialism," if it will help solve the problem. But in 1919 the old self-confidence was gone. The specter of Bolshevism stalked the land, and men like Utah's Senator William King, who had cried "socialism" as often as the little boy cried "wolf" and with as little effect, were now listened to with more respect. Altogether, it was too much for Blakslee's experiment, and Congress cut it off without a dime after July 1920.[38]

But the farm-to-table movement did not quite die here. When farm prosperity sagged in the 1920's, the idea was dusted off and presented to Congress again. In 1925 the Postmaster General was authorized to reduce postage rates on a number of experimental rural mail routes to any level he thought necessary to induce farmers to start mailing their produce to city consumers. Rural carriers were even allowed to solicit business for the first time since 1904 and were to be given a certain percentage of the postage on all such business they encouraged.[39]

Again, hardly anyone was really interested. Times were changing fast. By then buyers were going out to the farms in their own trucks and hauling produce to their stores, or else the farmers themselves carried their crops to market in their own trucks. After a year's trial the experiment ended, and although here and there people still talked about it in the 1930's and tried to get farmers to mail their produce to the cities, it was only talk. The Post Office Department tried no more farm-to-table experiments.[40]

Trying to make the farm-to-table movement work had been like trying to make water run uphill. Apparently nothing would make trade flow over rural mail routes from the farm to the city. In fact, the natural flow was the other way around, and parcel post kept rural mailmen busy carrying packages not from farm to city but from city to farm. And this, as it turned out, was the package service's great contribution to rural life. To appreciate what this meant to the average farmer a few years before and after World War I, one needs only to recall how the farmer bought the necessities of life before there was a parcel post.

It seems longer, but it was not much more than a generation or so ago that the farmer's trade area was no larger than the distance he could drive his team and spring wagon from chore time to chore time. This may have been as far as ten miles when the roads were good but not much farther. Even this was a twenty-mile round trip and taking time out for shopping, eating, and caring for his team at noon, it was more miles than most farmers wanted to go in a day to trade. Within this ten-mile area, give or take a mile or so, the farmer had to buy almost everything he did not produce.

Within the area itself, he may have had some choice in the stores with which he wished to trade. Take a farmer living near Cleves, Iowa, say, in 1901, when the rural agent was laying out rural routes there. He could trade at the one store at Cleves or go a mile and half farther to Abbott or six miles west to Robertson or six miles north to Ackley. On occasion, he might even go to Eldora, the county seat, some ten miles from Cleves, but probably never in the winter or spring. According to the rural agent, the

Iowa River was something of a problem to cross. Besides there were almost no gravel roads in Hardin County in 1901, and the mud roads in spring and winter were virtually bottomless.[41]

Eliminating Eldora then, that gave the Cleves farmer a choice of perhaps six or seven stores with which to trade. This was a greater selection than many farmers of the period had at that, but even so it was probably not very helpful. For most stores in the towns and villages of rural America were much alike. In any given locality storekeepers usually bought from the same traveling man, and their wares were similar. There was little difference in the service they offered and even their stores, particularly inside, wore the same tired expression. And so, the chances are that, unless the Cleves farmer harbored a mighty grudge against him, he traded with his nearest storekeeper Saturday after Saturday, taking what the merchant had to offer at prices he set.

Much has been written and more said about yesterday's stores and merchants in rural America. They have been pictured as the backbone of the rural economy, the lifeblood of small rural towns. The storekeepers, it has been pointed out, provided farmers with credit to pull them through the lean years. They accommodated him by taking his eggs and butter and cream in exchange for manufactured goods. They gave him sitting room near a pot-bellied stove in their stores, so he could chat with his neighbors on a wintry day and spit in the fire when his plug of Horse Shoe made it necessary. Nor have the favors they did for farmers and their communities gone unnoticed. They gave free advice and loaned money and turned their stores into a kind of dispatch center where messages passed back and forth among families and friends before there were any rural telephones. And they made donations to the Methodist Church and to just about every other church in the community.[42]

But somehow the farmers were never quite as enchanted with the system as were the storekeepers and their biographers. For these merchants never did all they did for nothing. Their prices were high, their goods unvaried, and their credit often exorbitant. The farmers generally regarded them as parasites who sucked up their money yet created no real wealth, and the history of the post-Civil War period is filled with the "do-it-yourself" cooperatives they established to break the local merchants' monopoly of their trade. Most of them failed, of course, and when they did the only other possible way the farmers had of breaking the monopoly was to trade with the mail-order stores.[43]

Farmers had been doing this to some extent ever since 1872 when Montgomery Ward founded his store, called it "The Original Grange Supply Store," and convinced farmers that his store by buying direct from the manufacturers in large quantities and selling for cash at a small profit was, in effect, eliminating the middleman. It was an inspired idea, and the mail-order market proved to be as broad as the country and as rich as Iowa farmland. To help tap it in the 1880's and 1890's came a number of other stores, Spiegel's, the Stern Company, the National Cloak and Suit Company, among others, and finally in 1893, the store destined to be the greatest of them all, Sears, Roebuck and Company.

Sears, Roebuck and Company made its mark by advertising. Its catalogue was like a barker at a sideshow. "The Cheapest Supply House on Earth," it yelled from its cover in 1894, and if this was not altogether true, it was at least the loudest, and no better proof of that old slogan "it pays to advertise" exists than this company's success. By 1897, it boasted of selling four suits a minute, one buggy every 10 minutes, a watch a minute, a revolver every two minutes, and three years later it had overtaken and surpassed in sales and revenues Montgomery Ward and Company, its closest competitor. But the market was big enough for both of them in those years, and both flourished, helped on immeasurably by the growth of the R F D.[44]

Rural free delivery did for the mail-order business what the Sears catalogue said its tonic, VIN VITAE, did for the human being; it produced "a wonderful exhilarating result" and left "no ill effects." R F D gave the mail-order stores a direct pipeline into every farm home on a rural route, and compared to the old mail service, it was like being invited into the family parlor instead of having to stand outside the kitchen door. Rural delivery meant faster service, more letters, and inevitably more orders. The farmer and his wife who studied the mail-order catalogue at night and decided on the spur of the moment to buy something, wrote out the order and gave it to their mailman next morning. No delay, no stopping to think it over. In the old days the order would probably have rested on the grandfather clock until the farmer had time to take it to town to mail. By then, "The Boss Pig Extractor and Tooth Forceps, No. 8T1946," listed at 79 cents, might have seemed less necessary than it had, and the chances were reasonably good the order would be thrown in the woodbox and used as a starter for the morning fire.[45]

Rural delivery made ordering by mail seem so much easier too. The process of making out orders and sending money orders had always been a little baffling to some farm people, so about 1904 the Sears catalogue began giving its customers a few simple rules for ordering. Among other things, it urged farmers to "tell us in your own way what you want" and "don't be afraid you will make a mistake." The next year the catalogue added another friendly word of advice destined to remain on the instruction page for years and to make ordering by mail as simple as milking a cow. "If you live on a rural route," said the catalogue, "just give the letter and the money to the mail carrier and he will get the money order at the post office and mail it in the letter for you."[46]

Still there remained the problem of shipping the farmer's orders to him. They could be sent by mail, express, or freight, but all these had their shortcomings which were reflected in the Sears catalogue. Before 1913 the catalogue always recommended shipping by express or freight instead of by mail. The mails, it pointed out, were expensive, limited to four-pound packages, had no insurance, except the company's own, and no C.O.D. They were to be used, the catalogue said, mainly for small and valuable parcels.[47]

On the other hand, the company's customers had to be warned about certain flaws in shipping by express and freight too. One was the cost, and for years the catalogue assured suspicious farmers that though they had to pay the express and freight charges on their packages, these would "amount to almost nothing" compared with "what you will save in price." Changing rates were also a bother. Listed in the catalogue were the freight and express rates from Chicago to points around the country and also a warning, needed by no farmer who knew the railroad and express companies, that all rates listed were subject to changes "likely to occur at any time." And with the express companies particularly, there was a problem of long standing. "Wherever a customer suspects an overcharge on the part of the transportation company," ran the catalogue's instructions, "we will be pleased to give same our most prompt and careful attention in his behalf, if he will send us the expense bill received from the agent, after he has paid the charge."[48]

But inconvenience was the worst feature about shipping express or freight, and the catalogue's constant reminder that a customer must send along with his order both his shipping address and mailing address, if they were different, suggested how clumsy the old system really was. As often as not, they were different which usually meant his post office was as far away from a railroad as he was, and he would have to go no telling how far to a station to pick up his package.

Here is where the old transportation system broke down, and limited the farmers' use of mail-order stores. One may imagine the long, slow buggy drive, the muddy roads, the bitter weather, or the long summer work day when every hand was needed on the farm from sunup to sundown that delayed the farmers' trips to town and prompted Sears, Roebuck to put this express note in their catalogue: "Always respond promptly to the notification of the Express Agent as to arrival of merchandise. We are constantly in receipt of requests from them for disposition of packages by reason of the fact that consignee does not reply to postal notices promptly."[49]

All this, parcel post changed. It pulled the stopper out of the transportation system, sped the farmer's merchandise over steel rail and rural routes from Chicago directly to the farm, and revolutionized the farmers' buying habits. Again, the Sears catalogue for 1913 told the story. "Packages up to 11 pounds in weight," it read, "will be handled just like any other mail matter. They will be delivered to your box by your rural mail carrier if you live on a rural route, or delivered to your door if you live in a city where there is carrier service, or delivered to your local post office if you live in a town where there is no carrier service."[50]

Never before had the farmers had such a convenient method of breaking the rural merchants' monopoly of their trade, and they wasted no time taking advantage of it. In 1920, of the 787 Wisconsin farm families questioned about their buying habits, 38 per cent were buying an average of $58.91 worth of goods a year from mail-order stores. That same year, 102,416,466 packages were delivered into farm homes over rural mail routes. Averaged out, this meant every family served by a rural route had about 17 packages sticking out of its mailbox at some time or other during the year.[51]

Even toward the close of the decade, when the automobile was already breaking up the old pattern of rural life and farmers were traveling farther than ever to shop, they were still ordering extensively from mail-order stores. In the same area in Wisconsin where the 1920 poll had been conducted, another was made in 1928. This time the poll showed that although they were now traveling from 20 to 80 miles from home to shop, three-fifths of the farm families were still using the mail-order stores with each family spending an average of $59.00 a year that way. Two years later, the year after the stock market collapsed, the average family on one of Uncle Sam's rural routes was still receiving about 17 packages a year from the rural mailman.[52]

Seventeen packages in the mail, one about every three weeks if evenly spaced, and every one a new thrill for farm families of the period. For as many an urban American can still remember, a package from Sears or Montgomery Ward was more than just a package. It represented a farm boy's corn-hoeing savings perhaps, or some prized labor-saving device for the farm, or possibly a promise made by a farmer to his wife. A week or more of anxious waiting was invested in that package, a week or more of watching for the rural mailman and running to the mailbox when his buggy or Model T showed up down the road. And when at last it came, it might mean a family gathering in the dining room or kitchen to see the unveiling. The package might contain a pair of curlers, long underwear, or a .22 rifle, but no matter; it was new, all the way from Chicago probably, and everyone in the family was interested.

Twice a year, spring and fall, the rural mailman also brought the fabulous mail-order catalogues to the farmers along his route, and in some ways they were more important to the farmers than the packages themselves. For the store came right to the farm with the catalogue, increasing the farmers' desires and showing them thousands of articles they would never find in the cluttered shelves of their local stores. Young women discovered new dress and hat styles in the catalogue and reveled in the possibility of buying Seroco Perfume or Milk of Cucumber for oily skins and even perhaps considered hopefully the "Princess Bust Developer and Food" for the "swelling, rounded, firm, bosom," while little girls found the catalogue filled with hundreds of potential paper dolls. And how many rural mothers, having moved their sick children from cold bedrooms to pallets placed close to the dining-room stove, placated them with the mail-order catalogue is nowhere recorded though it was a common enough occurrence in rural America to have been noted in the census.[53]

A book of many uses, the mail-order catalogue was equally useful for feeding dreams, replacing a textbook, or stirring the heart of a country bachelor. More than once Sears, Roebuck and Company received a letter from some lonely male asking the name of a particular model pictured on a particular page under a particular hat with a particular number. Next to the Bible, the most important book in the household, the catalogue was often called the "Homesteader's Bible," and it could have been an honest mistake that prompted the little boy, in answer to his Sunday school teacher's query as to where the ten commandments came from, to reply that they came from Sears, Roebuck.[54]

An inevitable byproduct of parcel post was, of course, the rapid rise of the mail-order stores, and it was one of the little ironies of the period that the mechanism established primarily for farmers should have been so valuable to city stores. Even more ironic was the fact that the farm-to-table movement was more valuable to the mail-order stores in the long run than to the farmers. For the more the Postmaster General juggled the parcel-post regulations, raising weight limits and reducing postage rates to lure farmers into sending their produce to the cities, the larger the packages the mail-order houses could send back to the farmers and at cheaper rates. By 1920, they could send a 50-pound package by parcel post from Chicago anywhere in the country and a 70-pound package anywhere in the first three zones.[55]

One could see the the results of all this in the soaring sales of the mail-order stores. In parcel post's first year, Sears, Roebuck and Company, received five times the number of orders it had received in 1912, and the company's shipping department was all but submerged. That year its revenues jumped from $77,116,859 to $91,357,276 and in just five years tripled those of 1912. While Montgomery Ward and Company's totals were less spectacular, its revenues, too, tripled from 1912 to 1920. Farmers were prosperous in those years, true, and mail-order sales rose because of it. But without the R F D and parcel post much less of their prosperity would have poured into Chicago. They were, as one advertiser noted, the "very life" of the system.[56]

But as the fortunes of the mail-order stores rose, those of the rural merchants fell. This came as no surprise to them. Everything was working out just as they had feared when they had begun their fight against parcel post years before. The idea of a rural parcel post had led to a general parcel post, as they had said it would, and a general parcel post was leading them to ruin. The service was no more than two years old when a journalist's survey showed that 95 out of 100 small-town merchants wanted to sell out, and sell out not for a profit but simply for their inventories and equipment. An exaggeration perhaps, but there was no doubt that parcel post had hit the rural merchants hard. The way they were striking back at the mail-order stores at the time the nation entered World War I made this clear.[57]

Some of the local merchants fought as they had always fought, with no holds barred. They made frontal assaults on the opposition in their local newspapers, spread stories about cheap stores, and put pressure on their congressmen to do something for them. And eventually in the 1920's when reaction against government in business had set in, Congress did lay a special tax on all parcels not mailed on rural routes and might have gone even further had the farmers' friends in Congress not come to parcel post's rescue.[58]

A gentler approach to the problem, however, was the loyalty campaign. The campaign's purpose was to make buying by mail seem subversive, and in the decade split by World War I, rural towns and villages were so saturated with "buy at home" from "home-owned store" slogans, some people felt as guilty sending an order to Montgomery Ward and Company as a union man crossing a picket line. Old arguments about the local merchant's value to the community—arguments of real merit, to be sure—were used again and again. One's dollar, it was said, must remain in the community where it could be spent for the community's welfare. Cooperation was the thing, and once in 1916, in a great show of "togetherness" the merchants at Cadillac, Michigan, closed up their stores, slung potato forks over their shoulders, and went out to help short-handed farmers harvest their potatoes before the freeze came.[59]

The farmers' reaction to this particular bid for their good will went largely unrecorded, but loyalty campaigns in general had little effect on the farmers. The old antagonism between town and country, not entirely the result of economic causes by any means, was not that easy to heal, and now that the shoe was on the other foot, farmers were no more inclined to buy at home when they could buy more cheaply some place else than the rural merchants had been to reduce prices in their better days.

The wiser among the rural merchants saw that the farmers' loyalty to them would be more likely if their stores were tidier, their goods more interesting, and their prices more reasonable, and they began to look inward for the seat of their trouble rather than to the mail-order stores. In Elyria, Ohio, in 1917, the "buy-at-home" division of the Chamber of Commerce sent out questionnaires to 500 householders to find out what they thought about shopping in local stores. Perhaps the merchants were shocked to learn their customers resented the fact that store clerks talked about them to other customers, that their stores were short on merchandise, that meat was handled by dirty-handed clerks, that their goods were inferior, their prices high, and that certain customers received special treatment, but it was the kind of shock they needed. Those who were willing to face the facts in Elyria and in rural towns all over the nation took such surveys seriously and began cleaning up their stores, arranging attractive displays, giving up certain lines of merchandise, and specializing in others. More and more this became the pattern as first parcel post and then the automobile swept across rural America, changing its face, its institutions, and the habits of its people. By accommodating themselves to the new order of things, rural merchants found they could compete with mail-order stores after all. But they had to compete. Their monopoly of the farmers' trade was gone forever.[60]

Gone too, or fast fading by 1930, was the old general store. That old institution, so dearly remembered by so many, could no more hold on to its regular customers in the new age than a farmer could keep from buying a Model T, and it must have been a wistful postmaster-storekeeper in the 1920's who made out money orders for Montgomery Ward and Company and watched that company's packages come through his post-office store addressed to former customers whose names were still on the debit side of his ledger.

Some of these merchants made an attempt to change their stores and hang on to their trade. One eager storekeeper was even willing to learn from the hated mail-order catalogue. "I sent for a mail-order catalogue myself and began to study it . . . ," he wrote. "I cleaned up my store, put in new windows, and gradually increased my stock and brought it more up to date. I poured over the Mail-order catalogues day and night. I studied the people of the community, and tried to figure out what they would like: Inside of a year I was doing twice as much business as when I began."[61]

This was the old rural merchant's spirit at its best, but he was playing a losing game. The decline of the old general store began the day parcel post went into effect. True it lingered on for some years in a kind of twilight period until the automobile came along. Then it changed completely or went out of business altogether. And now where the farmer once stopped to buy almost all his goods, his sons and grandsons stop, if indeed there is still a place to stop, only for a loaf of bread and hurry on to the city to buy everything else they need.

As the roads improved and automobiles multiplied and the farmers' reliance on parcel post lessened, the system was used more and more by city people. Especially was this true after World War II when express rates went sky-high and parcel-post rates remained comparatively low. When the parcel-post business leaped upward while the express business sank, the Railway Express Company begged Congress to change the parcel-post regulations. And this was done in 1951. Whereas a generation before congressmen had stood denouncing the greedy express companies, they now talked of saving this private business lest it and other businesses as well be nationalized, and passed a law reducing the weight limit on mailable packages from 70 to 40 pounds in the first two zones and from 70 to 20 in all the others.[62]

But Congress was not allowed to forget that in an urban world there were still thousands of rural people who had no service but parcel post, and this law did not apply to packages mailed on rural routes or to those mailed to or from second-, third-, and fourth-class post offices. Here, seventy-pound packages were still in order, and even in this missile age, isolated farm families still thumb through their mail-order catalogues, mail in their orders, and wait anxiously for their rural mailman to bring them their packages.[63]

First delivery of farm produce by mail truck

Bringing the city store to the farmer's mailbox

Bureau of Agricultural Economics

Parcel-post delivery

Bureau of Public Roads

Row of RFD mailboxes

Bureau of Public Roads

Delivering mail today

11

BACK TO THE FARM

"What do I think of the joys uv farmin'?" snorted the old farmer. *"What do I think about a hen's hind legs? I think there ain't no sech things."*

A. P. Hitchcock, "The Joys of Being a Farmer," *Country Life in America,* 20 (July 1, 1911), 46

RURAL free delivery was an expensive service. There was no doubt of that. Between 1900 and 1920, when a million dollar appropriation for anything was still a large sum, the government poured more than half a billion dollars into the rural delivery system, and the old Populist who watched the expenditure of all this money must have thought it the irony of ironies. Back in the 1890's when times were hard on the farm and mortgages were his best crop, the government had been unwilling to do much for him in spite of the noisy and vigorous political organization that spoke for him. But now in the prosperous 1900's when his old political party lay in ruins, the government was spending millions just to bring him his mail.[1]

Some of this money came back to the government as the farmers bought stamps and postcards. But even during President Taft's administration the R F D was credited with an annual loss of $28,000,000 and an estimated $40,000,000 loss in President Wilson's day—enough to have built more than three first-class battleships for the great American fleet. All these losses were of necessity absorbed by the government, and were, in effect, a kind of subsidy to the farmers.[2]

Congress did not always appropriate all this money unquestioningly, and sometimes the debate over what was to be spent on the R F D was as bitter as it was wordy. But in the end, year in and out, each annual appropriation was almost always larger than the previous year's and sometimes even larger than the Post Office Department asked for.

The reason for this was not primarily because the National Rural Letter Carriers' Association put pressure on Congress, although this helped. Nor was it because the farmers were better organized in this period or overrepresented in Congress. What brought the appropriations for rural delivery year after year was the same thing that brought so much farm legislation in these years: others besides the farmer had at last become concerned about what was happening in rural America.

Some of the men concerned were politicians, some were editors of magazines and newspapers, some were specialists in agricultural problems, and some were journalists, and all were men who helped mold public opinion. Most of them lived or at least worked in the cities, and oddly enough it was what they saw in the cities that aroused their interest in the country.

Like the nation's industrial empire, the American cities had grown with incredible speed in the last years of the nineteenth and early twentieth centuries. Only 28.6 per cent of the nation's people lived in towns or cities with populations larger that 2,500 in 1880. Twenty years later 40 per cent lived in such areas, and by 1910 the number had increased to almost 46 per cent or more than 42,000,000 people, and a nation that had never worried much about cities before now had an urban problem on its hands.[3]

The urban problem was not one but many problems ranging

all the way from corrupt politics to prostitution. Yet among them all there was a connection, and in one way or another many of them could be traced to the rise of city slums.

As more and more people flocked to the cities—people without money, jobs, or prospects—they gravitated naturally to the poorest parts of the cities, and there, in a land renowned for its abundant spaces, they huddled together in unbelievable squalor. So crowded were parts of New York City in 1908, according to one journalist, that all the people in the world could have lived in the State of Delaware and been no more pressed for space than they were in eleven of the city's most crowded blocks. "In the territory bounded by Catharine, Market, Hamilton and Monroe streets," he wrote, "1,672 people are jammed together—sleeping, cooking, and raising families in one acre of ground. . . . If they died, there would scarcely be room to bury them on the space on which New York's tenement-house laws permit them to live."[4]

New York City was the glaring example of overcrowded conditions, but it was by no means the only city in the nation troubled by the problem. The cities had grown so fast between 1900 and 1910 that all the large ones had slums, and congestion was a national problem.

City slums were the seedbed of many of those problems Americans at the turn of the century had not yet become inured to—organized crime, vice, machine politics, sweatshops, ill health. In fact, most Americans had only a vague conception of such things and no idea at all of how bad urban conditions really were until their innocence was shattered by a series of exposés that appeared in their magazines in the early 1900's.

The new century was not yet three years along when a group of young writers began to probe the dark spots of city life. Lincoln Steffens led off in *McClure's Magazine* with a number of articles about the political corruption of the cities. About the same time Ray Stannard Baker was writing on the growth of labor racketeering in the cities, and in 1907 George Kibbe Turner, examining the fleshpots in Chicago, discovered one saloon for every 150 people in some of the city's poorest wards and 10,000 prostitutes plying their trade in brothels, cheap dance halls, and hotels. "The City—from scarlet Babylon to smoky Chicago—has always been the great marketplace of dissipation," he wrote. "In the Jungle you would call this thing savagery. In the city there is a new side to it. The dweller of the city,—true to the instincts of city life,—has made it a financial transaction."[5]

No doubt the young muckrakers, as President Roosevelt called them—Steffens and Baker and Turner and many others—uncovered the sordidness of the cities because they were paid to and because people were anxious to read what they wrote. But, just as many of the reformers of the period came originally from farms and small-town rural America, so did many of the muckrakers, and it was this rural background that gave them zeal for their task and breathed sincerity into their articles.

Unlike those who had lived their lives in the great cities and had grown used to city misery, many of the muckrakers saw the cities with fresh eyes that looked at life with old agrarian values, and when they wrote of vice and political corruption and crime, even cold facts and statistics did not completely mask their indignation that such things could take place in America. "Indeed I think now," wrote Lincoln Steffens looking back on his days as a muckraker, "that my writings of that period were effective because I set out on my search with all the taught ignorance of my day. It was this that put the astonishment, shame, and patriotic indignation in my reports."

And in much the same vein Ray Stannard Baker, viewing his work in retrospect, wrote: "The articles do give an impression of sincerity and authenticity. They have much in them of what Ida Tarbell used to call 'righteous indignation'—and I realize now, even more keenly than I did then, how much of that they had; for we were ourselves personally astonished, personally ashamed, personally indignant at what we found, and we wrote earnestly, even hotly."[6]

One journalist, Seymour Deming, who saw the cities from the small-town, rural point of view, could not, of course, speak for them all, but his comments seem close to what most of the important muckrakers probably felt as they told their tales of the corrupt cities. "And then to our new-opened eyes," he wrote, "the tragedy of the city begins to reveal itself. . . . This is now not a stage play or a story book. . . . This is real blood and tears. These shrieks are genuine; this despair is the hollow throat-rattle of exhaustion; this sin is vile; this suffering unbearable. We see it now, we small-towners, with eyes washed clean by our own temptations, defeats, self-conquests, and with hearts that know from the sweet, wholesome neighborly intercourse in which we were reared that people were never meant to live like this. The drawn-underlip of the rouged woman in the cafe; . . . the sodden face of the pawer-over of garbage barrels; the haggard glare of the drug fiend. . . . The child struck by a motor truck. . . . A scream, a pool of blood, a limp little body, a mother's shriek. . . . I do not say that the city bred are invariably desensitized to such sights. What I say is that we of the small-towns look on them with sensitiveness to the human side of things which sharpens our capacities for suffering and stimulates our consciences to seek a remedy. We know that if such things had happened in our home towns we could and would have 'done something' about it."[7]

Bad as it was, the urban problem was only one horn of the American dilemma in the early 1900's. For while the population of the cities expanded rapidly, the rural population seemed to be declining, and putting two and two together, it appeared that the reason for the first was the result of the latter. Actually this was not entirely the case. The rural population itself had increased from 1900 to 1910, and most of the growth of the city population had come not from the rural areas but from an increase of births over deaths and from successive freshets of immigrants.

Nevertheless, the immigrants had been joined in the cities by increasing numbers of farm folk, and the 11 per cent rate of increase of farm population in the century's first decade compared to the city's rate of nearly 35 per cent made it plain that before another decade had passed more people would be living in cities than in rural America. In fact, the sun had already set on the face of agrarian America.[8]

This was the other horn of the dilemma and even more disturbing than the first. For this had always been a rural nation. Its history was rooted in the soil. Its most precious documents—the Declaration of Independence and the Constitution—had been drawn for an agrarian society by men who knew and loved the land. Even the symbol of the nation, Uncle Sam himself, was a kind of shrewd, rustic fellow who epitomized the rural character of the country. And out of the rural past had come an agrarian tradition whose principles were subscribed to by thousands of Americans who had taken them in with their mothers' milk.[9]

Of all the nation's people, the farmers traditionally were believed to be the healthiest and most virtuous, and the greatest exponent of this belief in America was Thomas Jefferson whose classic description of farmers has echoed down through the years. "Those who labor in the earth," he had written, "are the chosen people of God, if ever He had a chosen people, whose breasts He has made His peculiar deposit for substantial and genuine virtue. It is the focus in which He keeps alive that sacred fire, which otherwise might escape from the face of the earth. Corruption of morals in the mass of cultivators is a phenomenon of which no age nor nation has furnished an example."[10]

The incorruptible man, at least in the mass, this was Jefferson's farmer, and upon his shoulders rested democracy itself. For the farmer, to paraphrase the master of Monticello, looked only to heaven, to his soil, and to his own hard work for his existence. His farm which produced his food and his living was his security, and he was dependent upon no man. And this was good. For "dependence," wrote Jefferson, "begets subservience and venality, suffocates the germ of virtue, and prepares fit tools for the designs of ambition."[11]

Just as democracy was dependent upon him for its strength, so too were the cities with their teeming millions. By "the application of brain and muscle to the natural resources," as William Jennings Bryan had said, the farmer created the nation's real wealth, and the economic livelihood of all depended upon the fruits of his toil. "Let the farmer withhold his hand from the plow for two seasons," said a congressman expanding on Bryan's Cross of Gold speech, "and the grass will grow in your thoroughfares; barnacles and bilge water will rot your ships as they lie idle at your docks; cobwebs will festoon your counting houses; owls and bats will usurp your warehouses; your children will clamor to you for bread, and we will gather in this Chamber with pallor in our faces."[12]

Nor was food for the cities all the farms produced. The belief was general that they also produced the nation's best people—its soldiers in time or war, its most solid citizens in time of peace, and its natural leaders in time of war and peace. A Georgia congressman once summed it up this way: "The country is the pure fountain that sends forth our best men and women. . . . Our great men do not come from the gilded palaces where lives of ease, comfort, and elegance are spent; nor from the cities where vice, dissipation, and immorality reign supreme; but from the industrious, Christian, country homes that are uncontaminated by evil influences."[13]

It was as natural for the congressman to have spoken of vice in the cities as to have thought of the country as the pure fountain. For those who believed that the country was man's natural habitat, the ancient and normal place for those created in God's image, more than likely believed just as firmly that the cities were sinkholes of sin. Evil lurked in their shadowy places and draped windows looking out upon the streets hid from view the countless crimes and immoralities of degenerate people. Cities to them were great labyrinths—crowded, unhealthy, unnatural, impersonal—where life lost its meaning. Willa Cather expressed the feeling in her book, *O Pioneers*, when one of her characters who had been living in the city said to the country girl, Alexandra: "Here you are an individual, you have a background of your own, you would be missed. But off there in the cities there are thousands of rolling stones like me. We are all alike; we have no ties, we know nobody, we own nothing. When one of us dies, they scarcely know where to bury him. Our landlady and the delicatessen man are our mourners, and we leave nothing behind us but a frock coat and a fiddle or an easel, or a typewriter, or whatever tool we got our living by."[14]

Moreover, cities were regarded as dangerous to the nation's institutions. ". . . God save this country," said an Iowa congressmen in 1912, "if we ever reach a time when the majority of our citizenship comes from the cesspools of a congested city population," and this was only a variation of the theme Jefferson had suggested to James Madison in 1787 when he wrote that we would be a virtuous people "as long as agriculture is our principal object, which will be the case, while there remain vacant lands in any part of America. When we get piled up on one another in large cities, as in Europe, we shall become corrupt as in Europe, and go to eating one another as they do there."[15]

Jefferson, it was true, had put most of these ideas in imperishable prose for his fellow countrymen, and he in turn could have drawn upon the writing of poets, statesmen, and philosophers from Cicero and Virgil to the French philosophers of the eighteenth century and to his own contemporaries like Benjamin Franklin for support. But the ideas would never have been so deeply imbedded in the American mind, had they not been as simple, logical, and as rooted in the American experience as they were.

Being a practical people, observation not rhetoric had convinced

Americans that their cities rested on the country's "broad and fertile plains"; that real wealth was the product of a Kansas wheat field or a Southern cotton farm; that country air and open spaces were healthier than smoky cities and squalid slums; that organized crime and vice were fruits of the cities; and that most of the nation's leaders—American Presidents, for example—came from the country. According to one official in the Department of Agriculture, 23 of the 25 presidents up to Theodore Roosevelt's time, had rural origins.[16]

Experience also confirmed the old tradition of the farmer's independence, even in the twentieth century. True, he had become something of a businessman with a cash crop to sell and with a businessman's worries about money with which to pay the mortgage and to buy new machinery. And it was true, too, that he bought more of his goods at the store and was less self-sufficient than he once had been. But anyone who knew the farmers in the early 1900's, knew they were still Jefferson's independent citizens in many respects. Their farms still produced a large share of their living just as they always had. Farmers still did their own butchering and raised their own chickens and geese. Their orchards as in biblical times "brought forth their fruit in due season." And their gardens supplied their tables with an abundance of fresh foods in summer and canned foods in winter. In some places farmers still took their corn to the mill to be ground and their wheat to be exchanged for flour.

A survey made of 483 farm families in the South, Midwest, and the East in 1912 showed that 62 per cent of all the food these families consumed in a year was produced on their farms. For food, fuel, and home, they spent an average of $595.08 a year per family, only $68.00 less than the total wages of an unskilled laborer in a steel plant for that year. But the farmers' farms produced nearly three-fourths of this amount, $421.17, while the steelworker had to buy, at considerably higher prices than those the farmers received for his goods at the market, all his food, fuel, and home payments out of his salary of $663.00. Said one South Carolina farmer, commenting on the self-sufficiency of farmers in his area, ". . . we are proud of the fact in this section that we go to Columbia and other market places with our wagons full of produce, and we come back with our wagons empty, except for such few things as cannot be produced in this section."[17]

Farming, then, was still a way of life and the farmer more self-sufficient than is usually thought, and if his farm were clear, he was still subservient to no one. But even if the moneylender was pressing him as he often was, still the farmer continued to work for himself. No one told him when to plant and when to harvest, what machinery to buy and what he must sow here and what there. His hours were his to spend as he pleased, a privilege that induced the dedicated farmer to stay on the farm through panic and prosperity. Years of being his own boss had made him dread working for another with a passion incomprehensible to the city man. "I have seen a gray hue steal over the face of a settler," wrote the sociologist Edward Ross, "when speaking of some one who has 'lost his farm' and 'had to go out by day.' "[18]

Deeply rooted in the American mind, these ideas were simply taken for granted in the years after the Civil War, and most people saw no particular threat to the old ideals in the nation's rising industrial empire. They assumed that rural people, like the poor, would be with them always, and Populist admonitions that the agrarian tradition and the agrarian way of life were in danger had fallen on deaf ears.

But the cities, brimming with immigrants and folks from the farm and wrestling with problems too big to handle, made serious-minded men stop to wonder if perhaps Oliver Goldsmith had not been right when he wrote,

> Ill fares the land to hast'ning ills a prey,
> Where wealth accumulates and men decay.

For if the farmers moved to the city, who would create the wealth and who would feed a nation of city people? "An ever-decreasing rural population," said a congressman, "will not always be able to sustain an ever-increasing urban population." Worse still, what would happen to the vigor and virtue and independence which had been so much a part of the American character if the country were completely drained of its young? For the vigor and enterprise the American cities had in 1910, suggested the English observer, Sir Horace Plunkett, they owed to the influx of people from the country. But this would not always continue. "You cannot," he warned the American people, "keep on indefinitely skimming the pan and have equally good milk left. In America the drain may continue a while longer without the inevitable consequences becoming plainly visible; but sooner or later, if the balance of trade in this human traffic be not adjusted, the raw material out of which urban society is made will be seriously deteriorated. When that time comes, the symptoms of National degeneracy will be properly charged against those who failed to foresee the evil and treat the cause."[19]

Nothing but time of course could prove or disprove the theory, but it seemed logical to men in those days to believe that by moving from the farms to the cities, the farm people were cutting the umbilical cord that had nourished the nation spiritually and physically. "Our great cities are augmenting their population in an accelerated ratio," warned a congressman. "Some day, without warning, they may tell a tale of disaster, and then there will be no escape or refuge save in the immunity, the stability, and the conservatism of the country."[20]

So the problem was—how to keep the farmers on the farm. And the answer was—improve farm life even with the aid of national legislation if need be. The willingness of Congress to enact farm legislation, everything from postal savings to the Federal Highway Act, in those prosperous days before World War I, can only be understood against this background of rising cities and declining rural areas and the fears both quickened in the minds of the American people.[21]

This was the crisis into which the R F D had been born, and from the beginning it had been presented as a means of keeping the boys on the farm. In 1891, the year after Jacob Riis wrote about the terrible conditions in the New York tenement districts in his book, *How the Other Half Lives*, that old country boy, John Wanamaker, had written in support of his plan to deliver the mail to farmers that "the regular arrival of the papers and magazines . . . will not only keep many of the boys and girls at home and make them more contented there, but add to their ambition and determination to make the old farm pay."[22]

But it was really only after the turn of the century that this became a major argument in support of rural delivery, and the more congested the cities became, the better the argument, and the R F D hurdled obstacle after obstacle on the strength of what it would do to save the countryside. "Mr. Chairman," said a congressman in 1902 as he argued against letting the rural routes out to contract, "let us go forward in extending this service until its benefits and blessings shall extend to every community and to every home. Let us destroy the isolation and loneliness of country life and stop the constant and deplorable drift from country to town. We can never do too much for the rural sections of this great country, whose people feed and clothe the world."[23]

This was always the argument, and it had helped secure appropriations large enough by 1907 to build 37,728 rural mail routes. But in spite of the routes, farm people were still pouring into the cities in that year when the economic panic struck throwing men out of work and spreading misery throughout the great cities.[24]

Now, more than ever, attention was drawn to the overcrowded cities. While hungry, idle men lined the city streets, the farmers had a scarcity of labor. But the unemployed in the cities apparently had no desire to work on farms and, according to one journalist, they would not have known how to get to the country if they had wanted to go. Too much effort, he thought, had been spent on making city life comfortable while the country had been forgotten with the result that city people dreaded the country. "These city dwellers on the lower levels of industrial life," he wrote, "never find out what American citizenship means nor what American life offers. They are the victims of bad city government. They are the victims of hard employment. They are the victims of degrading class distinctions such as arise wherever the very rich live. . . . To be men and to see the horizon all around are impossible to them. Two or three generations of such life will produce a distinctly degenerate type." There was need, he thought, for "a larger, stronger, franker, leadership; and need to come back to the old truth that the normal life is on the soil."[25]

President Theodore Roosevelt, city-born but agrarian-minded, shared this view. Deeply worried about the drift of the farm population to the city, he asked Professor Liberty Hyde Bailey of Cornell University in 1908 to head a commission to study country life and make recommendations for the improvement of life on the farm.[26]

The sincerity of Roosevelt's concern with this problem was beyond question. His term of office was almost over. He was trying neither to win farm votes nor to secure favorable farm legislation. Nor did he have anything at all to gain politically by the appointment of the commission. Quite simply, he was genuinely concerned about what was happening in the cities and on the farms, because he believed in the agrarian tradition.

Roosevelt had been instructed on the farm problem by Sir Horace Plunkett, the English agrarian reformer, who had ranched in Wyoming, farmed in Nebraska, and as an official of the British government had helped develop a suitable farm program in Ireland. But the President's own understanding of the American past, his love of the outdoors and the strenuous life, the kind of life lived on American farms, and his vast reading had shaped his agrarian philosophy and made him responsive to Plunkett's suggestions.

A constant reader of history, Roosevelt could not help comparing what was happening in the United States to what had happened in older, fallen civilizations. "Wherever civilizations have hitherto sprung up," he told a group of New York Grangers in 1910, "they have always tended to go through certain stages and then to fall. No nation can develop a real civilization without cities. Up to a certain point the city movement is thoroughly healthy; yet it is a strange and lamentable fact that always hitherto after this point has been reached the city has tended to develop at the expense of the country by draining the country of what is best in it, and making an insignificant return for this best. In consequence, in the past, every civilization in its later stages has tended really to witness those conditions under which 'the cities prosper and the men decay.'" And there were signs, he thought, suggesting these tendencies were at work in the United States.[27]

The problem was not in the mere growth of cities, Roosevelt had told the Grangers. It was the growth of cities fed by people who ought to live on the land that worried him because, as he said, "from the beginning of time it has been the man raised in the country—and usually the man born in the country—who has been most apt to render the services which every nation most needs."[28]

Like a bad dream, the drift of country people to the cities seemed to haunt him, and he recurred again and again to the problem. "No growth of cities, no growth of wealth can make up for the loss in either the number or the character of the farming population," he had said in 1908. Three years later he wrote that "the men of the open country have always been the real backbone of the Nation, and it will be a National calamity of the very gravest sort if they are permitted to sink in moral and physical well-being relatively to the dwellers of the city." And the next year, 1912, he pointed out that while England had let her farm population drift to the cities, the militaristic nations who knew the value of the farm population to the nation's welfare had not allowed their farmers to suffer. Borrowing ideas from Sir Horace

Plunkett, he wrote: "Our city populations have been physically and morally sustained by the constant inflow of the best country blood. This cannot go on indefinitely. If the human reservoir from which the cities have drawn, and must continue to draw, so much of their best citizenship becomes depleted and deteriorated, the cities themselves will be the greatest sufferers from the evils which always threaten a nation which as a whole abandons the country for the town. National degeneracy will then proceed apace."[29]

President Roosevelt's Country Life Commission seemed utter foolishness to some of his fellow countrymen. Members of Congress who disliked the President's habit of appointing commissions thought this was at last one too many, and Mr. Dooley poked fun at the President for investigating unhappiness on the farm. "Onhappiness," he said, "is a very gen'ral complaint," and he thought it strange that "iv all th' men who have governed countries, f'm Solomon down, Tiddy Rosenfelt is the first to undhertake a scientific invistigation of the subject."[30]

But the commission went on with its work anyway and received an overwhelming response from the farmers who met in their country schoolhouses to write reports on farm conditions for the commission or poured out their individual stories in some 125,000 letters they sent the commissioners.

The commission found that much was already being done to improve farm life. It singled out for particular attention the R F D as one of the factors that was already helping to correct the social sterility of farm life and recommended that "as rapidly as possible the rural free delivery of mails should be extended."

But the commission was looking for the unsmiling aspects of farm life and it found them. Asked if there was a sufficient labor supply on the farm, one plainspoken farmer wrote: "No; because the people have gone out of the baby business." And when asked whether sanitary conditions were satisfactory in his neighborhood, he replied: "No; to[o] careless about chickens (and the like) and poorly covered wells, in one Well in a Neighbor's farm I counted seven snakes in the Wall of the Well, and they used the Watter daily, his wife dead now and he is looking for another."

And so it went. The commission found poor roads in rural America, poor schools, poverty, intemperance, isolation, and even poor health—especially in the South; and when President Roosevelt submitted the commission's report to Congress and asked for $25,000 to publish it, he wrote: "I warn my fellow countrymen that the great recent progress made in city life is not a full measure of our civilization; for our civilization rests at bottom on the wholesomeness, the attractiveness, and the completeness, as well as the prosperity, of life in the country. The men and women on the farm stand for what is fundamentally best and most needed in our American life. Upon the development of country life rests ultimately our ability . . . to continue to feed and clothe the hungry nations; to supply the city with fresh blood, clean bodies, and clear brains that can endure the terrific strain of modern life; we need the development of men in the open country, who will be in the future, as in the past, the stay and strength of the nation in time of war, and its guiding and controlling spirit in time of peace."[31]

Out of the Country Life Commission's work came its famous report, published in 1909 with no thanks to Congress which had refused to appropriate the money for the printing, and two movements concerned with country life. One was the annual Country Life Conferences to study and discuss country life; the other was the back-to-the-farm movement.

The goals of the back-to-the-farm movement were to encourage farmers to remain on their farms as well as to lure city people countryward, so that the cities would be less congested, democracy strengthened, and the nation assured of a continuing supply of farm people. "People are wanted on the farms," wrote one man capturing the spirit of the movement, "to raise corn and grow stock for the markets; but they are wanted there far more for the training of manhood and womanhood in moral worth, in religious sensibility, in all the traits of a strong upright personality. In the future as never heretofore, our cities with their multiplying wealth and lavish luxury are likely to need the country for that steady renewal of their better life which shall keep them from relaxing into sensuality and sinking into decay."[32]

There was very little organization about the movement; almost none in fact. Here and there urban groups, trying to build up the farms about their cities, helped would-be farmers get started on the land, but this was never done on a large scale. Much more important was the work of the Department of Agriculture's Office of Farm Management under the direction of William J. Spillman. It was his business to give expert advice on going back to the farm to questioning city men, and by 1911 he was receiving thousands of letters of inquiry a year.

Spillman believed city people would save the countryside. "Country boys will continue to crowd into the cities, perhaps always," he reasoned. "To them the city offers excitement and novelty, while to the man who knows the city thoroughly country life offers a refuge from the turmoil of the city and the uncertainty of city employments. But the cities will continue to grow until the limit of food production in the country is reached. Conditions in the cities will continue to grow harder for laboring men. . . . In time the flow of population from the city back to the farm will equal the current which flows in the opposite direction. Then and not till then will the ratio of urban and rural population become approximately stable."[33]

Spillman's office passed out vast quantities of information to "back-to-the-landers" who sought advice, but it did not promote the movement vigorously. This work was taken over by periodicals, such as *World's Work,* and its editor, Walter Hines Page. Reared in a rural community in North Carolina, Page was devoted to the agrarian tradition, and to the improvement of farm conditions in his native South. Near the turn of the century he had become a partner in Doubleday, Page and Company and shortly afterwards the Company had founded two magazines, *World's Work* and *Country Life in America.* In 1908 Page served as a commissioner on the Country Life Commission, and in 1911 he began to give organized leadership to the back-to-the-farm movement through the pages of *World's Work.*

By that time, after all that had been done to encourage people to go back to the farm, it was only too apparent there had been no headlong rush to the country, and *World's Work* wondered why. "Is the trouble," it asked, "the lack of information about good farm land and a lack of ways and means of getting back to the soil? Or is 'back-to-the-land' all cry and no wool? Do people prefer to remain in town and to keep flocking to town?" *World's Work* proposed to find out. It offered its pages as a clearing house to anyone interested in knowing where to buy land, the price of land, the possibilities of success on the farm, where to get specialized information on farming or on any question about going "forward-to-the-land," as the magazine liked to say. All one had to do was to write to the magazine's "Land Inquiry" department, and whatever questions they had would be answered.[34]

The back-to-the-farm movement stirred the imagination of thousands of Americans. Nostalgia for the "good old days," the impersonality of city life, frustrations in their jobs, ill health, insecurity, usually not one but a combination of these turned men's minds back to the land. "Men walk the hot asphalt streets," noted one writer after discussing the letters of those who inquired about going back to the land, "working in a narrow groove for a mere pittance; and in their hearts they long for brawny-armed freedom of life on a farm, where they can know that at least a little piece of old earth belongs to them."[35]

Going back to the farm they saw themselves returning to independence, security, and release from the tensions of city life. To them the farm meant fresh food grown in one's own garden, fresh eggs, and fresh milk. It meant fresh air and health—"firm-fleshed, steady-nerved, ostrich-stomached health," as one man said—for themselves and their children. Above all, it meant independence. "The farmer is his own employer, his own boss," they read in the pages of the *Country Life in America* in 1911. "His only timetable is that kept by the sun and marked by the toot of the dinner-horn. He has not 'hours of labor,' no fixed work day. His sense of duty is his only taskmaster—that and his responsibility for results. . . . He may lean his hoe against the fence and go fishing if a ruffling breeze on the brook surface tells him the fish will bite, or he may drop his fish-pole and hurry his mown clover into the barn if a rising 'thunderhead' promises a wetting."[36] Not to dream of the open country, not to long for a farm of their own when they read such things was impossible for Americans whose traditions harked back to the land.

In the course of time thousands of letters of inquiry from city-worn men were sent to the *World's Work* and the Office of Farm Management, letters that told stories of ill-health and tensions and the insecurity men felt in the cities in those seemingly halcyon years before the Great War. "I am an employe of a large manufacturing establishment," one man wrote. "My wife, mother and sister are dependent upon my salary which is $1,000 a year. I have saved $2,000. I do not know what time some relative of a high official of the company may need my place. I desire to own a farm and to live on it, so that I may feel the sense of proprietorship."[37]

In the meantime, while men wrote and talked and dreamed about going back to the farm, the R F D was reaping the benefits of the back-to-the-farm movement. For what else, unless it was better roads and rural telephones, could make farm life more attractive in those years than rural delivery? And what else would be more likely to help keep the boys on the farm? Said one congressman: "Nothing has been done in your lifetime or mine that has done more to make country life attractive than the rural mail system. . . ."[38]

It followed, therefore, that rural free delivery must be extended as the Country Life Commission had recommended and that nothing must be done to injure it. "Let the routes be extended . . . ," said a Virginia congressman as he argued for a larger R F D appropriation. "Let the daily paper be each night handed to the farmer, with tired muscles and limbs, but rested brain. . . . It is worth more to us in war, as well as in peace, to have a prosperous, patriotic people, free from excessive taxes from without and more internal improvements from within. This law is for the plain people, who will defend us in time of war, who will love us in times of peace. This service must never be reduced, but rather extended and increased. Carve other appropriations. Yea, carve them all rather than to touch one hair in the head of this appropriation for the producers of the country."[39]

Reducing the extension of rural delivery, however, was just what the Post Office Department had in mind at the time the congressman was speaking, and it was fortunate for the R F D that the back-to-the-farm movement was in full swing when the Department began to cut back on rural route organizing.

Rural routes had been established so rapidly there were more than 40,000 of them by 1909, and the R F D appropriations since 1900 had increased on the average of two and a half million dollars annually. But that year the government faced a deficit, and President Taft sent word to the Departments to cut expenses. At the Post Office Department this meant cutting the R F D, the costliest program in sight, and from then on fewer and fewer routes were laid out, as petitions for routes piled up in the Department unanswered or were returned with an adverse report.

But the rural delivery system would have suffered even more if people had not been as concerned about the drift of farmers to the cities as they were. Year after year for more than a decade, Congress fought the Post Office Department's retrenchment program and urged the extension of rural delivery on the ground that it would help keep the boys on the farm. Said one congressman protesting against an insignificant increase in the R F D appropriation in 1910: "But certainly, my friends . . . , it is bad policy to begin retrenchment with the bone and sinew of our land—the sturdy farmers. One of the crying evils of this day is the fact that the country people are flocking into the cities. . . . It is our business so to legislate as to encourage the people to go into the country, rather than to leave the country, and nothing has encouraged country people to be satisfied with their lot more than the Rural Free Delivery Service."[40]

This now was the main argument in support of R F D just as it was for most of the farm legislation passed in this period; and to improve country life and keep the boys on the farm, Congress not only appropriated more money for the R F D than the Postmaster General requested each year, it also saved the rural routes from being let out to contract as Postmaster General Burleson wanted to do.[41]

Congressmen were bound to use the arguments that came readiest to hand, of course, and no one could claim they were always sincere. But to dismiss the back-to-the-farm movement and the arguments that centered about it as of no fundamental importance would be to misread the spirit of the times and to ignore the evidence. One need only glance at the debates on farm issues from parcel post to the Federal Farm Loan Act to see the real concern with which Americans viewed the loss of their farm population. One congressman said he had "believed for years that the real question in this country was and is the country life question," and this sentiment was shared by numerous Americans outside Congress who wrote books on the subject, filled the magazines with their articles, and even composed poems that tugged at the emotions of farm-bred city dwellers.

Even Jacob Riis, escaping from the city to live in the country as many of the muckrakers did, wrote an article to tell how he and his wife found their farm. And Ray Stannard Baker fled the city life he had written so much about to write a series of novels under the pseudonym of David Grayson which glorified the agrarian way of life and touched approvingly on every tenet of the agrarian tradition from the hatred of the city, which he called "a monster," to the idea that the best men come from the country. "It was good," said David Grayson, "to escape that place of hurrying strangers. It was good to be in a place where things *are* because they *grow*. . . ! Oh, my friend, say what you please, argue how you like, this crowding together of men and women in unnatural surroundings, this haste to be rich in material things, this attempt to enjoy without production, this removal from firsthand life, is irrational, and the end of it is ruin. If our cities were not recruited constantly with fresh, clean blood of the country, with boys who still retain some of the power and vision drawn from the soil, where would they be!"[42]

Nor was the back-to-the-farm movement all talk. People did go back to the farm in these years. Not nearly as many went as dreamed of going, of course, for it took both courage and capital to cut loose from the city, and the long-time urban resident who longed to leave often lacked one prerequisite or the other and sometimes both. Nevertheless, a report prepared by George K. Holmes of the Department of Agriculture in 1912, and based on information compiled from 45,000 crop correspondents, showed that people were moving back to the land everywhere, and east of the Mississippi River near large urban centers, the movement was particularly strong.

Many had gone back to farm, cutting their ties with the city completely, and some had gone simply to live on the farm and to work in the cities. A few had even gone to be farm laborers, and many wealthy people merely bought farms for their summer residences.

Poor health drove many of these people back to the land; others went for the sake of their children, and some for the pure pleasure of country living. But the majority—the businessmen who had done poorly or become discouraged by the futility of their city occupations, the unemployed mechanics, common laborers, and salesmen—went back to the country for the economic security the land would bring.

Holmes concluded, however, that the kind of people who were going back to the farm were not, in many instances, the kind who were leaving, and that the movement poorly offset "the loss to agriculture of the farmers' sturdy sons who leave that occupation to enter industry, trade, the professions, and other occupations."[43]

Apparently nothing could be done to stop this drift of country boys to the cities. "Every highway in the country might be made as good as a Roman road," wrote Seaman Knapp, field representative for the Department of Agriculture, "with a free delivery mailbox . . . at every crossing, and a box stuffed with newspapers . . . and the flow of young men from the country to the city would not be arrested in the least, so long as the earning capacity of the average city laborer, or clerk, or professional man, is at least five fold what the same talent can command in the country."[44]

Dr. Knapp had it right. The attractive city salary, or the city salary that seemed attractive, led the boys to the city. A study made of farm boys at Cornell University showed most of them were leaving the farm for economic reasons. For them the city was the end of the rainbow, and they hurried there by the thousands to find their pot of gold. "Why does the boy . . . leave the farm. . . ?" asked Harvey Wiley, the crusader for Pure Food and Drugs. "Because of his desire for greater opportunity. . . . I remember my own mental attitude. I was born near the Ohio River, and could hear the whistle and see the smoke of the passing boats. When I lay under the wide-spreading beech-tree during my midday rest, I did not dream of a future on the farm. My thoughts followed the southward-moving steamboat down to the Mississippi, down past Memphis and Vicksburg, down to the canefields of Louisiana, to New Orleans and the gulf. My ambition was some day to get a passage on one of those boats and seek my career and my fortune in the South."[45]

Thoughts like these filled the minds of many a farm boy as he drove his cows along a country lane or shocked hay in the meadow or followed barefooted in the dusty wake of the harrow. Born into an isolated life, shouldered with responsibility at an early age, and nurtured on hard work, he was often ambitious, self-reliant, and independent, and these very traits which farm life had fostered in him were the traits that drove him to the cities.

And herein lay the paradox of the R F D. Independence, self-reliance, and ambition were always considered among the most valuable characteristics of rural people, and it was to keep people on the farm where these virtues might be continually developed for the good of the nation, that men supported rural delivery. But independence and self-reliance were in part the product of the farmer's isolation, and to improve his system of communication by developing the free delivery system was to run the risk of breaking down barriers that might weaken his independence and even lead him away from the country altogether.

Theodore Roosevelt saw the problem. "In all this," he wrote, "we have to grapple with one fact which has made both the strength and weakness of the American farmer, and that is, his isolation. This isolation implies a lack both of the pleasure and of the inspiration which comes from closer contact between people, and from a well-developed organization for social pleasures, for religious life, for education. On the other hand, it is to this isolation more than to anything else that we owe the strength of character so typical of the American farmer, who lives under a peculiarly individualistic system in the management alike of the farm and of the farm home. . . . Our object must be . . . to do away with the disadvantages which are due to the isolation of the family farm, while conserving its many and great advantages. . . ."[46]

Perhaps this was an impossible goal. At any rate, while the R F D was doing away with the isolation of the family farm, it may also have been a significant factor in doing away with the future family farmers. For the more newspapers farm boys and girls read, the more circulars, the more magazines, the more they learned of city life and the more attractive it seemed. Furthermore, the R F D contributed greatly to the elimination of rural America's small neighborhoods, and the breakdown of community life with its old-fashioned entertainment that followed their disappearance had perhaps some small part to play in the exodus of young people from the farm.

Before the R F D was established, there were hundreds of little communities in rural America, most of them identifiable by their local post offices, and people who lived within their boundaries had a sense of belonging and a community spirit which showed itself in their occasional social meetings. "Formerly," wrote one observer of the old community life, "frequent social gatherings were held, when the whole neighborhood would 'turn out,'—the women and children gathering in the afternoon, and the men both old and young, joining them in the evenings. The sons of farmers married daughters of farmers, and the new farm homes were established, thus perpetuating the community."[47]

But the rural delivery system had the effect of expanding the community, loosening up old, familiar relationships, and often wiping out long established neighborhoods altogether. For when rural routes came through an area, many of the little fourth-class post offices disappeared, and with them went the identity of the community and finally the community itself. In Reno County, Kansas, for example, rural delivery eliminated sixteen post offices in ten years. "Some of these localities are completely off the map now," the *Hutchinson News* reported in 1912, "not even a country store being left to mark their sites. Others still have country stores and maintain their identity but they all now get mail by rural routes."[48]

A study of the southern half of Courtland County, New York, in 1929, showed in detail what happened to little communities when rural routes came through them. At the turn of the century, separate neighborhoods existed at each of the places located on the map on the following page. Freetown, Texas Valley, Hunts Corners, Marathon, and Messengerville had post offices and active businesses and social organizations.

Shortly after 1900, three rural routes were established at Marathon. The post offices at Freetown, Texas Valley, and Hunts Corners were closed, and gradually the businesses at these little villages deteriorated. Of the two stores that had existed at Freetown, only one was left in 1917, and it operated only intermittently. The store at Texas Valley was rarely open in 1917, while the one at Hunts Corners had been closed and reopened several times in the decades between 1919 and 1929. The churches in the communities held on into the twenties but with declining attendance, and the same was true of such social organizations as the Grange. By 1929 the small tightly knit communities had almost disappeared, and Marathon had become the main shopping center of the area.[49]

All this is not to say that the R F D was of no help at all in keeping people on the farm. How many people might have gone to the cities but stayed on the farm because of the convenience of rural free delivery, no one knows or ever will. Nor can one say the R F D played no part in luring people back to the farm. Perhaps it did.

But the R F D could not do the impossible. Probably nothing short of blowing up the cities would have kept the young people on the farms. The city was a woman, beautiful and alluring, a promise for the isolated farm boy, and as the years passed, the economic reasons for his leaving the farm became more and more compelling. Farm life was changing rapidly in the days before World War I. The frontier was gone, the price of land was rising

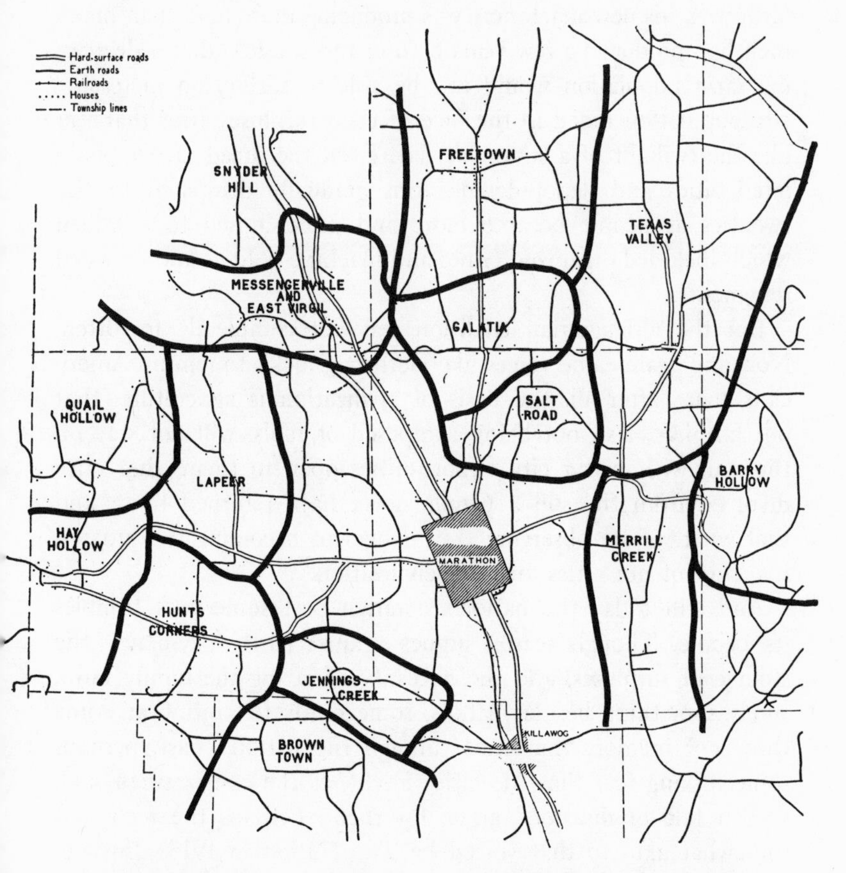

Neighborhoods in Courtland County, New York, about 1900
(Map reproduced from Bruce L. Melvin, *The Sociology of a Village and a Surrounding Territory*, Cornell University Experiment Station, Bulletin No. 523, p. 128.)

steadily, and with each passing year it took more capital to go into the business of farming.

Besides there was no longer room on the farms for everyone, even if they wished to stay. By World War I, one man on the farm with his new machinery was producing more food than many men had produced a few years before, and the fear that a decreasing farm population would not be able to sustain an increasing city population faded in the face of farm surpluses after that war like the twilight of a summer's day. Even the dread of overpopulated cities and depopulated farms gradually dissipated in the twenties as people became more and more inured to a milieu which included organized crime and machine politics and crowded tenements.

But the old agrarian tradition was not completely forgotten. Now and again came voices like Herbert Quick's to remind Americans that "after all, the basis of civilization is agriculture; that our farming class, not being composed of fools, will not stay on the soil, with better city opportunities open to them; that once divorced from the soil a people never have returned to it; and that what we are observing is in danger of becoming the progressive ruin of our cities and our civilization."[50]

And still today the nation's agrarian past sometimes troubles its people. Though reason argues against parity payments, the storage of surpluses, and the necessity of saving the family farm, surely something besides ballots, some dimly felt intuition, some thread of memory that runs through the nation's past, perhaps some lurking fear that the cities might, as the congressman said, "tell a tale of disaster," argue for them. Perhaps the feeling is somewhat akin to that voiced by *The Nation* in 1913: "Specifically, we know that good can come out of the city. . . . City schools are better than country schools. City food is often more wholesome than country food. Hours of labor in the great city are shorter than in the small town or on the farm. . . . Great enthusiasms and great charities flourish in the cities. So one will argue point by point; and having so argued will unquestioningly subscribe to the hereditary faith that man was made for the land and lives in cities for his sins."[51]

12

THE PASSING OF RURAL ISOLATION

"A physician riding with the Fourth Assistant Postmaster General over the hills of Vermont in the early 1900's saw a rural mail carrier surrounded by his patrons as he delivered the daily mail. 'There, Mr. Postmaster General,' said the doctor . . . , 'is one of the blessings of the rural delivery service. The mail carrier is probably the only traveler along this road for days . . . that these poor people have . . . an opportunity to talk with. . . .

" 'Not only is rural delivery a godsend to these people, but it is a cure for melancholia . . . and the official statistics of this region and other equally isolated sections of the country show that there has been a great reduction in the number of suicides since rural free delivery became general throughout the country.' "

As quoted in the *Congressional Record*, 59th Cong., 1st sess., 5251

IF THE farmer had any one problem greater than another when rural free delivery of mail began, it was isolation. Certainly none of his other problems were as pervasive. For isolation had shaped his life as surely as the weather shaped his crops. It marked the way he spoke, the way he dressed, the way he thought, and the way he looked, and as late as World War I, at least, one could still tell a farmer from the city man in any crowd.

There was a long-standing belief in America that isolation was the source of the rugged independence and self-reliance that had always characterized the American farmer. It had, wrote one rural sociologist, "fostered the independence of the farmer's thought . . . ," and that was undoubtedly true. In the solitude of his farm he was able to think his own thoughts and form his own opinions, and in the open spaces separating him from his neighbors he had room to feel free and independent. He was never confused by an excess of reading material, nor was his loneliness the loneliness of a man lost in a crowd that neither knew nor appreciated him.[1]

But if he was independent and self-reliant, the farmer was also provincial, and, as Lord Bryce shrewdly observed in his famous work on the American commonwealth, he was "obstinate, tenacious of his habits, not readily accessible to argument." And these traits he also owed to the isolation that restricted his knowledge largely to the things he experienced directly. "Experience," he would say, "is the best teacher." Perhaps he believed it, but he also said it partly in self-defense, because, isolated as he was, it was the way he had learned most of what he knew.[2]

Isolation was perhaps not the principal reason farm youth left the farm for the cities, but it was one important reason. It was this that made farm life seem drab and monotonous to young men and women, and it was also this that helped age the farmer's wife beyond her years. Indeed, rural isolation was even harder on the farmer's wife than it was on the farmer, and stamped her as indelibly as it did him. Even Hamlin Garland who wrote so realistically about farm life on the prairies, admitted he did not adequately describe the woman's lot on those farms. "Even my youthful zeal faltered in the midst of a revelation of the lives led by the women on the farms of the middle border," he wrote. "Before the tragic futility of their suffering, my pen refused to shed its ink." In the loneliness of their life insanity, particularly among the Scandinavian women in Minnesota and the Dakotas, was not uncommon, and Beret Hansa in O. E. Rölvaag's novel, *Giants in the Earth*, stands as a prototype of all those women whose minds were shattered by the loneliness and hardship of life on the prairies. Wrote one observer of farm life in the 1890's: "Each separate farmhouse is an isolated community and a law unto itself. From this waste of social energy comes the hunger of the human heart and too often the atrophy of the intellect. From this too comes that abiding soul-weariness suffered by so many farmers' sons and, most of all, by so many farmers' wives."[3]

One measure of the farmer's isolation in the early 1900's was the distance he lived from his nearest neighbor, and aside from the farmer himself, no one realized better just how far this was or what it meant to the farmer than the rural agents who were laying out rural mail routes in those years. Riding up and down country roads, mapping schoolhouses and houses and churches and bridges, they could travel mile upon mile and never see two farmhouses standing nearer one another than a quarter of a mile and often no nearer than a mile. They were, in fact, so far apart in many places that agent after agent had to establish rural routes with less than four families to the mile in violation of postal regulations. "The people are not there to be served," wrote one frustrated agent from Hardin County, Iowa, in 1902, "unless the routes be extended to a length where it would be impossible for a carrier to make a trip. . . ."[4]

Route 2 from Eldora in Hardin County illustrated the rural agent's point exactly. Passing those landmarks familiar to all rural Americans, the route ran east from Eldora past the Frank school to the county line, down and across the line to Ivester and Schoolhouse Number 9, northerly to the southwest corner of section 21 in Melrose Township, over to Finster's Corner and back to the post office. Altogether it covered twenty-five and three-fourths miles, but in all that distance it served only seventy-one families. This meant of course that a farmer living in that part of Hardin County would have to travel at least one-third of a mile, if all farms were evenly spaced, to visit his nearest neighbor, and Iowa roads being what they were, this was something he may have thought twice about doing at certain seasons of the year.[5]

At that these farmers were better off than those in the larger prairie states like Kansas and Nebraska where farms were sometimes as large as sections and most were at least 160 acres. Add to the long stretches between such large farms the distance resulting from the helter-skelter fashion of settling, the skipping of a half section here and the school section there, and it is evident why the farmer here was lucky if he were within a mile or two of his neighbor. In Sumner County, Kansas, where in 1905 the rural routes averaged twenty-four and one-half miles apiece, there were but forty-five families to the route.[6]

This was less than two families to the mile and a graphic illustration of what the writer in the *Atlantic Monthly* meant when he wrote in 1893 that "in no civilized country have cultivators of the soil adapted their home life so badly to the conditions of nature as have the people of our great northwestern prairies." European farmers, he pointed out, had settled in villages where they could have companionship, and he urged the American farmers to leave their farms and follow the European example. "There is," he wrote, "but one remedy for the dreariness of farm life on the prairie: the isolated farmhouse must be abandoned and the people must draw together in villages."[7]

But this was about as practical as a twenty-acre dryland farm in Nebraska. For more than 200 years American farmers had been living on their individual farms almost everywhere except in colonial New England, and isolated farmhouses were as characteristic of rural America as barbed-wire fences. These were family farms, and the American farmer, unlike the European, was no peasant. He was, instead, Thomas Jefferson's independent farmer, bone and sinew of the nation as he liked to be called, lord of all he surveyed when he looked out his kitchen window, and he was no more likely to leave his farm for the village in 1893 than he was to stop complaining about the weather and the middleman.

The farmer's isolation would have been more bearable in spite of poor roads and the distances between himself and his neighbor if only his mail service had been better. But it too was geared to rural America's slow-paced ways, and the scarcity of mail the farmer received through the pre-R F D mail system was another measure of his isolation.

In the 1890's when a farmer went to his post office once a week or so to pick up his mail, he never expected very much, and he was rarely surprised. He wrote few letters and he received few, and altogether his first-class mail was usually as scarce as the money in his pocket. Even circulars came infrequently, and such was the farmer's scarcity of mail and his eagerness to read that, when business houses advertised in farm papers "Lots of mail for ten cents," they were able to build up impressive mailing lists from farmers who sent in their dimes and their names.[8]

As for news, one newspaperman who knew rural America in the 1880's and 1890's very well, estimated that not one farmer in 300 took a daily newspaper in the 1890's, and he could not have been far wrong. Only farmers who lived close enough to a post office to get their mail every day could take full advantage of a daily. Otherwise, daily papers came a "sackful at a time," as one pioneer Nebraska woman once remarked, and under the circumstances it was more sensible to take a county weekly than a daily that arrived weekly.[9]

Even the county weekly was a rarity in many communities. "I remember very well in the country community where I was reared," said a congressman in 1916, "when but a single newspaper came to the local post office. It was a weekly publication, and I can . . . remember how almost that entire neighborhood depended on the substantial old farmer who enjoyed the luxury of a weekly newspaper for their information about current events. A daily paper or a high-class magazine was a thing unknown in that community."[10]

In this respect there was not much difference between the congressman's neighborhood in Illinois and the average rural community in the great farm states of the South and other places in the Midwest. Many were the farmers in those areas who first heard of the Homestead strike in 1892 and Cleveland's election that same year from a neighbor on his way home from town or from someone like the congressman's substantial old gentleman who read the news to them from his weekly paper. In those days, newspapers and magazines were still scarce enough in country neighborhoods to be saved and passed around as they had been a few years earlier when boys like Herbert Quick and Hamlin Garland, growing up on the Iowa prairies, had borrowed such story magazines as the *New York Ledger* and the *New York Saturday Night* from their neighbors.[11]

In an entire month then before the R F D was established, a farmer's mail might contain, as one newspaper noted in 1891, no more than "one letter from the old folks, one letter from John, one notice of interest on the mortgage falling due, one dun from the bank, three steam threshing-machine pamphlets, and some sample leaves from the Farmers' Guide to Hygiene and Politics, in twenty-four parts"; and considering that this mail was one of their principal sources of information, it is remarkable, not that the rebellious farmers of the 1890's knew so little about the state of the nation and the reasons for their unhappy plight in those years, but that they knew so much.

It was into this world of poor roads and isolated farmhouses and poor mail service that the R F D came to help revolutionize the farmer's life, and as early as 1903 one journalist foresaw its impact on rural America. "The invention of the harvester," he wrote, "produced a revolution in American agriculture. The establishment of the rural free delivery, however, may cause a transformation of far more significance, for it means a social revolution which will enlighten and elevate the farm home, making its life more than the isolated existence which thousands of families are compelled of necessity to endure." By 1930 one could look back and see that the journalist had been a discerning prophet. There had indeed been a social revolution in farm life. The farmer's isolation had been pierced and his understanding of his world had been broadened, and nothing except the automobile had done more to bring this about than the R F D.[12]

The statistics alone suggest how effective rural delivery had been in breaking up rural isolation. In 1898, two years after its establishment, rural mailmen delivered about 2,753,581 or about 18,000 pieces of mail for every rural route, and in 1903, 40,932 pieces per route. In 1929 the average amount of mail per mail route was a little more than 101,315 pieces and totaled some 4,441,656,000 items, a figure that stands as a kind of monument to the disappearance of the farmer's isolation.[13]

To be sure, the R F D was only partly responsible for this swelling of the mails. Some of the increase came from the natural growth produced by the nation's expanding population and rapid business development. But the R F D quickened the flow of mail to farm homes far beyond what would have been the natural increase. An experiment that the Post Office Department ran in 1900, comparing the increase in mail at 35 rural route post offices with 35 post offices without rural routes, showed that the increase in one year was 6.4 per cent greater at the rural route post offices than it was at the others.[14]

Significantly, by far the largest percentage of all the mail that poured into farm homes over rural routes before and between the two great wars was second class—newspapers and magazines—the kind of mail that did the most to relieve the farmer's isolation. And of all the second-class mail, the daily newspapers produced the greatest change in the farmer's life.

The difference the daily newspaper made on the farm was explained by an editor of a country newspaper in 1907. "Out in the

Middle West the other morning," he wrote, "a dozen miles from town, a farmer rode on a sulky plough turning over brown furrows for the new crop.

" 'I see by today's Kansas City papers,' he began as a visitor came alongside, 'that there is trouble in Russia again.'

" 'What do you know about what is in today's Kansas City papers?'

" 'Oh, we got them from the carrier an hour ago.' "

The farmer, the editor noted, was 200 miles west of the Missouri River and 12 miles from a railroad. It was not quite noon, and yet he was in touch with the news of the world up to one o'clock that morning![15]

To the farmers of the horse-and-buggy generation this was as much a revolution in communication as the telegraph had been. Said one congressman of the RFD: "It has brought the daily paper to tens of thousands of homes where it could not have appeared before," and this was exactly the point. The old mail service might have brought the farmers more letters and circulars in time, but only rural delivery could bring him the daily newspapers.[16]

If their enthusiasm for daily newspapers was any indication, no one in the nation was more eager to know what was going on in the world than the farmers. No sooner were their rural routes established and their mailboxes planted than they began to subscribe for daily newspapers for the first time in their lives. On the eve of the establishment of rural free delivery in Sumner County, Kansas, in 1902 a rural agent wrote: "The county has been thoroughly canvassed by the *Kansas City Star, Kansas City Journal, Topeka Daily Capital* at Topeka and I estimate that at least 2,500 daily newspapers will go out in the first delivery made by the service. . . ."[17]

Many news-starved farmers signed up for two or three daily papers, and by 1902 the newspaper boom was so great the *Editor and Publisher* magazine reported that "the daily newspapers have never had such a boom in circulation as they have since the free rural delivery was established. . . ." By 1911 over a billion newspapers and magazines were delivered along rural routes, and this was more than the combined total of all other classes of mail delivered. First-class mail had narrowed this gap between itself and second-class mail considerably by 1929, but the nearly two billion newspapers and magazines that went into farm homes by rural delivery in that year still composed the largest single class of mail delivered.[18]

One had only to look at what happened to the farmers' reading habits in Nebraska and Missouri in the 1920's to see how thoroughly the R F D had saturated the countryside with daily newspapers. Studies made in these two states—Nebraska in 1921 and Missouri in 1928—showed that in both places almost three fourths of the farmers took daily newspapers, and in Missouri one third of all the families studied took two. These percentages might have been even higher, particularly in Nebraska, if there had been more rural mail routes. In Perkins County, Nebraska, there were no rural routes at all, and fewer dailies were taken than in any other community in the state. Cass County, on the other hand, where seven out of eight farmers took daily newspapers had twenty-three rural routes.[19]

Besides the daily, the rural mail carriers also brought the farmers the old weekly newspapers. There had been much speculation about the effect the R F D would have on this old hallmark of rural America. Some thought weeklies were doomed to disappear with the coming of the rural routes, and over the period from 1900 to 1930 their numbers did decline from 14,743 to 11,205.[20]

This decrease was particularly noticeable in towns where the dailies and weeklies had been in competition. In 1900 Titusville, Pennsylvania, for example, had one daily and three weekly newspapers. In February of the next year five rural routes ran from the town, and two years later the total circulation of the weeklies was 4,400. But at the same time, the town now had two dailies with a combined circulation of 2,675. In 1910 only one weekly newspaper remained. Its circulation was only 2,000 while the two dailies now circulated 4,750 newspapers. Just one decade later the one weekly had disappeared, and only one daily, with a circulation of 4,750 papers, was still in business.[21]

That daily newspaper, however, if it resembled most small-town dailies, was no replica of the big city daily, for it provided much the same fare that the old country weekly had, and the farmers could read it with satisfaction, because it was still a country newspaper. "Our papers, our little country papers, seem drab and miserably provincial to strangers," wrote William Allen White in 1916. "Yet we who read them read in their lines the sweet, intimate story of life. . . . When the girl at the glove-counter marries the boy in the wholesale house, the news of their wedding is good for a forty-line wedding notice, and the forty lines in the country paper gives them self-respect. When in due course we know that their baby is a twelve-pounder named Grover or Theodore or Woodrow, we have that neighborly feeling that breeds real democracy. When we read of death in that home we can mourn with them that mourn. . . . Therefore, men and brethren, when you are riding through this vale of tears upon the California Limited, and by chance pick up the little country newspaper . . . ; when you see its array of countryside items; its interminable local stories; its tiresome editorials on the waterworks, the schools, the street railroad, the crops, and the city printing, don't throw down the contemptible little rag with the verdict that there is nothing in it. But know this, and know it well; if you could take the clay from your eyes and read the little paper as it is written, you would find all of God's beautiful, sorrowing, struggling, aspiring world in it, and what you saw would make you touch the little paper with reverent hands."[22]

In the proud and, perhaps, self-conscious words of one editor, this was the country daily that took over the chores of the old weekly when the R F D came along, and William Allen White had as good reason as any country editor to thank the R F D for boosting the subscriptions to his *Emporia Gazette*. Looking back on the year 1908, he wrote in his autobiography: "And here is a curious thing: The same number of people—not a thousand more—who less than two decades before had supported meagerly the Gazette and its rival, the Republican, with not more than twelve-hundred subscribers between them . . . now this same population was supporting the Gazette with three times as many subscribers taking a daily paper in Lyon County as had taken daily papers before." Of course the R F D had made the difference. There were thirty rural mail routes in Lyon County in 1908, ten of them emanating from Emporia alone.[23]

But where weekly and daily papers were not published in the same town the R F D usually did no damage at all to the weeklies. Instead, it seems to have stimulated their circulations just as it did the dailies. For example, three rural routes were established at Olathe, Kansas, in 1900 when the circulation of the town's weekly *Mirror* was about 1,800. Some two years later the *Mirror*'s circulation had risen to 2,300 and to 3,200 by 1920, although Olathe itself was only 25 miles from Kansas City and the *Mirror* had to compete with the dailies delivered from that city.[24]

Unlike William Allen White's *Emporia Gazette*, however, the Kansas City dailies did not give the rural people all they wanted to read, and so the *Olathe Mirror*, carrying some of the news the farmers valued most, circulated side by side with them. The *Kansas City Star* might tell a farmer in detail about Theodore Roosevelt's fight with the trusts, but it would not tell him, as the *Olathe Mirror* might, that a school picnic had been held at Pretty Prairie or that William Jones was in the harvest. Nor was he as likely to see his own name in the *Star* as he was in the *Olathe Mirror*, and farmers were as eager as the next man to see their names in print. One country editor even remembered a farmer who wanted to cancel his subscription to the local paper because his name had not appeared in its pages for two years.[25]

So when the rural routes came, and the farmers could take a daily newspaper instead of a weekly if they wished, they usually took both. The study in Boone County, Missouri, in 1928, showed that all but nine of the seventy families interviewed took the local weekly. Often, even those who had grown up in rural communities and moved to the cities, continued to subscribe to the old country weekly just to be able, as one man said, "to smell the new mown hay."[26]

The old country weekly, however, was different from what it had been before the coming of the R F D. Unable to compete with the dailies in bringing the farmers the news, it ceased to try. As the rural routes came in, the old warmed-over news reports in the weeklies went out. Even the space so long reserved for patent insides, fiction, and boiler plates, those old staples of weekly newspapers, was cut. More and more the weeklies were filled with matters of local interest. Some 70 per cent of the space in 243 weekly newspapers in Missouri was devoted to items of local interest according to a survey made in 1919. Only 37.18 per cent of the papers' space was given over to news, and of this 58.16 per cent was local.[27]

But room was still left in the country weeklies for editorials and more, much more, for advertising. Periodically some burning issue—a school-board election perhaps or the removal of hitching posts from the town's streets—might tie up a page or two, and notices of death, delinquent taxes, and estate settlements were always to be found in their special corners. But mostly, week in and week out, the weekly was filled with columns—community columns, 4-H columns, church columns—and these made the news that held the farmer's interest as they do today.

Since the R F D wiped out the handicaps of the old rural mail service and made it possible for farmers to broaden their selection of reading material for the first time, the second-class mail matter the rural carriers brought them may be used as a kind of mirror reflecting their interests and aspirations. Studying that reflection one may judge that the average farmer, especially in the Midwest where the most studies of his reading habits have been made, was as middle class as a city banker, at least in attitude if not in income.

From the number of newspapers he received, it was plain the farmer had a healthy middle-class enthusiasm for keeping up with the news of the world and an abiding interest in local affairs. His middle-class interest in orthodox Christianity, traditionally a characteristic of rural people, was suggested in part by the religious papers that came to his home. In 1905 a writer counted nine different religious papers, everything from the *World-Wide Mission* to the *Ram's Horn,* circulating through rural homes in one community. The Nebraska study sixteen years later showed only a handful of strictly religious papers going into farm homes, but weekly papers—*Capper's Weekly,* for instance—with their Bible verses and sermons made up for the absence of the old religious papers. And, of course, the editors of the country dailies who catered to the farmers' interests felt compelled to carry various religious items in their newspapers which even to this day distinguish the small-town daily.[28]

The itch to get ahead in this world was as much a middle-class trait as one's interest in community affairs and religion, and the never-ending stream of farm papers and farm magazines farmers pulled out of their mailboxes in the years between 1900 and 1930, gave evidence of their enthusiasm for their vocation and their desire to improve their lot in life. In what was probably the broadest survey of its kind ever made, a number of agents from the Department of Agriculture interviewed 3,698 farmers in the Midwest, the South, and the Middle Atlantic states in 1912, and found that 65.5 per cent of them subscribed to farm papers. By section, the number of farmers taking agricultural papers ranged from 75 per cent in the Midwest, where, incidentally, the rural routes were thickest, to 45 per cent in the South where they were thinnest.[29]

Subsequent studies only verified the farmers' interest in farm papers. They were found in three out of every four homes in Nebraska in 1921, and in 90 per cent of the homes studied in Missouri. In Nebraska there were twice as many farm papers in farm homes as trade and professional journals in town homes, suggesting that Nebraska farmers at least were possibly even more anxious to "do well," as the saying went, in their profession than were the higher paid professional groups in the towns.

Nor was the farmer's wife any less middle class than her husband if second-class mail is a valid yardstick to measure such things. While the farmer was keeping up with the farming world through his farm papers, his wife was reading the middle-class women's magazines. As early as 1905 such magazines as *Harper's Bazaar, Good Housekeeping,* and the *Modern Priscilla* were being read in rural homes, and in Nebraska in 1921 women's magazines were being delivered to almost 30 per cent of the farm homes. But the 1920's was the heyday of these periodicals on the farm. In 1928 they were read by 64.3 per cent of the families studied in Missouri.[30]

All this mail which the farmers found lying on the pantry shelf or dining-room table when they came in for their noon-day meal helped mold their minds as their isolation had molded them in the past, and people who watched the R F D at work regarded it as an educator second only to the schools themselves. A congressman once called it a "great university in which 36,000,000 of our people receive their daily lessons from the newspapers and magazines of the country," and in a way it was. One of its great achievements in fact was its part in educating farmers to farm better.[31]

Before World War I a farmer with a good formal education was about as rare as an indoor toilet in a farmhouse. In the 1912 survey of 3,698 farmers, 3,258 had nothing more than a common-school education and only 440 had attended high school or college. Moreover, in a world as isolated as theirs, there were almost no avenues of education except the schools open to them.

But the R F D made it possible for them to learn by mail, and the most enterprising among them did. When the 3,698 farmers were asked what agency had been most helpful to them in their farming, a large percentage, 43.7, upholding one of their cherished beliefs, refused to admit that anything but experience had helped. Of the others, 6.5 per cent believed farm bulletins had been the most helpful, 3.6 per cent said the farmer's institutes, and 4.5 per cent said all agencies had been helpful. But the rest—more than 40 per cent of all farmers questioned—agreed that the agricultural papers the rural mailmen brought them had helped the most. "So far as this survey is an indication," wrote an agent from the Department of Agriculture, "the agricultural press would seem to be the most efficient of our agricultural extension agencies in reaching the farmer!" It was an unspoken tribute to the R F D that had helped make it possible.[32]

The farmer's education by mail was not restricted to newspapers and magazines, however. Every piece of mail that came his way helped shatter his isolation and broaden his perspective, and this included the advertisements that came to his farm through the R F D as well as the newspapers.

Because the farmer had a penchant for buying through the mails, and maybe because he was not always too careful to read the fine print, men with something to sell were always circularizing him and plaguing the Post Office Department or the local postmasters for their rural route rosters. The Department never gave out such information, but the third-class mail came anyway—297,613,383 pieces in 1911 and almost a billion pieces in 1929—and in addition there were all the advertisements that went first class or that were to be found in newspapers and periodicals. Obviously the day had passed when the farmer needed to sign a card indicating he would like lots of mail for ten cents.[33]

This was the mail that taught the farmers to "send no money" and to ask for a "free trial." It was the mail that opened up the world of gadgets to him, put him privy to the latest inventions, gave him bright-pictured calendars to hang on the pantry door or the spring porch, and urged him to buy NOW!

Third-class mail came from far and near but mostly near as local merchants circularized the farmers unmercifully. How they did it was described by a Pennsylvania merchant. Being an enterprising businessman, this merchant had stocked his store with a variety of new products, among which were kitchen pumps. But the farmers, accustomed to the old open well, were slow to buy the pumps. "A pump costs too much," they said. "My mother carried water all her life; so I guess my wife can. And if you put a pipe in the water it will spoil the taste."

So the merchant prepared a circular and sent it to the farmers' wives. It pointed out that a farm woman traveled 3,800 miles in her lifetime going to and from the well and that she was robbed of her youth by the hundreds of thousands of pounds of water she carried. When the farmers still balked, the merchant, noticing that health inspectors were just then forcing the farmers to provide more sanitary quarters for their cows, slyly suggested the farmers thought more of their cows than they did their wives. If this was true, the farmers apparently did not want the community to know it, for in the end, according to the merchant's account, the farmers bought the pumps.[34]

Probably many of the improvements made in farm living from 1900 to 1930 owed their existence to some such circular as the Pennsylvania merchant devised, and there was no question but that this mail along with the rest the R F D brought to the farm was helpful in bringing "the man living in the city and the fellow living in the country in close conjunction with one another . . . ," as one congressman said. But advertisements sometimes had the opposite effect. For farmers learned by experience that not all advertisements were honest, and the discovery that some city slicker had tricked them with a misleading circular did nothing to improve their traditional suspicions of city people and their ways.[35]

Take the advertisement from Professor A. H. Thole of McCook,

Nebraska, for example. It seemed particularly directed to rural young men, and probably found its way into a number of rural mailboxes. Captioned "THE GREAT SECRET" it read: "How you can make your lover or sweetheart love you. . . . This secret is based on scientific principles and cannot fail. Send 25 cents in silver. . . ."

To the lovelorn young man who invested came this reply which perhaps in a fever of excitement he read behind the barn: "Your letter of recent date at hand, and in reply will say to win the woman you love you must constantly think with your whole soul's intensity that you want her to love you; in addition you must not drink. . . . Flattery goes a long way to win a woman, but don't overdo it. Don't be bashful, as women hate bashfulness in men, but love bold men." The letter was signed, "Yours for suckers, Prof. A. H. Thole."[36]

Possibly this letter was worth the price to some shy young man on the farm even if the scientific principles mentioned in the advertisement fell short of expectations. At least it was mail to break the monotony of farm life, and it cost only 25 cents.

Unfortunately, not all fraudulent advertisements were as harmless. During Theodore Roosevelt's administration when rural routes were being established by the thousands, farmers were frequently induced by the advertisements they found in their new mailboxes to send their butter and cheese and maple syrup to some buyer in the city who offered them high prices he never intended to pay and never did. And there were always circulars from big operators like the Burr brothers who in 1910 were caught selling stocks in 32 fictitious corporations and bilking city people as well as farmers of some $20,000 a day.[37]

It was one of the ironies of life that the R F D which was doing so much to alleviate the loneliness of farm life should also have been the means of accelerating the spread of fraudulent advertising, and, worse still, that it should have been a valuable accessory to the patent-medicine trade that plied the country with its deceitful balms. But this was the way it was. For the more newspapers and circulars the rural mail carriers brought the farmers the more patent-medicine advertisements, complete with testimonials, there were to mislead them.

"There are none so credulous as sufferers from disease," wrote President Taft, and he might have added that among all sufferers none were more credulous than those rural people who were either too poor or too isolated to have a doctor's care. In the papers that came to their farms, even in their religious papers, they would find advertisements promising to cure everything from cancer to consumption. In desperation they would answer the advertisements and back would come circulars, pamphlets, and testimonials, all relating to the wonders of some particular patent medicine which in truth would relieve the sufferer of nothing but his money.

In this material would be included a question blank on which the potential patient was to list his symptoms and a letter of reassurance like this one from the Dr. Curry Cancer Cure Co.: "We are in receipt of your inquiry, requesting information as to our method of treatment of cancer. It certainly gives us pleasure to be able to say to you that we have a positive cure for this, one of the most dreadful diseases that afflicts the human race. We are sending you free the necessary information that will show you how to cure yourself at home in from 10 to 20 days without the aid of a physician or surgeon and at little expense."[38]

Regardless of the company or cure it offered, the pattern of salesmanship was almost always the same. If the prospective patient did not immediately respond to the pamphlets and circulars, follow-up letters were sent, as many as five or more, each stressing a little more urgently the absolute necessity of taking the cure before it was too late, and at the same time reducing its price. Letter Number 7 from Dr. Bertha C. Day, Specialist in Diseases of Women, for example, began: "This is the MOST IMPORTANT letter I have ever written to you. . . . NOW LISTEN: If you can't see your way clear to accept the Special Treatment on the low terms

I quoted you, simply send $1.50 and start using the remedies."[39]

Women were the readiest victims of the patent-medicine trade. Plagued by symptoms both real and imagined, insecure in their poverty, fear, and inexperience, they would read in their newspapers that a woman of their own station in life with an address similar to their own had been cured of some dread disease and promptly believe they too could be cured. An eye-catching testimonial like this one, for instance, may have convinced thousands of farm women of the efficiency of McElree's Wine of Cardui: "MY WOMB CAME DOWN almost as large as my fist," writes Mrs. John B. Justice of R. F. D. No. 1, Pedro, Ohio. "I had dreadful pains in my back and was so weak that I could scarcely stand on my feet. Finally I became so bad that my son, who is a physician, wanted to perform an operation, but I fought him off and tried the Cardui Home Treatment. It has done me more good than anything else I have taken, during the 35 years in which I suffered. Only a few days after I commenced with Cardui, I became stronger, the womb went back and Cardui took away the inflammation and pain. The Cardui Home Treatment has done great things for me."[40]

Women were urged to write to Dr. So and So, giving him their symptoms, so he could prescribe for them, and many a time when the red flag was up on a rural mailbox and the rural carrier stopped to pick up the mail, inside the box was a letter the farmer's wife had written with painstaking care to some patent-medicine doctor revealing the most intimate details of her trouble. When the letter arrived at its destination, there was no doctor to read it; there were only clerks who often laughed at the woman's symptoms, filed her letter in one category or another, and sent her a bottle numbered one, two, or three, whichever was prescribed for her particular ailment.

In time, the lady's confidential letter and address may have been sold to a letter-broker who rented them out to other patent-medicine men who in turn sent their own circulars to the afflicted woman. One company dealing in this kind of business claimed to have for rent more than 140,000 confidential letters worried women had written Harriet M. Richards of Joliet, Illinois, pouring out their troubles and asking to try her Balm of Figs for their condition.[41]

Among the patent medicines most widely advertised along rural routes in the early 1900's besides McElree's Wine of Cardui and Lydia Pinkham's Vegetable Compound, which were on everyone's list, were Peruna and Dr. Pierce's Favorite Prescription, all prepared especially to cure female trouble of one kind or another. For anyone, man, woman, or child, who had fits there was Dr. Kline's Great Nerve Restorer and for those with tuberculosis there was Nature's Creation, Yonkerman's "Tuberculozyne," Lung Germine, and the Hill Consumption Cure. And then there were hundreds of others like Brown's Vegetable Cure, Absorbine, and Dr. Garbutt's Antox, which were good for almost every frailty of the human flesh.[42]

All these medicines were fraudulently advertised in one way or another. Certainly no cure, except psychological ones, was ever effected by such nostrums as Dr. Kline's Nerve Restorer. The cocaine, morphine, or opium found in many of them were enough to relieve pain temporarily, and their alcoholic content—20.6 per cent in Lydia Pinkham's Vegetable Compound and 28.5 in Peruna—could take an imbiber's mind from his illness until the effect wore off, but that was all. Sometimes, the after-effects of these medicines—drunkenness and dope addiction—were worse than the disease they had been designed to cure.[43]

Perhaps the patent-medicine fraud had to get worse before it could get better, and if the R F D helped make it worse by spreading the news of miraculous cures to people who had not heard of them before, it was also partly responsible for arousing the American public to the menace of the medicine men. In 1903, probably because rural mailmen were bringing them to more and more people, the Post Office Department began a vigorous campaign to exclude fraudulent patent-medicine advertisements from the mails. This was the same year the Bureau of Chemistry in the Department of Agriculture began testing patent medicines and turning over the results of the tests to the Post Office Department to be used in the prosecution of those who were defrauding the public through the mails. And it was also the year patent-medicine nostrums were added to the list of products to be controlled by the government in the pending Pure Food and Drug bill.[44]

Furthermore, by scattering patent-medicine advertisements broadside among the people, the R F D undoubtedly contributed in its own way to the enactment of the Pure Food and Drug Act in 1906. Rural congressmen and senators, were well aware of the fraudulent patent-medicine advertisements their people were taking from their rural mailboxes and of the need for protecting them from spending money on the cures they promised. "And yet, Mr. President," said North Dakota's Senator Porter J. McCumber as he argued for the Pure Food and Drug Act in 1906, "one can not look over the United States, viewing . . . the great number of advertisements in every magazine and every paper in the United States, declaring the wonderful medicinal qualities of an innumerable character and kind of cure-alls, without becoming convinced that the health of the people themselves is a material thing that should be looked after by legislation."[45]

Unfortunately, the Pure Food and Drug Act did not put an end to the "Great American Fraud," for nothing in the Act prevented the medicine men from making exaggerated claims for their medicines as they had always done. In 1912 Congress tried to prevent this by outlawing false statements about a medicine's curative powers, but this applied only to the label on the bottle, and so false advertising continued. Of course, the Post Office Department could exclude such advertising from the mails, and it worked hard to do so. But it was an uphill battle. By the time postal inspectors could find and stop those who used the mails for this purpose, thousands and thousands of false advertisements would already have gone through the mails.[46]

Sometime in the early 1900's, for example, Professor H. Samuels had developed the novel idea that most diseases could be cured through the eye, and he prepared a medicine to be funneled through the eye to the rest of the body. According to the advertisement, a few drops of his medicine in the eye would cure tuberculosis, rheumatism, bronchitis, diabetes, tumors, and almost all common diseases.

His medicine was branded false in the *Journal of the American Medical Association* as early as 1910. But it was 1914 before the postal inspectors caught up with the Professor and issued fraud orders denying him the use of the mails. By that time, his advertisements had already attracted enough attention to bring him in an estimated income of between $10,000 and $16,000 a month. And no wonder! His medicine consisted of 10 ounces of sugar and ten ounces of salt to a gallon of water. It cost 6 cents a gallon to make and sold for $25.00 an ounce. How many customers he had along rural routes was not a matter of record, but his location in Wichita, Kansas, suggests that people with R F D addresses may have been among his best customers.[47]

The patent-medicine advertisements rural carriers brought the farmers did far more to relieve their isolation than the medicine did to relieve their pains. Certainly they provided reading matter aplenty, and even an education of sorts for the farmer and his family. From such material a farmer and his wife could accumulate enough information about diseases, symptoms, bodily functions, and cures to keep a conversation going almost endlessly.

And one of the strange things about this patent-medicine literature was that it was so very explicit about the most intimate details of human life in a day when a leg was still a limb to most people. Indeed, there was not much about the facts of life curious farm boys could not glean from, say, the 178-page booklet entitled

Viavi Hygiene or from that other little booklet *Perfect Manhood*, provided of course they got to the mailbox ahead of their mothers. *Perfect Manhood* was, in fact, so disturbing that when a physician was asked what he thought such a book might do to a farmer's boy, he replied: "I think the effect would be to cause a nervous condition in that person. . . . He would think he had something the matter with him which he did not have."[48]

If R F D brought unsavory mail along with the good at least this was mail that helped the farmer fulfill an enduring ambition to be like his "city cousin." For in spite of his disdain and mistrust of the city and city people, beneath the surface he envied the city man his worldly wisdom. So prevalent was this feeling that even a farm boy who had gone to live in the city was treated, according to one caustic critic, "as if some aura of glory now radiated from his person," when he returned to the country for a visit.[49]

As well as anyone the farmer realized his isolation made the difference between himself and the man from the city, and his enthusiasm for the R F D sprang partly from the belief that it would erase this difference. "Free delivery is the greatest benefactor we farmers receive," wrote an Indiana farmer in 1898. "Our country is a complete network of gravel roads, and for the past five years one can scarcely draw the line on country and city people when in a gathering. This, I think, is due to the convenience of travel enjoyed by country people. Now, if we can have the advantage of daily mail, we can converse with our 'city cousins,' and the line will then not be drawn."[50]

By the time World War I came along, the line was fast disappearing, thanks to the R F D. The farmer may still have been something less than sophisticated by city standards, but he was considerably wiser in the ways of the world than he had been before his mail was delivered to him. A little jingle in the *R.F.D. News* summed it up this way:

> We've read of the farmer in papers and books
> In regard to his manner, his clothing and looks

When they'd visit the city, how they'd gawk and they'd stare,
With pants in their boots, hay seed in their hair.
How they'd travel all day the sights to admire,
And blow out the gas when they'd go to retire.
How some, in order to raise money quick,
Would mortgage their farms to buy a gold brick.

Now such things were common a few years ago,
But the farmers are improving in a way that's not slow,
Since Uncle Sam delivers the mail at their gate,
They read the best papers and are right up-to-date.
They are building good houses, improving their lands,
By using their brains, as well as their hands.
In a year or two more 'twill be only the drones
Who will not buy mailboxes and have telephones.[51]

As an educator, however, the R F D had its limitations. A congressman once predicted that when the rural delivery system was completed "books on biography, travel, history, and fiction," would "find their way into the smallest farmhouse in the country." At the time it was made, there was nothing illogical about this prophecy. There were virtually no country libraries in rural America in those years, and it was natural enough to suppose the rural mailman would become a kind of traveling library taking "the farmer around the world," as someone put it, with the books he brought him.[52]

Alas, this never happened. The farmer was a practical man, much more interested in reading about where to market his crops and whether he should sell directly from the threshing machine at harvest time or store his grain than he was in Booth Tarkington's *The Conquest of Canaan* or *The Spoilers* by Rex Beach. He even had a practical dollars-and-cents use for the daily newspapers he took. "I get two dailies every morning . . . ," wrote one farmer. "On November 16, 1900, I saw a big jump in the potato market. Next day I left a postal card in the United States postal box at the crossroads for a farmer three miles distant to 'hold your big potato crop . . . ; don't sell too soon.' In two weeks from that date, he sold 1,000 bushels at 20 cents above the October market."[53]

While it was true the farmer was no reader of books and only one farmer in twenty-four, according to the 1912 survey, had a library of farm books, nevertheless, it must be said that the Post Office Department never really tried to make a traveling library out of the mailman in spite of several individual attempts to promote the idea.

In 1920 an enthusiastic rural mailman on Route 1 at Greenwood, New York, conducted his own experiment in circulating library books on his route. Over a ten weeks' period, he carried an average of two and a half books each way and concluded that "farm people will use the public library facilities very much the same as other people once the distance is overcome." But when he suggested a reduction in the postage on books going to and from the library over a rural route, the Post Office Department was not interested, and nothing was heard of the experiment again. Nor did rural mailmen ever take many books to the farmers, and after more than thirty years of delivering the mail to the farmers, it was clear that the R F D had been much less successful in taking the farmer around the world in books than it had been in giving him a better understanding of his own back yard.[54]

Like his reading habits, the farmer's writing habits also showed up in the R F D statistics and essentially confirmed the fact that the practical reader was also a practical writer. In the R F D's younger days, those who supported the service liked to say it would pay for itself when the farmers got used to it, because then they would write more letters and of course buy more stamps. And at first this seemed to be the case. In 1903 rural carriers collected from the farmers along their routes roughly 15 letters and postcards for every person served by rural delivery that year. Eight years later they collected almost twenty per person, and if the trend had continued, R F D might have become self-sustaining.

But in 1929, when the farmers mailed 514,990,439 pieces of first-class mail, this was only 21 per rural route patron, just slightly more than the 1911 figure.[55]

Apparently the farmers had a certain number of letters to write in a year and these they wrote year in and year out, and not even the convenience of rural delivery could induce them to write more.

Another facet of the farmers' letter-writing habits revealed in the R F D reports and as characteristic of them as their early rising was their use of postcards. They used these by the thousands, and almost no one could get more information on a penny postcard than a farm woman writing to tell her daughter in a neighboring community what to bring to the Thanksgiving dinner. This again was a practical matter. Farm people were not necessarily stingy, but as Lord Bryce noticed, they were "sparing," and a postcard was the best bargain the Post Office Department had. But their use of postcards as well as their failure to write more letters ruined the chances of making R F D self-sustaining.

The volume of first-class mail the farmers received belied the old adage that "you have to write a letter to get a letter." For at the time that those who lived on rural routes were writing about 20 letters and postcards per person in 1911 and 1929, they were receiving approximately 34 pieces of first-class mail in 1911 and 61 pieces in 1929.[56]

One reason for this was the great use they made of the R F D for business purposes. A congressman once explained to his colleagues how in only one transaction with a mail-order house, the farmer's first-class mail increased. "There is the letter advertising goods," he said, "then the letter acknowledging receipt of orders, then the letter making prices on specific articles, then the letter notifying that the article has been sent," all of which meant the farmer received four first-class letters, assuming the original advertisement came first class, to the one or possibly two he wrote.[57]

Actually, the R F D helped revolutionize the farmer's business methods just as it had his reading habits. Not long after rural delivery was established it was pointed out that with this service a farmer, for the first time, "could answer an important business letter on the day of its receipt, with the assurance of immediate dispatch," and this made a big difference in the way he carried on his business.[58]

In the pre-R F D days he had to go to his local banker or his lawyer or the man at the grain elevator if he had business dealings with them. And by the same token, they had to go to his farm to see him if an emergency arose. But the rural route running by his farm made it possible to conduct almost all his business by mail if he wished, and the value he put on this convenience, especially in the horse-and-buggy days, can best be appreciated by his stubborn determination to have his mail route begin at his trade center.

First-class mail was the cherished mail on the farm, and more than one and a half billion pieces of it came to homes along the rural routes in 1929. This was the mail that brought sorrow and joy, that came to the farmers from their children in the cities, from their sons in the trenches in France in World War I and from all over the world in World War II, and it was the mail that made the farmer and his family watch for the mailman and run to the mailbox when they saw him coming. And like the newspapers and advertisements, it too contributed to the passing of the farmer's isolation.

Even as late as 1947, when the radio and automobile had made the country and city virtually one, a farm woman could still write: "Of all the good things of country life, I love best the delivery of the mail. . . . Each morning as I look out on the new day, my eye seeks out the mailbox, and I wonder what the carrier will bring us. From that time on my mind and heart are filled with anticipation. My housework gets finished more easily and with more zest in order that I may be free to enjoy the mail when it comes—letters from kinfolks and friends, bringing news of pleasant events, or letting us know how distant loved ones are faring. . . . Another thing about the free delivery; it never really disappoints you. Even when there are no letters there is always the daily paper, telling us the happenings of our community as well as those of the nation and the world. Let me say, 'Thank God and our Government for rural free delivery.' "[59]

A NOTE ON SOURCES

The primary source material on rural free delivery and related subjects is voluminous, but the nucleus of the story may be found in the debates in the *Congressional Record*, particularly the debates on the annual Post Office appropriation bills, and in the Senate and House reports and documents containing summaries of bills, committee hearings, and the findings of congressional committees that studied such problems as the R F D, parcel post, and good roads.

The *Annual Reports of the Postmaster General*, referred to in this study as the *Postmaster General's Report* but actually published under a variety of titles, were invaluable to an understanding of the establishment and operation of the rural delivery system. For other aspects of the study, particularly on good roads, parcel post, the back-to-the-farm movement, and the farm-to-table movement, the *Annual Reports of the Secretary of Agriculture*, the Department of Agriculture's *Yearbook*, *Farmer's Bulletins*, and bulletins published under the auspices of the Office of Public Road Inquiry and the Bureau of Public Roads were of great importance. Among the other significant government publications used were the *Annual Reports of the Civil Service Commission* which were most helpful in developing the story of the rural mailman.

Some of the most interesting material on the R F D is located in the postal records in the National Archives. Among these valuable records are the reports of the rural agents who laid out the rural mail routes and the correspondence of farmers, fourth-class postmasters, small-town businessmen, senators, and congressmen, all of whom were interested in the R F D for one reason or another. As a record of rural America in the early 1900's, many of these documents are priceless.

In this section of the Archives are also located the records of the rural carriers dating from 1900 to 1920 and the correspondence of James I. Blakslee. The former was especially valuable in rounding out the two chapters on the rural mailman, and the Blakslee correspondence for the chapter dealing with the farm-to-table movement. Important information on the good-roads movement turned up in the Agriculture Branch of the Social and Economic Division of the National Archives. These are basically the old records of the Office of Public Road Inquiry and the Bureau of Public Roads and essential for any thorough study of the good-roads movement. From this Division, too, came the report on what the farmers were reading in 1912 which was of importance to the chapter on the passing of rural isolation.

Aside from the familiar periodicals of the period, such as *The Outlook*, the *Review of Reviews*, *Atlantic Monthly*, *The Century*, *World's Work*, *Literary Digest*, and *The Independent*, all of which contained important articles dealing with the various aspects of the study, the most important were the *R.F.D. News* and *The National Rural Letter Carrier*, both on file at the headquarters of the National Rural Letter Carriers' Association in Washington. *The R.F.D. News* dates from 1903 to 1927, and its successor *The National Rural Letter Carrier* from then to the present. Of especial interest is the Golden Anniversary issue of the *National Rural Letter Carrier* published in August 1953, to commemorate the fiftieth year of the National Rural Letter Carriers' Association.

Though they are in no sense a new or unused source, the *Sears, Roebuck Catalogues* were particularly useful for the two chapters relating to the parcel post.

NOTES

CHAPTER 1

1. *American State Papers: Post Office Department* (Washington, D.C., 1834), 16.

2. *Ibid.*, 17.

3. *Ibid.*, 42-43.

4. R. Carlyle Buley, *The Old Northwest: The Pioneer Period, 1815-1840* (2 vols.; Indianapolis, 1950, and Bloomington, 1951, 1962), I, 467-68. See also *Postmaster General's Report*, 1859, 1400-2.

5. *Annals of Congress*, 1st Cong., 1st sess., 2180.

6. Quoted in Leonard D. White, *The Federalists: A Study in Administrative History* (New York, 1948), 175-76. For letters from the Postmaster General to Rufus Putnam see Clarence E. Carter (ed.), *The Territorial Papers of the United States* (26 vols.; Washington, D.C., 1934——), II, 482-83. For the political importance attached to the mail service see Louis P. Bretz, "Some Aspects of Postal Extension into the West," American Historical Association, *Annual Report*, 1909, 143-49.

7. *American State Papers: Post Office*, 17-18; Fortescue Cuming, *Sketches of a Tour to the Western Country*, reprinted in Reuben Gold Thwaites (ed.), *Early Western Travels, 1748-1846* (32 vols.; Cleveland, 1904-7), IV, 196.

8. L. D. White, *The Federalists*, 188.

9. *Annals of Congress*, 2d Cong., 1st sess., 1333-41.

10. Thomas Jefferson to John Taylor, Nov. 26, 1798, in Andrew A. Lipscomb and Albert E. Bergh (eds.), *The Writings of Thomas Jefferson* (20 vols.; Washington, D.C., 1903-4), X, 63.

11. *American State Papers: Post Office*, 1-12.

12. *Annals of Congress*, 2d Cong., 1st sess., 1334; 3d Cong., 1st sess., 1434; 4th Cong., 2d sess., 2959.

13. See Leroy R. Hafen, *The Overland Mail, 1849-1869: Promoter of Settlement, Precursor of Railroads* (Cleveland, 1926).

14. *U. S. Statutes at Large*, 3 (1794), 357, for the first authorized use of the stage.

15. Mark Twain, *Roughing It*, in *The Writings of Mark Twain* (25 vols.; New York, 1913), VII, 7; James Flint, *Letters from America . . .*, reprinted in R. G. Thwaites (ed.), *Early Western Travels*, IX, 65; *American State Papers: Post Office*, 42.

16. *Postmaster General's Report*, 1834, in *Register of Debates*, 23d Cong., 2d sess., 20; *U. S. Statutes at Large*, 5 (1845), 738.

17. *U. S. Statutes at Large*, 2 (1813), 805; and 5 (1838), 283.

18. *Ibid.*, 10 (1855), 641.

19. *Ibid.*, 4 (1825), 112-13.

20. *Postmaster General's Report*, 1834, in *Congressional Globe*, 28th Cong., 2d sess., 15-16; quoted in *Niles' Weekly Register*, 69 (1845), 37.

21. *Niles' Weekly Register*, 73 (1847), 65, 68.

22. *Register of Debates*, 31st Cong., 2d sess., 270.

23. "Cheap Postage," *Harper's New Monthly Magazine*, 3 (Nov. 1851), 837-39, gives the argument for free delivery of mail, and *Postmaster General's Report*, 1859, in *Congressional Globe*, 36th Cong., 1st sess., 20, contains the Postmaster General's statement.

24. *U. S. Statutes at Large*, 12 (1863), 703.

25. *Postmaster General's Report*, 1892, 223.

26. Henry Castle, "Dissatisfaction in the Country Post Office," *Lippincott's Magazine*, 78 (Sept. 1906), 330-31.

CHAPTER 2

1. John Stahl, *Growing with the West* (New York, 1930), 141.

2. Charles M. Gardner, *The Grange—Friend of the Farmer* (Washington, 1949), 113.

3. *Postmaster General's Report*, 1891, 83; 1892, 1-7, 68; see also Herbert Adams Gibbons, *John Wanamaker* (2 vols.; New York, 1926), I, 277-78.

4. H. A. Gibbons, *John Wanamaker*, I, 279-80; and "Free Delivery Service," S. Doc. 92, 52d Cong., 1st sess., 180.

5. See H. A. Gibbons, *John Wanamaker*, Vol. II, for a satisfactory treatment of Wanamaker's business activities, and for a eulogistic account see Russell H. Conwell, *The Romantic Rise of a Great American* (New York, 1924).

6. For varying views on the campaign fund see Gibbons, *John Wanamaker*, I, 257-61, and Matthew Josephson, *The Politicos, 1865-1896* (New York, 1938), 422-25, 440.

7. H. A. Gibbons, *John Wanamaker*, I, 268-75.

8. *Ibid.*, 332.

9. See "Free Delivery Service," S. Doc. 92, and *Congressional Record*, 52d Cong., 1st sess., 4769.

10. *Postmaster General's Report*, 1891, 6.

11. See National Grange, *Journal of Proceedings, 1891* (Philadelphia, 1892), 150-60.

12. *Journal of Proceedings, 1891*, 155.

13. *Journal of Proceedings, 1891*, 98-99, 166; see also "Free Delivery Service," S. Doc. 92, 48-56; *Congressional Record*, 52d Cong., 1st sess., 282, 1358, 1580, 1711, 1858.

14. *Congressional Record*, 52d Cong., 1st sess., 4769.

15. *Ibid.*, 4768.

16. H. A. Gibbons, *John Wanamaker*, I, 281; *Congressional Record*, 52d Cong., 1st sess., 4786.

17. *Congressional Record*, 52d Cong., 1st sess., 4768.

18. *U. S. Statutes at Large*, 27 (1893), 732.

19. *Congressional Record*, 52d Cong., 2d sess., 1759; and C. Vann Woodward, *Tom Watson, Agrarian Rebel* (New York, 1938), 244.

20. *Postmaster General's Report*, 1894, 50; and R. M. Steele, "Rural Free Delivery," *San Francisco Chronicle*, Magazine Section, Oct. 19, 1902, 2.

21. Carl Vrooman, "Meeting the Farmers Halfway," U. S. Department of Agriculture, *Yearbook*, *1916*, 71.

22. Hamlin Garland, A *Son of the Middle Border* (New York, 1917), 363.

23. C. Vrooman, "Meeting the Farmers Halfway," 71.

24. Selected items on the plight of the farmer from 1870 to 1896 are: John D. Hicks, *The Populist Revolt* (Minneapolis, 1931); Solon J. Buck, *The Agrarian Crusade* (New Haven, 1920); Fred Shannon, *The Farmers' Last Frontier* (New York, 1945); Alex Mathews Arnett, *The Populist Movement in Georgia* (New York, 1922); Francis Butler Simkins, *The Tillman Movement in South Carolina* (Durham,

N.C., 1926); Russel B. Nye, *Midwestern Progressive Politics* (East Lansing, 1951), Chap. II; Nelson A. Dunning (ed.), *The Farmers' Alliance History and Agriculture Digest* (Washington, 1891).

25. Kirk H. Porter and Donald B. Johnson (eds.), *National Party Platforms, 1840-1956* (Urbana, 1956), 94.

26. F. Shannon, *Farmers' Last Frontier*, 417.

27. *Postmaster General's Report, 1893*, ix.

28. *Congressional Record*, 53d Cong., 2d sess., 3235.

29. *Ibid.*, 3240-41.

30. National Grange, *Proceedings, 1891*, 152-53, 158-59.

31. *Postmaster General's Report, 1895*, 117.

32. *U. S. Statutes at Large*, 28 (1894), 104-5.

33. *The National Cyclopedia of American Biography* (44 vols.; New York 1893-1951), XIII, 117; see also Theodore Roosevelt to Carl Schurz, Aug. 9, 1893, and Theodore Roosevelt to Lucius Burrie Swift, Oct. 13, 1894, in Elting E. Morison, et al. (ed.), *The Letters of Theodore Roosevelt* (8 vols.; Cambridge, Mass., 1951-54), I, 328-30, 404, 406.

34. Champ Clark, *My Quarter Century of American Politics* (2 vols.; New York, 1920), I, 350; and Festus P. Summers, *William L. Wilson and Tariff Reform* (New Brunswick, N.J., 1953), Chap. 14.

35. *Postmaster General's Report, 1895*, 8; F. P. Summers, *Wilson and Tariff Reform*, 234; *Congressional Record*, 54th Cong., 2d sess., 1778.

36. *Congressional Record*, 54th Cong., 1st sess., 3670-71, 5949.

37. *Postmaster General's Report, 1897*, 123-24; *The Virginia Free Press*, Oct. 7, 1896; see also R. M. Steele, "Rural Free Delivery," 2.

CHAPTER 3

1. *Postmaster General's Report, 1897*, 117.

2. *Postmaster General's Report, 1897*, 104-17; and 1931, chart, 114.

3. *Postmaster General's Report, 1897*, 114-18; and 1898, 228.

4. *Postmaster General's Report, 1899*, 224.

5. *Postmaster General's Report, 1897*, 123.

6. *Postmaster General's Report, 1896*, 25.

7. *Postmaster General's Report, 1899*, 198; see also F. P. Summers, *William L. Wilson and Tariff Reform*, 231-36.

8. "Rural Free Delivery," H. Doc. 324, 54th Cong., 2d sess., 1-2.

9. *The National Cyclopedia of American Biography*, XVI, 204, and *The National Rural Letter Carrier*, 47 (Apr. 3, 1948), 5-6; "Investigation of the Post-Office Department," S. Doc. 151, 58th Cong., 2d sess., 80.

10. For Heath's relations with McKinley see Dorothy Ganfield Fowler, *The Cabinet Politician* (New York, 1943), 249; on Machen see "'Investigation of the Post-Office Department," S. Doc. 141, 80 ff., and R. M. Steele, "Rural Free Delivery," 1.

11. *Postmaster General's Report*, 1897, 114.

12. *Postmaster General's Report*, 1897, 12-13; *Congressional Record*, 54th Cong., 2d sess., 1778.

13. *Postmaster General's Report*, 1898, 155; and 1899, 203.

14. *Postmaster General's Report*, 1931, 114.

15. *Postmaster General's Report*, 1899, 203; *Congressional Record*, 55th Cong., 2d sess., 2938 ff.

16. Mark Sullivan, *Pre-War America* (*Our Times* [6 vols.; New York, 1923-35], III, 1930), 347-48.

17. Many of the rural route agents' reports are on file in the National Archives. See, for example, Report of Rural Agent Thomas Houpt, May 15, 1903, McLean County, Ill., Rural Mail Service, County Files (Post Office Department Records, National Archives). Hereafter referred to as County Files, N. A.

18. Champaign County, Ill., County Files, N. A.

19. *Postmaster General's Report*, 1899, 203.

20. Sen. A. S. Clay to Fourth Assistant Postmaster General, July 29, 1908, Cobb County, Ga., County Files, N. A.

21. S. B. Rathbone to W. R. Spilman, Apr. 24, 1905, Clermont County, Ohio, County Files, N. A.

22. *Postmaster General's Report*, 1899, 203.

23. *Postmaster General's Report*, 1899, 206; and 1901, 122-23; *Congressional Record*, 57th Cong., 1st sess., 2794, 3930, 6716; "Uniform Metal Lock Boxes," S. Doc. 378, 57th Cong., 1st sess.; and *U. S. Statutes at Large*, 32 (1902), 113.

24. *Postmaster General's Report*, 1899, 245.

25. *Postmaster General's Report*, 1901, 117-18.

26. *Postmaster General's Report*, 1906, 33-34.

27. *Postmaster General's Report*, 1899, 212-13; "Rural Delivery in Carroll County, Maryland," H. Doc. 691, 56th Cong., 1st sess., passim.

28. "Rural Delivery in Carroll County, Maryland," H. Doc. 691, 1-12.

29. *Ibid.*, 12; Rural Agents A. H. Cousins and G. P. Conway to H. Conquest Clarke, May 26, 1906, Carroll County, Md., County Files, N. A.

30. *Postmaster General's Report*, 1902, 112.

31. *Congressional Record*, 56th Cong., 1st sess., 4636.

32. *Ibid.*, 55th Cong., 2d sess., 4611; C. M. Gardner, *The Grange*, 188; *U. S. Statutes at Large*, 30 (1898), 2514.

33. *Congressional Record*, 52d Cong., 1st sess., 4876-79; 53d Cong., 2d sess., 3238; and 54th Cong., 1st sess., 2617 ff.; "Rural Free Delivery Service," H. Rept. 597, 57th Cong., 1st sess., 1-2; for Loud's own account of his support of the R F D see *Congressional Record*, 57th Cong., 1st sess., 943, 2310.

34. *Congressional Record*, 57th Cong., 1st sess., 2329.

35. *Ibid.*, 2364.

36. *Ibid.*, 2359, 2362.

37. *U. S. Statutes at Large*, 9 (1851), 587-91.

38. *Congressional Record*, 57th Cong., 1st sess., 2417, 2452, 2503.

39. *U. S. Statutes at Large*, 32 (1902), 164.

40. R. M. Steele, "Rural Free Delivery," 1.

41. "Investigation of the Post-Office Department," S. Doc. 151, 6, 10 ff.

42. *Ibid.*, 122.

43. William Ward Wight, *Henry Clay Payne: A Life* (Milwaukee, 1907), 32; *Postmaster General's Report*, 1903, 608.

44. *Postmaster General's Report*, 1931, 114; and 1960, 148.

CHAPTER 4

1. *R.F.D. News*, 3 (Jan. 1905), 7.

2. Quoted in *ibid.*, 1 (Sept. 1903), 225.

3. *Postmaster General's Report*, 1899, 203; and 1901, 109.

4. *Congressional Record*, 58th Cong., 2d sess., 263.

5. E. D. Crumpacker to J. Bristow, Aug. 5, 1903, Benton County, Ind.; C. Landis to J. Bristow, July 23, 1903, Cass County, Ind.; Jonathan Dolliver to P. V. DeGraw, Mar. 8, 1907, Webster County, Iowa, County Files, N. A.

6. *Congressional Record,* 58th Cong., 2d sess., 263-64; *R.F.D. News,* 1 (Dec. 1903), 319; *Postmaster General's Report,* 1904, 585-86.

7. *Congressional Record,* 58th Cong., 2d sess., 264; *Postmaster General's Report,* 1903, 610; for material on the South and the politics of the R F D already in print see Wayne E. Fuller, "The South and the Rural Free Delivery of Mail," *The Journal of Southern History,* 25 (Nov. 1959), 499-521. Copyright 1959 by the Southern Historical Association and used here by permission of the managing editor of the *Journal.*

8. *Congressional Record,* 59th Cong., 1st sess., 5084.

9. *Ibid.,* 58th Cong., 2d sess., 262.

10. *Postmaster General's Report,* 1906, 328-29.

11. U. S. Department of Commerce, U. S. Census, *Statistical Abstract,* 1907, 64; *Congressional Record,* 58th Cong., 2d sess., 3647.

12. *Congressional Record,* 58th Cong., 2d sess., 3643-45.

13. *Ibid.,* 59th Cong., 1st sess., 5084.

14. *Postmaster General's Report,* 1902, 114.

15. S. B. Rathbone to A. W. Machen, Apr. 25, 1902, Tippecanoe County, Ind., County Files, N. A. For the political situation in Indiana before the election see the *New York Times,* Nov. 2, 1902, 11.

16. Reports of Rural Agent Edwin W. Shriver on Posey County, Ind., Mar. 18, and on Gibson County, Ind., Apr. 1, 1902, County Files, N. A.

17. C. Landis to A. W. Machen, Oct. 4, 1902, Hamilton County, Ind., County Files, N. A.

18. A. L. Brick to A. W. Machen, Oct. 4, 1902, Kosciusko County, Ind., County Files, N. A.; *New York Times,* Nov. 2, 1902, 14.

19. A. Beveridge to A. W. Machen, Apr. 5, and C. Fairbanks to A. W. Machen, Mar. 31, 1902, Bartholomew County, Ind.; Report of Rural Agent W. C. Ela, Apr. 4, 1903, Jefferson County, Ind., County Files, N. A.

20. S. B. Rathbone to A. W. Machen, May 15, 1902, Tippecanoe County, Ind.; A. W. Machen to A. L. Brick, Oct. 7, 11, 1902, Kosciusko County, Ind., County Files, N. A.

21. E. D. Crumpacker to A. W. Machen, Aug. 13, 1902, Tippecanoe County, Ind.; and C. Landis to A. W. Machen, Sept. 19, 1902, Hamilton County, Ind., County Files, N. A.

22. *Postmaster General's Report,* 1903, 611.

23. M. Garber to C. Fairbanks, Oct. 18, 1902, Jefferson County, Ind.; W. Stevens to C. Fairbanks, Sept. 10, 1902, Bartholomew County, Ind., County Files, N. A.

24. C. Fairbanks to A. W. Machen, Oct. 20, 1902, Jefferson County, Ind.; C. Fairbanks to A. W. Machen, Sept. 12, A. W. Machen to C. Fairbanks, Sept. 20, and C. Fairbanks to A. W. Machen, Oct. 17, 1902, Bartholomew County, Ind., County Files, N. A.

25. A. W. Machen to C. Fairbanks, Oct. 18, 1902, Bartholomew County, Ind., County Files, N. A.

26. *San Francisco Call*, Nov. 5, 1902, 1, 7; *Official Congressional Directory*, 58th Congress (Washington, D.C., 1903), 29-30.

27. *Postmaster General's Report*, 1902, 114.

28. *Postmaster General's Report*, 1902, 114.

29. *Postmaster General's Report*, 1902, 114; and 1903, 608-12; *R.F.D. News*, 3 (Aug. 1905), 371.

30. Frank C. Lockwood, "Senator Bristow of Kansas," *The Outlook*, 90 (Nov. 21, 1908), 617-21; Clarence H. Matson, "Joseph L. Bristow, The Argus of the Post Office Department," *Review of Reviews*, 29 (Jan. 1904), 45-48; *R.F.D. News*, 2 (Apr. 1904), 112, and 3 (Feb. 1905), 53.

31. *Postmaster General's Report*, 1903, 608-12; J. Bristow to E. D. Crumpacker, Aug. 13, 1903, Benton County, Ind., County Files, N. A.

32. C. Fairbanks to J. Bristow, Aug. 11, N. Gilbert to C. Fairbanks, July 31, C. Fairbanks to J. Bristow, Aug. 26, 1903, Steuben County, Ind., County Files, N. A.

33. E. D. Crumpacker to J. Bristow, Aug. 17, 1903, Benton County, Ind., County Files, N. A.

34. J. Overstreet to J. Bristow, Aug. 20, 1903, Johnson County, Ind.; S. Cullom to J. Bristow, Mar. 22, 1904, Christian County, Illinois; J. Foraker to the Postmaster General, Nov. 10, 1903, Clinton County, Ohio; J. Bristow to E. D. Crumpacker, Aug. 27, 1903, Benton County, Ind., County Files, N. A.

35. *Postmaster General's Report*, 1904, 585-86.

36. J. Bristow to B. Caldwell, Mar. 15, 1904, Christian County, Ill., County Files, N. A.; *Postmaster General's Report*, 1904, 584-85; T. Roosevelt to G. Cortelyou, Sept. 29, and T. Roosevelt to W. H. Taft, Sept. 29, 1904, in E. E. Morison (ed.), *The Letters of Theodore Roosevelt*, IV, 959-60.

37. James E. Watson to J. Bristow, Oct. 25, 1904, Shelby County,

Ind.; T. Hedge to J. Bristow, Aug. 20, 1904, Washington County, Iowa; Robert Nevin to J. Bristow, May 22, 1904, Montgomery County, Ohio, County Files, N. A.

38. David Oldham to C. Dick, July 27, C. Dick to J. Bristow, July 29, 1904, Shelby County, Ohio, County Files, N. A.

39. Memorandum to W. R. Spilman, Apr. 12, W. D. Page to C. Fairbanks, Feb. 29, and E. Leonard to C. Fairbanks, Feb. 29, 1904, Allen County, Ind., County Files, N. A.

40. *Postmaster General's Report*, 1905, 672.

41. J. H. Mathews to Charles Lynn, Sept. 6, and Postmaster at Huntertown to Department, Oct. 29, 1904, Allen County, Ind., County Files, N. A.

42. *Postmaster General's Report*, 1907, 350-51.

43. *Congressional Record*, 61st Cong., 2d sess., 29, 32.

44. *Postmaster General's Report*, 1931, 114.

45. *U. S. Statutes at Large*, 39 (1916), 423; *Congressional Record*, 64th Cong., 1st sess., 9631; *Postmaster General's Report*, 1920, 166; and 1950, 179.

46. *Postmaster General's Report*, 1950, 179; U. S. Census, *Statistical Abstract*, 1953, 28-29.

CHAPTER 5

1. On DeGraw see D. G. Fowler, *The Cabinet Politician*, 287; *R.F.D. News*, 3 (June 1905), 269; *Who's Who*, 1906, 456-57; and "Rural Delivery Service," H. Doc. 651, 62d Cong., 2d sess., passim.

2. C. Landis to P. V. DeGraw, July 26, and C. Landis to Inspector Holmes, Sept. 23, 1908, Fountain County, Ind.; A. L. Brick to P. V. DeGraw, Sept. 17, 1907, Kosciusko County, Ind.; P. T. Chapman to P. V. DeGraw, Sept. 10, 1906, Edwards County, Ill., County Files, N. A.

3. *Postmaster General's Report*, 1899, 823.

4. Thomas D. Clark, *Pills, Petticoats, and Plows: The Southern Country Store* (Indianapolis, 1944), 90-108; Gerald Carson, *The Old Country Store* (New York, 1954), 116-34.

5. "Rural Free Delivery in Carroll County," H. Doc. 691, 4-5; Report of Rural Agents A. H. Cousins and G. P. Conroy, Jan. 8, 1906, Carroll County, Md., County Files, N. A.

6. U. S. Civil Service Commission, *Thirtieth Report*, 1912-1913, 15; D. G. Fowler, *The Cabinet Politician*, 99, 194.

7. R. Bartholdt to R. Wynne, May 12, 1903, St. Louis County, Mo., County Files, N. A.

8. Report on Madison County, Ill., n.d., County Files, N. A.

9. *Postmaster General's Report*, 1901, 111.

10. Report on Madison County, Ill., County Files, N. A.

11. Report of Rural Agent Alex Charles on Ogle County, Ill., Aug. 16, 1905, County Files, N. A.

12. "Rural Free Delivery in Carroll County," H. Doc. 691, 4; P. V. DeGraw to James McKinney, May 11, and Report of Rural Agent Alex Charles on Rock Island County, Ill., July 2, 1906, County Files, N. A.

13. On the evils of the contract system see *Postmaster General's Report*, 1896, 291-94.

14. J. L. Canterbury to Second Assistant Postmaster General, Nov. 3, Henry Bannon to P. V. DeGraw, Mar. 15, P. V. DeGraw to H. Bannon, Mar. 30, and W. R. Spilman to E. H. Hathaway, Oct. 3, 1905, Gallia County, Ohio, County Files, N. A.

15. Report of Rural Agent William F. Heck on Gallia County, Aug. 14, C. W. Lanier to H. Bannon, Oct. 16 and 17, 1905, and C. L. Carter to President Roosevelt, Feb. 1, 1907, Gallia County, Ohio, County Files, N. A.

16. Fourth Assistant Postmaster General to H. Bannon, Oct. 26 and 17, and W. R. Spilman to Division of Appointments, Nov. 22, 1905, Gallia County, Ohio, County Files, N. A.

17. C. L. Carter to President Roosevelt, Feb. 1, 1907, Gallia County, Ohio, County Files, N. A.

18. *U. S. Official Postal Guide*, 1916, 605.

19. P. V. DeGraw to C. Lindbergh, Nov. 16, P. V. DeGraw to Postmaster at Little Falls, Minn., Nov. 16, W. M. Fuller to P. V. DeGraw, Nov. 21, C. Lindbergh to P. V. DeGraw, Dec. 6, 1907, W. M. Fuller to John T. Boylan, July 13, 1908, Report of Inspector Fosness, July 24, 1908, Morrison County, Minn., County Files, N. A.

20. Owaneco Postmaster to P. V. DeGraw, Mar. 7, 1905, Christian County, Ill., County Files, N. A.

21. J. L. Kellar to Department, n.d., Jefferson County, Wis.; E. E. McColm to Sen. A. J. Hopkins, May 3, 1905, Marion County, Ill., County Files, N. A.

22. E. E. McColm to Sen. A. J. Hopkins, May 3, 1905, Marion County, Ill., County Files, N. A.

23. Owaneco Postmaster to P. V. DeGraw, Mar. 7, 1905, Christian County, Ill., County Files, N. A.

24. Supplementary Report of Rural Agent Frank Nevins on Christian County, Mar. 9, 1905; clipping from the *Owaneco News*, n.d., Christian County, Ill., County Files, N. A.

25. Supplementary Report of Rural Agent J. F. Grote on Marshall County, Kans., May 1, 1905; Report of Rural Agent W. F. Heck on Fountain County, Ind., May 1, 1905, County Files, N. A.

26. Supplementary Report of Rural Agent Frank Nevins on Marion County, May 11, and F. Nevins to Judson P. Walker, June 8 and 13, 1905, Marion County, Ill., County Files, N. A.

27. Supplementary Report of Rural Agent Frank Nevins on Christian County, Ill., Mar. 9, 1905, County Files, N. A.

28. Report of Rural Agent R. V. Leahy on Lincoln County, Okla., Nov. 30, 1909, County Files, N. A.

29. Supplementary Report of Rural Agent W. J. Munro on Mower County, Apr. 19, 1904; M. O. Wilsie to J. A. Tawney, Apr. 6, W. A. Nolan to J. A. Tawney, Apr. 2, R. E. Crane to J. A. Tawney, Apr. 5, and Supplementary Report of Rural Agent Charles Mason on Mower County, Minn., Apr. 23, 1904, County Files, N. A.

30. Report of Rural Agent Thomas Houpt on McLean County, May 15, 1903; A. W. Machen to E. H. Hathaway, Feb. 21, G. W. Stubblefield to A. W. Machen, Feb. 2, S. M. Cullom to A. W. Machen, Feb. 4, 1903, and J. P. Walker to W. R. Spilman, May 20, 1904, McLean County, Ill., County Files, N. A.

31. Report of Rural Agent F. W. Smith on Maury County, Tenn., June 30, 1906, County Files, N. A.

32. P. V. DeGraw to Chief Inspector, Jan. 23, P. V. DeGraw to G. N. Haugen, Feb. 24, Mar. 2, and Apr. 27, 1906, Lafayette County, Iowa, County Files, N. A.

33. A. W. Machen to A. L. Brick, Oct. 11, 1902, P. V. DeGraw to A. L. Brick, Sept. 25, Memo for W. R. Spilman, Nov. 26, 1907, P. V. DeGraw to A. L. Brick, Jan. 23, Memo of the Fourth Assistant Postmaster General, Aug. 5, 1908, and clipping from the Warsaw newspaper, n.d., Kosciusko County, Ind., County Files, N. A.

34. Report of Rural Agent Frank Nevins on Jackson County, Ill., July 29, 1906, County Files, N. A.; *U. S. Official Postal Guide*, 1936, lists the Raddle post office for the last time.

CHAPTER 6

1. *Instructions for the Guidance of Postmasters and Carriers in the Conduct of the Rural Delivery Service* (1907), 1-78; James I. Blakslee (ed.), *Postal Laws and Regulations Applicable to the Rural Mail Service* (1915), passim.

2. Edward Snyder, "My 21 Years as an R F D Carrier," *American Magazine*, 98 (Dec. 1924), 59; *R.F.D. News*, 1 (Sept. 1903), 231; and U. S. Civil Service Commission, *Twenty-ninth Report*, 1911-12, 15-16.

3. *Instructions for the Guidance of Carriers*, 7; *Postmaster General's Report*, 1901, 119; Patrons' petition, received in Department, June 16, 1910, Okla., Records relating to Rural Carriers, 1901-1920, Bureau of the Fourth Assistant Postmaster General (Post Office Department Records, National Archives), and hereafter referred to as Rural Carrier Records, N. A.; Woodrow Wilson to Albert Burleson, Mar. 13, and A. Burleson to the President, May 10, 1916, in Albert Burleson Papers, Library of Congress.

4. James Hausman to P. V. DeGraw, Feb. 24, and (acting) Fourth Assistant Postmaster General to Postmaster at Jordan, Pa., Apr. 3, 1911, and Fourth Assistant Postmaster General to Samuel J. Buckner, Feb. 4, 1907, Rural Carrier Records, N. A.

5. U. S. Civil Service Commission, *Nineteenth Report*, 1901-2, 9-12; and *Twenty-ninth Report*, 1911-12, 48; *R.F.D. News*, 4 (Jan. 1906), 10; Fred White to J. Blakslee, May 4, 1916, in Correspondence of James I. Blakslee, Fourth Assistant Postmaster General (Post Office Department Records, National Archives). Hereafter referred to as Blakslee Correspondence, N. A. See also "Final Report of the Joint Committee on Postal Salaries," S. Doc. 422, 66th Cong., 3d sess., 265.

6. *Congressional Record*, 63d Cong., 3d sess., 659-60; "Rural Free Delivery," H. Doc. 651, 62d Cong., 2d sess., 28; *R.F.D. News*, 8 (Jan. 1910), 6.

7. *Congressional Record*, 63d Cong., 3d sess., 660.

8. E. Snyder, "My Years as an R F D Carrier," 58.

9. *R.F.D. News*, 5 (Feb. 1907), 68.

10. H. King to Fourth Assistant Postmaster General, Feb. 21, 1913, Iowa, Rural Carrier Records, N. A.; "Point of View," *Scribner's Magazine*, 57 (May 1915), 645-46.

11. *R.F.D. News,* 1 (Sept. 1903), 225; *The National Rural Letter Carrier,* 38 (Sept. 2, 1939), 4-5, and 54 (Oct. 8, 1955), passim.

12. *The National Rural Letter Carrier,* 46 (June 28, 1947), 10; *R.F.D. News,* 10 (Sept. 28, 1912), 962.

13. *R.F.D. News,* 3 (June 1905), 298; E. Snyder, "My Years as an R F D Carrier," 58.

14. E. W. to Rena Booher, June 15, 1908, Okla., Rural Carrier Records, N. A.; *The National Rural Letter Carrier,* 51 (May 10, 1952), 11.

15. E. Snyder, "My Years as an R F D Carrier," 58, and *R.F.D. News,* 4 (Mar. 1906), 109.

16. *The National Rural Letter Carrier,* 55 (Feb. 4, 1956), 10, and 48 (Nov. 19, 1949), 10.

17. *R.F.D. News,* 1 (Sept. 1903), 303; *Congressional Record,* 58th Cong., 2d sess., 2939.

18. "Day with a Rural Mail Carrier," *World's Work,* 6 (Sept. 1903), 3928; *R.F.D. News,* 1 (Apr. 1903), 6, and (May 1903), 90.

19. Quoted in *Congressional Record,* 58th Cong., 2d sess., 3717-18.

20. *Ibid.,* 4368, 3715; see also *R.F.D. News,* 2 (Apr. 1904), 112.

21. *Postmaster General's Report,* 1903, 26-27; *Instructions for the Guidance of Carriers,* 28; *U. S. Postal Laws and Regulations* (Washington, D.C., 1948), 390.

22. *Congressional Record,* 57th Cong., 1st sess., 2408.

23. Mark Whalon, *Rural Free Delivery: Recollections of a Rural Mailman* (Brattleboro, Vt., 1942), 52; Max Bennett Thrasher, "Thirty Miles with a Rural Mail Carrier," *The Independent,* 55 (Feb. 5, 1903), 311-17.

24. *R.F.D. News,* 1 (May 1903), 106.

25. Anonymous to Fourth Assistant Postmaster General, Jan. 2, 1909, Pa., Rural Carrier Records, N. A.

26. A. W. Russell to Fourth Assistant Postmaster General, Mar. 1, 1912, Tenn., Rural Carrier Records, N. A.

27. Jacob Perry to Postmaster General, Mar. 9, 1914, Mich.; Anonymous to Fourth Assistant Postmaster General, Mar. 3, 1906, Ga.; Daisie Shook to Fourth Assistant Postmaster General, June 1910, Okla., Rural Carrier Records, N. A.

28. Emil Johnson to Fourth Assistant Postmaster General, Feb. 4, 1910, Iowa, Rural Carrier Records, N. A.

29. Inspector's Report on James Ray, July 13, 1906, N. C., Rural Carrier Records, N. A.

30. E. Snyder, "My Years as an R F D Carrier," 59, and *The National Rural Letter Carrier*, 47 (Jan. 10, 1948), 8.

31. *R.F.D. News*, 3 (May 1905), 237.

32. H. E. Steffey to Fourth Assistant Postmaster General, n.d., Pa., Rural Carrier Records, N. A.

33. *Congressional Record*, 58th Cong., 2d sess., 161 (Appendix); *R.F.D. News*, 1 (Apr. 1903), 68.

34. *Congressional Record*, 62d Cong., 2d sess., 10720; *R.F.D. News*, 7 (Mar. 1909), 134, and 16 (Sept. 14, 1918), 10.

35. "Rural Free Delivery," H. Doc. 651, 207.

36. *R.F.D. News*, 20 (Sept. 16, 1922), 3.

37. *Congressional Record*, 63d Cong., 2d sess., 3174.

38. *Ibid.*, 61st Cong., 3d sess., 1364.

39. Fourth Assistant Postmaster General to Postmaster, Edge Moor, Del., Feb. 29, 1908, and Inspector M. S. Plummer to Inspector-in-charge, Mar. 19, 1913, Del., Rural Carrier Records, N. A.

40. *R.F.D. News*, 2 (Jan. 1904), 23; 1 (Jan. 1903), 7, 14; and 7 (Nov. 1909), 553-54; see also *Sears, Roebuck Catalogue*, No. 113 (Spring 1904), 219. A typical R F D mail buggy may be seen at the Davenport Historical Museum, Davenport, Iowa.

41. *Congressional Record*, 57th Cong., 1st sess., 940; 59th Cong., 2d sess., 3486; 62d Cong., 2d sess., 10719; "Final Report of the Joint Committee on Postal Salaries," S. Doc. 422, 265.

42. Figures drawn from speeches made in Congress showing the general trend of prices. *Congressional Record*, 58th Cong., 2d sess., 4362, and 61st Cong., 3d sess., 51; *R.F.D. News*, 1 (July 1903), 180, and (Aug. 1903), 211.

43. *R.F.D. News*, 1 (Apr. 1903), 60.

44. Fourth Assistant Postmaster General to Merlin North, Jan. 11, and to Postmaster, Benson, Nebr., Jan. 10, 1909, Rural Carrier Records, N. A.

45. *Postmaster General's Report*, 1904, 20-22.

46. "Day with a Rural Mail Carrier," 3928.

47. *Congressional Record*, 57th Cong., 1st sess., 939.

48. For the history of the National Rural Letter Carriers' Association see Gwendolyn M. Aaberg, *The R.F.D. Golden Jubilee, 1896-1946* (Washington, D.C., 1946).

49. *Congressional Record*, 57th Cong., 1st sess., 2317.

50. *Postmaster General's Report*, 1914, 39-40; *U. S. Statutes at Large*, 39 (1916), 424.

51. U. S. Civil Service Commission, *Thirty-second Report*, 1914-1915, 13; and *Thirty-fourth Report*, 1916-1917, 139-64.

52. *R.F.D. News*, 3 (Jan. 1905), 7; *Boston Evening Transcript*, Feb. 20, 1904, 15; *Postmaster General's Report*, 1902, 127-29.

53. U. S. Civil Service Commission, *Twentieth Report*, 1902-1903, 11; *Postmaster General's Report*, 1904, 20.

54. U. S. Civil Service Commission, *Twenty-second Report*, 1904-1905, 122.

55. U. S. Civil Service Commission, *Twenty-second Report*, 1904-1905, 18.

56. U. S. Civil Service Commission, *Twenty-ninth Report*, 1911-1912, 15-16; *R.F.D. News*, 10 (Jan. 6, 1912), 50-51; and (Feb. 3, 1912), 146, quoting the Calumet, Wis., *Reporter*.

57. U. S. Civil Service Commission, *Twenty-second Report*, 1904-1905, 118-19; *Congressional Record*, 58th Cong., 2d sess., 3314; see also *R.F.D. News*, 3 (Jan. 1905), 1 ff.

58. *R.F.D. News*, 3 (Mar. 1905), 150; U. S. Civil Service Commission, *Twenty-eighth Report*, 1910-1911, 119.

59. Acting President of the Civil Service Commission to Postmaster General, Oct. 4, 1912, Mich., Rural Letter Carrier Records, N. A.

60. *Instructions for Guidance of Carriers*, 15.

61. *R.F.D. News*, 5 (Feb. 1907), 68.

CHAPTER 7

1. U. S. Census, *Statistical Abstract*, 1920, 313; *Collier's*, 52 (Jan. 10, 1914), passim.

2. Mark Sullivan, *The War Begins*, 1909-1914 (*Our Times*, IV, 1932), 44-72; *R.F.D. News*, 10 (Sept. 14, 1912), 2.

3. *R.F.D. News*, 1 (Jan. 1903), 9; and (Apr. 1903), 60-61.

4. *Ibid.*, 3 (Aug. 1905), 375; and 4 (Feb. 1906), 53.

5. *Ibid.*, 4 (Sept. 1906), 420; (Dec. 1906), 638; and (Apr. 1906), 166.

6. *The National Rural Letter Carrier*, 54 (Nov. 12, 1955), 8; *Postmaster General's Report*, 1914, 316.

7. Suggestions on driving in their paper indicate some of the rural

mailman's problems. See *R.F.D. News*, 15 (Sept. 22, 1917), 9.

8. *Ibid.*, 3 (Aug. 1905), 374.

9. *The National Rural Letter Carrier*, 54 (Oct. 22, 1955), 11; *R.F.D. News*, 15 (Aug. 11, 1917), 14; (Aug. 18, 1917), 10; (Oct. 20, 1917), 9; 16 (Jan. 12, 1918), 11; (Apr. 27, 1918), 15.

10. *Collier's*, 52 (Jan. 10, 1914), 40; *The National Rural Letter Carrier*, 54 (Sept. 3, 1955), 8.

11. *Congressional Record*, 64th Cong., 1st sess., 2732.

12. On Burleson see *The National Cyclopedia of American Biography*, XXVIII, 386-87, and William Hard, "Mr. Burleson, Sweat-Shopper," *The New Republic*, 18 (Mar. 29, 1919), 267-69; on Blakslee see *R.F.D. News*, 11 (Mar. 29, 1913), 1; on motorization, *Postmaster General's Report*, 1915, 30.

13. J. Blakslee to A. Burleson, May 1, 1915, Buchanan County, Iowa, County Files, N. A.

14. *Postmaster General's Report*, 1931, 114.

15. Harry Shirley to Fourth Assistant Postmaster General, June 12, 1915, Mich., Rural Carrier Records, N. A.

16. Arch D. Smith to Postmaster General, July 15, and J. Blakslee to A. D. Smith, July 29, 1915, Mich., Rural Carrier Records, N. A.

17. *Congressional Record*, 64th Cong., 1st sess., 2747, 3081.

18. Gustave Roode, "Trip Report of Rural Carriers," Botkins, Ohio, Jan. 1917, Shelby County, Ohio, County Files, N. A.

19. M. B. Maring to Fourth Assistant Postmaster General, Mar. 20, 1916, Monroe County, Iowa, County Files, N. A.

20. Wood E. Eliason to Chief Inspector G. L. Wood, Jan. 20, 1916; J. C. Koons to A. C. Garrigus, Jan. 15, 1916; Report of Inspector A. C. Garrigus on the Revision of Wayne County, Ind., Feb. 18, 1916, County Files, N. A.

21. *Congressional Record*, 64th Cong., 1st sess., 3081.

22. *Ibid.*, 2606 ff.

23. R. R. Sherman to Burton E. Sweet, June 26, 1915, Buchanan County, Iowa, County Files, N. A.

24. See Clinton County, Iowa, and Wayne County, Ind., County Files, N. A.

25. Quoted from *Minneapolis Journal* in *Congressional Record*, 64th Cong., 1st sess., 370 (Appendix); see also *R.F.D. News*, 14 (June 3, 1916), 1.

26. *Congressional Record*, 64th Cong., 1st sess., 426-28.

27. *U. S. Statutes at Large*, 39 (1916), 423.

28. *Postmaster General's Report*, 1912, 323-24.

29. *R.F.D. News*, 12 (May 30, 1914), 1; *Congressional Record*, 63d Cong., 2d sess., 8903; U. S. Civil Service Commission, *Fortieth Report*, 1922-1923, xxviii.

30. *Congressional Record*, 63d Cong., 2d sess., 8925-27.

31. *Ibid.*, 8929.

32. Based on statistics drawn from the *Postmaster General's Reports* from 1913 through 1919.

33. U. S. Civil Service Commission, *Thirty-fourth Report*, 1916-1917, 146.

34. U. S. Civil Service Commission, *Thirty-first Report*, 1913-1914, 147, and *Thirty-fourth Report*, 1916-1917, 146-47.

35. *R.F.D. News* (Jan. 30, 1915), 2; (Feb. 6, 1915), 2, 8; (Feb. 27, 1915), 6.

36. U. S. Civil Service Commission, *Thirtieth Report*, 1912-1913, 142; *Thirty-fourth Report*, 1916-1917, 159; *Thirty-second Report*, 1914-1915, 143.

37. *Postmaster General's Report*, 1914, 36; *Congressional Record*, 63d Cong., 3d sess., 370.

38. *R.F.D. News*, 12 (Sept. 19, 1914), 4; 15 (May 5, 1917), 1; see also J. Blakslee to Sen. Hardwick, Apr. 25, 1917, Blakslee Correspondence, N. A.

39. Sterling D. Spero, *The Labor Movement in a Government Industry* (New York, 1924), 104; Willam Hard, "Mr. Burleson, Unionizer," *New Republic*, 18 (Apr. 5, 1919), 299-301.

40. For the attack on Burleson see "Mr. Burleson Under Fire," *Literary Digest*, 60 (Feb. 15, 1919), 18, and *ibid.*, 61 (Apr. 19, 1919), 14-15; for Burleson's defense see "Our Postal System under Mr. Burleson," *Review of Reviews*, 61 (Feb. 20, 1920), 172-79; on Norris's resolution, *Congressional Record*, 66th Cong., 1st sess., 5832-33; *R.F.D. News*, 17 (May 3, 1919), 1.

41. Based on figures taken from the *Postmaster General's Reports* from 1913 through 1920; see also *Postmaster General's Report*, 1919, 72.

42. K. H. Porter and D. B. Johnson (eds.), *National Party Platforms*, 237; *R.F.D. News*, 19 (Mar. 5, 1921), 4.

43. *Postmaster General's Report*, 1921, 69.

44. *Postmaster General's Report*, 1921, 50-51; U. S. Civil Service Commission, *Forty-first Report*, 1923-1924, xxii.

45. "Final Report of the Joint Commission on Postal Salaries,"

S. Doc. 422, 265; *Postmaster General's Report*, 1922, 36.

46. *U. S. Statutes at Large*, 43 (1925), 1063-64.

47. *Postmaster General's Report*, 1960, 149.

48. *Postmaster General's Report*, 1930, 29; *The National Rural Letter Carrier*, 29 (Aug. 1, 1931), 15.

49. *The National Rural Letter Carrier*, 55 (Feb. 4, 1956), 10; *Congressional Record*, 76th Cong., 3d sess., 3926.

50. *The National Rural Letter Carrier*, 54 (July 23, 1955), 9.

51. *R.F.D. News*, 22 (July 26, 1924), 3.

52. *The National Rural Letter Carrier*, 51 (Jan. 5, 1952), 8.

53. *Congressional Record*, 76th Cong., 3d sess., 3927; see John F. Ryan to J. Blakslee, Oct. 4, 1918, Blakslee Correspondence, N. A., for patrons' complaint that rural carriers in machines ran away from mailboxes before the patrons could purchase stamps.

54. *The National Rural Letter Carrier*, 54 (July 23, 1955), 9.

55. *U. S. Statutes at Large*, 41 (1920), 614; *The National Rural Letter Carrier*, 48 (Feb. 19, 1949), 11.

56. *Postmaster General's Report*, 1933, 10, and the *Postmaster General's Reports* from 1934 through 1940.

57. Charles Bailey in *The National Rural Letter Carrier*, 37 (June 4, 1938), 5.

58. Based on *Postmaster General's Reports* from 1930 through 1940.

59. *The National Rural Letter Carrier*, 58 (Sept. 26 & Oct. 3, 1959), 547.

60. *Ibid.*, 24 (Dec. 1926), 23-24; G. M. Aaberg, *The R.F.D. Golden Jubilee*, 84-88.

61. Cf. *The National Rural Letter Carrier*, 24 (Nov. 1926), 2, and 59 (Sept. 3, 1960), 518.

62. For the establishment and work of the Ladies' Auxiliary see G. M. Aaberg, *The R.F.D. Golden Jubilee*, 68-83.

63. *The National Rural Letter Carrier*, 58 (Sept. 26 & Oct. 3, 1959), 547, 585.

CHAPTER 8

1. Maurice O. Eldridge, *Public Road Mileage, Revenues, and Expenditures in the United States in 1904* (U. S. Department of Agriculture, Office of Public Roads, Bulletin No. 32: Washington, D.C.,

1907), 7. The major portion of the material for this chapter may be found in Wayne E. Fuller, "Good Roads and Rural Free Delivery of Mail," *The Mississippi Valley Historical Review*, 42 (June 1955), 67-83. Copyright by the Mississippi Valley Historical Association, 1955, and used here by permission of the managing editor of the *Review*.

2. For a good account of the old roads see George S. May, "The Good Roads Movement in Iowa," *The Palimpsest*, 35 (Jan. 1955), 1-6.

3. Herbert Quick, *One Man's Life* (Indianapolis, 1925), 191.

4. Martin Dodge (ed.), *Road Conventions in the Southern States* (Office of Public Road Inquiries, Bulletin No. 23: 1903), speech of S. L. Patterson, Commissioner of Agriculture, North Carolina.

5. *Postmaster General's Report*, 1901, 124.

6. Frank E. Nevins, Report on Macoupin County, Ill., n.d., County Records, N. A.; Archer Butler Hulbert, et al., *The Future of Road-Making in America: (Historic Highways of America* [16 vols.; Cleveland, 1902-5], 15, 1905), 97.

7. *Congressional Record*, 62d Cong., 2d sess., 5138; G. S. May, "The Good Roads Movement in Iowa," 5.

8. Harriet C. Brown, *Grandmother Brown's Hundred Years* (Boston, 1929), 113-14; National Grange, *Journal of Proceedings*, 1906, 100.

9. Roy Stone, "Address Delivered before the State Board of Agriculture, Augusta, Maine, Jan. 24, 1897," in *Addresses on Road Improvement in Maine, New York, North Carolina, and Illinois* (Office of Public Road Inquiry, Circular No. 28: 1897), 2; *U. S. Statutes at Large*, 27 (1892), 737.

10. The activities of the Office of Public Road Inquiry may be followed in the *Yearbooks* of the U. S. Department of Agriculture from 1894 on; Earl May, "The Good Roads Train," *World's Work*, 2 (July 1901), 956-60; see also Martin Dodge (ed.), *Road Conventions in Southern States*, passim.

11. *Postmaster General's Report*, 1899, 203; for adverse reports on rural route petitions see *Postmaster General's Report*, 1904, 584.

12. *Postmaster General's Report*, 1900, 118-20.

13. *R.F.D. News*, 4 (Oct. 1906), 591; George S. May, "The King Road Drag in Iowa," *Iowa Journal of History*, 53 (July 1955), 247-72.

14. *Postmaster General's Report*, 1908, 317.

15. Report of Rural Agent Charles P. Johnson on Jefferson County, Kans., Aug. 9, 1905, County Files, N. A.

16. *Ibid.*

17. *Ibid.*

18. Report of Rural Agent J. S. Swenson on DeKalb County, Sept. 14, and Jude Bray to J. S. Swenson, Dec. 27, 1905, DeKalb County, Mo., County Files, N. A.

19. *Postmaster General's Report,* 1900, 119-20.

20. *Postmaster General's Report,* 1906, 77, 331-32.

21. Jonathan T. Boylan to Postmasters, Apr. 2, 1910, Yanktown County, S. Dak., County Files, N. A.

22. *Postmaster General's Report,* 1906, 332; *R.F.D. News,* 4 (Dec. 1906), 596.

23. E. R. Knight, County Supervisor, to Fourth Assistant Postmaster General, June 12, 1907, Chesterfield County, S. C., County Files, N. A.

24. These laws may be followed in the annual reports of the Office of Public Road Inquiries and the Bureau of Public Roads in the *Yearbooks* of the U. S. Department of Agriculture.

25. *Postmaster General's Report,* 1907, 354; U. S. Department of Agriculture, *Yearbook,* 1907, 600.

26. James D. Richardson (ed.), *Compilation of the Messages and Papers of the Presidents,* 1789-1897 (10 vols., 1896-1899: H. Misc. Doc. 210, pts. 1-10, 53d Cong., 2d sess.), I, 584-85, and II, 142-43, 483-93; K. H. Porter and D. B. Johnson, (eds.), *National Party Platforms,* 2.

27. *Congressional Record,* 52d Cong., 2d sess., 1883.

28. Roy Stone in *Proceedings of the National Good Roads Convention* (Office of Public Road Inquiries, Bulletin No. 26: 1903), 46.

29. "Roads and Road Building," S. Doc. 204, 58th Cong., 2d sess., 30-31.

30. Walter P. Brownlow, "National Aid to Road Improvement," *Cosmopolitan,* 34 (Jan. 1903), 355-58.

31. M. Dodge, *Road Conventions in the Southern States,* 32.

32. "Roads and Road Building," S. Doc. 204, 79, 31.

33. *Proceedings of the National Good Roads Convention,* 22.

34. "Compensation for the Use of Highways," H. Rept. 538, 62d Cong,. 2d sess., 2-5.

35. *Ibid.; Congressional Record,* 62d Cong., 2d sess., 5752.

36. Harold Underwood Faulkner, *The Quest for Social Justice,*

1898-1914 (New York, 1931), 132; U. S. Census, *Statistical Abstract*, 1929, 385.

37. The Office of Public Road Inquiry became The Office of Public Road Inquiries, then the Office of Public Roads, and finally the Bureau of Public Roads; on the opposition of automobile interests see *Congressional Record*, 64th Cong., 1st sess., 7225, and American Automobile Association, *Proceedings of the First National Convention* (Washington, D.C., 1912), 84.

38. *Congressional Record*, 63d Cong., 2d sess., 196 (Appendix).

39. President Taft to Charles Hillis, Sept. 21, 1912, The Papers of President William H. Taft, Library of Congress.

40. *U. S. Statutes at Large*, 37 (1912), 551-52.

41. "Construction and Maintenance of Rural Post Roads," H. Rept. 168, 63d Cong., 2d sess., 2; *Congressional Record*, 64th Cong., 1st sess., 1479-80; and "Federal Aid in the Construction of Rural Post Roads," Rept. 250, 64th Cong., 1st sess., 1.

42. President Wilson to Sen. John Bankhead, June 28, 1916, The Papers of President Woodrow Wilson, Library of Congress.

43. President Wilson to Gov. W. Ferris of Mich., July 4, 1913, and Wilson to B. T. Galloway, Acting Secretary of Agriculture, Jan. 19, 1914, Wilson Papers.

44. *U. S. Statutes at Large*, 39 (1916), 355 ff.; Memo to J. P. Tumulty, July 3, 1916, Wilson Papers.

45. Fred White to J. Blakslee, Feb. 13, 1917, Blakslee Correspondence.

46. *U. S. Statutes at Large*, 42 (1921), 213.

47. *Ibid.*, 49 (1936), 1521.

CHAPTER 9

1. *Postmaster General's Report*, 1899, 25-26; and 1907, 9.

2. *Postmaster General's Report*, 1890, 24.

3. Alden Hatch, *American Express: A Century of Service* (New York, 1950), 15-29.

4. *Ibid.*, 60; Albert Atwood, "The Great Express Monopoly: The Seats of the Mighty," *American Magazine*, 71 (Mar. 1911), 620.

5. A. Hatch, *American Express*, 47; Albert Atwood, "The Great Express Monopoly: Might Makes Right," *American Magazine*, 71 (Apr. 1911), 758.

6. On the express monopoly and express profits see Albert Atwood,

"The Great Express Monopoly: Where the Money Came From," *American Magazine*, 71 (Feb. 1911), 427-39, and Frank Haigh Dixon, "Publicity for Express Companies," *Atlantic Monthly*, 101 (July 1905), 1-8; "Reforming the Express Business," *Literary Digest*, 44 (April 13, 1912), 741-42; Albert Atwood, "The Express Bonanza," *American Magazine*, 75 (Nov. 1912), 94-100, and "The Faults of the Express Companies," *The Outlook*, 100 (Feb. 17, 1912), 341, all of which discuss the shortcomings of the express companies; the rate structure of the express companies is covered in Report No. 4198, in Interstate Commerce Commission, *Reports*, 24 (1913), 380-541.

7. A. Atwood, "Express Bonanza," 96.

8. Interstate Commerce Commission Report No. 4198, 413, and *Postmaster General's Report*, 1912, 335.

9. *Postmaster General's Report*, 1880, 35-36; 1890, 20, 23-24; and 1891, 114.

10. *The National Cyclopedia of American Biography*, XIX, 41-42; J. Stahl, *Growing with the West*, 147; W. W. Young, "The Fighting Father of the Parcel Post," *Hearst's Magazine*, 23 (Jan. 1913), 122-23.

11. *Congressional Record*, 55th Cong., 3d sess., 208 (Appendix); and 56th Cong., 1st sess., 971.

12. Allan Nevins, "Thomas Platt," *Dictionary of American Biography* ed. Allen Johnson and Dumas Malone (22 vols.; New York, 1928-44), XV, 4-6, and hereafter referred to as *D.A.B.*; Don C. Seitz, "Chauncey Depew," *ibid.*, V, 244-47; C. M. Keyes, "Why Express Rates Must Come Down," *World's Work*, 21 (Apr. 1911), 14242-47.

13. On the Postal Progress League see the *San Francisco Call*, Jan. 22, 1904, 16, and National Grange, *Proceedings*, 1903, 117; on the rural mailman's express service see *Congressional Record*, 58th Cong., 2d sess., 2939.

14. *Congressional Record*, 58th Cong., 2d sess., 2939.

15. *Instructions for the Guidance of Carriers*, 15, 16, 28.

16. *Postmaster General's Report*, 1904, 22-23.

17. "Data Relating to the Proposed Extension of a Parcel Post," S. Doc. 266, 60th Cong., 1st sess., 2.

18. Paul H. Buck, "George von Lengerke Meyer," *D.A.B.*, XII, 587; *Postmaster General's Report*, 1907, 10-11, 62.

19. *Congressional Record*, 60th Cong., 1st sess., 77, 2834-35; 61st Cong., 3d sess., 26; National Grange, *Proceedings*, 1907, 128-29.

20. Gerald Carson, *The Old Country Store*, 161-90.

21. *Congressional Record*, 58th Cong., 3d sess., 1848.

22. *Ibid.*, 1847.

23. Quoted in *ibid.*, 60th Cong., 2d sess., 2331.

24. R. H. Killbuck to President Taft, Mar. 3, 1912, Taft Papers; "Why We Have No Parcels Post in America," *The Outlook*, 99 (Sept. 9, 1911), 56; *Congressional Record*, 61st Cong., 3d sess., 2005.

25. *Congressional Record*, 62d Cong., 2d sess., 4680.

26. *Ibid.*, 61st Cong., 3d sess., 1137.

27. *Ibid.*, 60th Cong., 1st sess., 2848; see also Sylvester Smith, "Parcel Post Again," *The Independent*, 70 (Jan. 26, 1911), 185.

28. *Congressional Record*, 62d Cong., 2d sess., 4761.

29. *Ibid.*, 61st Cong., 3d sess., 1139-40; 62d Cong., 2d sess., 4665; *San Francisco Call*, Dec. 19, 1910, 1.

30. *Congressional Record*, 61st Cong., 2d sess., 2905, 2911; 60th Cong., 2d sess., 2628.

31. *Ibid.*, 61st Cong., 2d sess., 2528.

32. *Ibid.*, 62nd Cong., 2d sess., 3834; "The People's Prayer," *The Independent*, 70 (Mar. 21, 1912), 637-38.

33. "Exit Platt," *The Nation*, 88 (Mar. 11, 1909), 241-42; *Biographical Directory of the American Congress, 1774-1949* (H. Doc. 607, 81st Cong., 2d sess.: Washington, D.C., 1950), 1077, 768.

34. John Weeks to Rudolph Foster [Forster], Sept. 11, 1911, Taft Papers.

35. John Wells Davidson (ed.), *A Crossroads of Freedom: The 1912 Campaign Speeches of Woodrow Wilson* (New Haven, 1956), 44.

36. "Parcel Post," S. Doc. 485, 62d Cong., 2d sess., 4.

37. "Postal Express," S. Doc. 379, 62d Cong., 2d sess., 4.

38. *Congressional Record*, 62d Cong., 2d sess., 4727, 4733.

39. "Reforming the Express Business," *Literary Digest*, 44 (Apr. 13, 1912), 741-42; A. Atwood, "The Great Express Monopoly: Where the Money Came From," 428, 435; see also Edward Hungerford, *Wells Fargo: Advancing the Frontier* (New York, 1949), 46, 221, and "Postal Express," S. Doc. 379, 11.

40. A. Atwood, "The Great Express Monopoly: Where the Money Came From," 428.

41. Washington State Grange, *Proceedings*, 1912, 39.

42. "Parcel Post System," S. Doc. 430, 62d Cong., 2d sess., 1-30.

43. *Congressional Record*, 62d Cong., 2d sess., 5641, 5651, 10714.

44. *Ibid.*, 10714.
45. *Ibid.*, 10807.
46. *Ibid.*, 10807-9.
47. President Taft to John Stahl (telegram), June 10, 1912, Taft Papers; "Memorial Relative to a Postal Express," S. Doc. 557, 62d Cong., 2d sess., 1-9, and "The Farmers' Position on Parcel Post," S. Doc. 895, 62d Cong., 2d sess., 1-13.
48. *Congressional Record*, 62d Cong., 2d sess., 11039-42.
49. *U. S. Statutes at Large*, 38 (1912), 557; William Howard Taft, "A Splendid Legacy," *Good Housekeeping*, 56 (Jan. 1913), 6.
50. *Congressional Record*, 62d Cong., 1st sess., 3087.

CHAPTER 10

1. *San Francisco Call*, Jan. 1, 1913, 1; *R.F.D. News*, 11 (Jan. 11, 1913), 1; *El Paso Morning Times*, Jan. 2, 1913, 12.
2. "Parcels Post at Last," *The Outlook*, 102 (Dec. 1912), 872-73; Wingrove Bathon, "How the Parcel Post Will Be Conducted," *Good Housekeeping*, 56 (Jan. 1913), 6-7.
3. "How the Parcel Post is Working," *Literary Digest*, 46 (Jan. 18, 1913), 118-19.
4. *Ibid.*, 118; *Congressional Record*, 63d Cong., 2d sess., 3964, 13337. The 17,000,000 figure included only those packages mailed from the fifty largest post offices.
5. "How the Parcel Post is Working," 118.
6. James Middleton, "Uncle Sam, Expressman," *World's Work*, 28 (June 1914), 165.
7. "How the Parcel Post is Working," 118.
8. "A Million a Day: The Progress and Prospects of the Parcel Post," *The Outlook*, 103 (Mar. 15, 1913), 580-85.
9. William Allen White, *The Autobiography of William Allen White* (New York, 1946), 377.
10. "The Parcel Post and the People," *The Outlook*, 104 (Aug. 2, 1913), 728-29; David Lewis to President Wilson, June 16, 1913, Wilson Papers; "The Farm-Products' Post," *Literary Digest*, 48 (Mar. 28, 1914), 685.
11. William B. Mellor, "Great Post Office Snafu in 1916," *American Mercury*, 78 (Mar. 1954), 95-97.
12. J. Middleton, "Uncle Sam, Expressman," 169; *Congressional Record*, 63d Cong., 2d sess., 85.

13. J. Middleton, "Uncle Sam, Expressman," 170-71.

14. *Postmaster General's Report*, 1914, 12-13.

15. *R.F.D. News*, 13 (May 22, 1915), 1-2.

16. *Postmaster General's Report*, 1915, 14; Lewis B. Flohr and C. T. More, "Suggestions for Parcel Post Marketing," U. S. Department of Agriculture, Farmers' Bulletin No. 703 (Jan. 1916), 1-19.

17. "The Farm-to-Family Movement," *The Outlook*, 107 (Aug. 1, 1914), 772-73; "Butter from the Postoffice," *The Independent*, 82 (April 19, 1915), 112-13.

18. J. Middleton, "Uncle Sam, Expressman," 163, 174; "What Express Companies Are Doing," *The Outlook*, 107 (Aug. 1, 1914), 773-74.

19. *Postmaster General's Report*, 1914, 12-13; L. B. Flohr and C. T. More, "Suggestions for Parcel Post Marketing," contains a list of the 35 post offices.

20. "Butter from the Postoffice," 113; *Congressional Record*, 64th Cong., 1st sess., 148, 153-54.

21. D. B. Traxler to J. Blakslee, Mar. 17, 1917, Blakslee Correspondence, N. A.

22. "Report of the Joint Committee to Investigate the Parcel Post," S. Doc. 944, 63d Cong., 3d sess., 31 ff.; *Postmaster General's Report*, 1916, 13014; *R.F.D. News*, 12 (July 4, 1914), 1.

23. Memo for Mr. Brand. Subject: Scheme of David Lubin for Marketing by Parcel Post, Jan. 11, 1916, in Blakslee Correspondence, N. A.; see also David Lubin, "Direct Dealing between Producer and Consumer," S. Doc. 240, 64th Cong., 1st sess., 1-6.

24. *San Francisco Examiner*, Feb. 29, 1916, 8.

25. *Ibid.*, May 19, 1916, 8; *U.S. Statutes at Large*, 39 (1916), 424.

26. Olivia Rosetti Agresti, *David Lubin: A Study in Practical Idealism* (Berkeley, 1941), 284; *Postmaster General's Report*, 1917, 52.

27. *Congressional Record*, 65th Cong., 2d sess., 4096; *U.S. Statutes at Large*, 40 (1918), 753.

28. U. S. Census, *Statistical Abstract*, 1920, 313.

29. John Eustis, "From Farm to Table by Motor Truck," *The Independent*, 94 (June 15, 1918), 446; "Parcel Post, 4,000 Miles by Truck," *Literary Digest*, 56 (Mar. 27, 1918), 27; J. Blakslee to Alexander Johnston, Apr. 25, and J. Blakslee to Albert Metz, Feb. 23, 1919, Blakslee Correspondence, N. A.

30. "Government Proves Feasibility of Long Distance Motor Parcel

Post Service," *The Outlook*, 119 (June 5, 1918), 234-45; *Congressional Record*, 65th Cong., 2d sess., 4097.

31. R. D. Bowen to A. Burleson, Dec. 23, 1919; Charles Stewart to J. Blakslee, Feb. 24, 1919; A. R. Miller to J. Blakslee, June 17, and J. Blakslee to A. R. Miller, July 1, 1919, Blakslee Correspondence, N. A.

32. Frank Laycock to Fourth Assistant Postmaster General, Apr. 14, 1920, Blakslee Correspondence, N. A.

33. J. Blakslee to L. H. Hall, Mar. 18, 1920; R. O. Waldorf to J. Blakslee, July 28, 1920, Blakslee Correspondence, N. A.

34. G. R. Cashdollar to Fourth Assistant Postmaster General, Aug. 3, 1920; John J. McLucas to J. Blakslee, Nov. 7, 1919; J. Blakslee to J. J. McLucas, Nov. 11 and 17, 1919; PM. C. Lamberson to Fourth Assistant Postmaster General, Nov. 25, 1919, Blakslee Correspondence, N. A.

35. M. R. Love to J. Blakslee, Feb. 11, 1920; clipping from the *Trades Unionist*, Apr. 30, 1920; C. L. Nace to J. Blakslee, Oct. 31, 1920, Blakslee Correspondence, N. A.

36. J. Blakslee to Robert Springsteen, Nov. 27, 1918, Blakslee Correspondence, N. A.

37. *Congressional Record*, 65th Cong., 3d sess., 634-36.

38. *Ibid.*, 386-87; 65th Cong., 1st sess., 5960; and *U.S. Statutes at Large*, 40 (1919), 1198.

39. "Food by Mail Not a Success," *Literary Digest*, 89 (Apr. 3, 1924), 73; *U.S. Statutes at Large*, 43 (1925), 1068.

40. "On Failure of Transportation of Food Products under Provision of Bill 11444," H. Doc. 126, 69th Cong., 1st sess., 1-4.

41. Report of Rural Agent J. F. Grote on Hardin County, Iowa, n.d., County Files, N. A.

42. For a sympathetic treatment of the small-town merchant see Lewis Atherton, *Main Street on the Middle Border* (Bloomington, 1954), 43-57.

43. For the small-town merchant's worst side see Thorstein Veblen, "The Independent Farmer," *The Freeman*, 7 (June 13, 1923), 321-40, and "The Country Town," *ibid.* (July 11, 1923), 417-30.

44. Boris Emmet and John E. Jeuck, *Catalogues and Counters: A History of Sears, Roebuck and Company* (Chicago, 1950), 19-22, 39-46; *Sears, Roebuck and Co., Catalogue*, 1894, cover, and *Catalogue*, No. 103 (Fall 1896), 758.

45. *Sears, Roebuck and Co., Catalogue*, No. 111 (Spring 1902),

448, and No. 112 (Fall 1902), 469; B. Emmet and J. E. Jeuck, *Catalogues and Counters,* 14.

46. *Sears, Roebuck and Co., Catalogue,* No. 113 (Spring 1904), 1, and No. 114 (Spring 1905), 1.

47. *Ibid.,* No. 110 (Fall 1900), 3.

48. *Ibid.,* No. 105 (Fall 1897), 5 and No. 112, 6.

49. *Ibid.,* No. 112, 5.

50. *Ibid.,* No. 126 (Spring 1913), 2.

51. J. H. Kolb, *Service Relations of Town and Country* (Wisconsin Agricultural Experiment Station, Research Bulletin No. 58, 1923), 73; *Congressional Record,* 68th Cong., 2d sess., 349.

52. Edmund de S. Brunner and J. H. Kolb, *Rural Social Trends* (New York, 1933), 156; *Congressional Record,* 71st Cong., 3d sess., 5040, and *Postmaster General's Report,* 1930, 29.

53. *Sears, Roebuck and Co., Catalogue,* No. 111, 457-61.

54. Viola I. Paradise, "By Mail," *Scribner's Magazine,* 69 (Apr. 1921), 473-80.

55. *Postmaster General's Report,* 1918, 84.

56. B. Emmet and J. E. Jeuck, *Catalogues and Counters,* 295, 301, 736, note 10.

57. John Allen Underwood, "What's the Matter with the Small-Town Store," *Current Opinion,* 59 (July 1915), 60.

58. B. Emmet and J. E. Jeuck, *Catalogues and Counters,* 150-68; David L. Cohn, *The Good Old Days* (New York, 1940), 510-17; *U.S. Statutes at Large,* 43 (1925), 1067-68.

59. "Seventy-Four American Towns Mobilize to Keep Trade at Home," *Current Opinion,* 62 (Apr. 19, 1917), 288.

60. *Ibid.,* 288-89.

61. Julian Rosenwald, "What We Have Learned from 6,000,000 Customers," *American Magazine,* 90 (July 1920), 34.

62. *Congressional Record,* 82d Cong., 1st sess., 12799.

63. *U.S. Statutes at Large,* 65 (1951), 610-11.

CHAPTER 11

1. *Postmaster General's Report,* 1931, 114.

2. *Congressional Record,* 61st Cong., 2d sess., 32; *Postmaster General's Report,* 1914, 35.

3. U. S. Census, *Statistical Abstract* 1930, 619.

4. Claude C. Miller, "The Menace of Crowded Cities," *World's Work*, 16 (May 1908), 10268, and "The Problems of Overcrowding and the Cures for Overcrowding," *The Outlook*, 88 (Mar. 21, 1908), 615-17.

5. Lincoln Steffens, "Tweed Days in St. Louis," *McClure's Magazine*, 20 (Mar. 1903), 545-60; Ray Stannard Baker, "The Trust's New Tool—The Labor Boss," *ibid.*, 22 (Nov. 1903), 30-43; George Kibbe Turner, "The City of Chicago: A Study of the Great Immoralities," *ibid.*, 28 (Apr. 1907), 576.

6. Lincoln Steffens, *The Autobiography of Lincoln Steffens* (2 vols.; New York, 1931), I, 375; Ray Stannard Baker, *American Chronicle: The Autobiography of Ray Stannard Baker* (New York, 1945), 183.

7. Seymour Deming, "Homestead Revisited," *Atlantic Monthly*, 118 (Oct. 1916), 531.

8. John M. Gillette, "The Drift to the City in Relation to the Rural Problem," *American Journal of Sociology*, 16 (Mar. 1911), 645; William B. Bailey, "Our Urban and Rural Growth," *The Independent*, 71 (Sept. 14, 1911), 591.

9. On the agrarian tradition in the nation's history see Henry Nash Smith, *Virgin Land* (Cambridge, 1950), Richard Hofstader, *Age of Reform* (New York, 1955), Dwight Griswold, *Farming and Democracy* (New Haven, 1952), and Paul Johnstone, "Old Ideals versus New Ideas in Farm Life," in U. S. Department of Agriculture, *Yearbook*, 1940.

10. A. A. Lipscomb and A. E. Bergh (eds.), *The Writings of Thomas Jefferson*, II, 229.

11. *Ibid.*

12. *Congressional Record*, 59th Cong., 2d sess., 77 (Appendix).

13. *Ibid.*, 57th Cong., 1st sess., 2591-92.

14. Willa Cather, *O Pioneers* (The Riverside Library; New York, 1929), 123.

15. *Congressional Record*, 62d Cong., 2d sess., 5205; A. A. Lipscomb and A. E. Bergh (eds.), *The Writings of Thomas Jefferson*, VI, 392-93.

16. William J. Spillman, "Letter to Editor," *Science*, 29 (May 7, 1909), 740.

17. W. C. Funk, *What the Farm Contributes Directly to the Farmers' Living* (U. S. Department of Agriculture, Farmers' Bulletin No. 635, 1914), 5-21; *Wages and Hours of Labor in the Iron and Steel Industry in the United States* (U. S. Department of Labor, Bureau of

Statistics, 1914), 143; "If We Raised What We Eat," *World's Work*, 24 (May 1912), 13.

18. Edward A. Ross, "The Middle West: Fiber of the People," *Century*, 83 (Feb. 1912), 612.

19. *Congressional Record*, 61st Cong., 2d sess., 2563; Sir Horace Plunkett, "The Neglected Farmer," *The Outlook*, 94 (Feb. 6, 1910), 299.

20. *Congressional Record*, 59th Cong., 2d sess., 78 (Appendix).

21. For a contrasting point of view see R. Hofstader, *Age of Reform*, 117-18, who implies that farm legislation came in this period because the farmers were better organized and because of overrepresentation of the farm population in Congress. See also Carl Degler, *Out of Our Past* (New York, 1959), who dates the collapse of the agrarian tradition in America with the election of 1896. "After the debacle of 1896," he writes on pp. 333-34, "the business side of the schizoid farmers' movement was dominant; thereafter we hear little of the Jeffersonian rhetoric but much of parity, export debenture, equity fees, and crop allotments."

22. *Postmaster General's Report, 1891*, 85.

23. *Congressional Record*, 57th Cong., 1st sess., 2506.

24. *Postmaster General's Report, 1931*, 114.

25. "Degenerate, Molly-coddled Town-Life," *World's Work*, 16 (May 1908), 10172-73.

26. Theodore Roosevelt to Liberty Hyde Bailey, Aug. 10, 1908, in E. E. Morison (ed.), *The Letters of Theodore Roosevelt*, VI, 1167-68.

27. For Roosevelt's own estimate of Plunkett's help see Theodore Roosevelt to William Howard Taft, Dec. 21, 1908, in *ibid.*, 1433-44; for Roosevelt's speech to the Grangers see Theodore Roosevelt, "Rural Life," *The Outlook*, 95 (Aug. 27, 1910), 919-22.

28. T. Roosevelt, "Rural Life," 920.

29. T. Roosevelt to L. H. Bailey, Aug. 10, 1908, in E. E. Morison (ed.), *The Letters of Theodore Roosevelt*, VI, 1168; Theodore Roosevelt, "American Worker in Country and Town," *The Outlook*, 97 (Apr. 22, 1911), 938, and "The Welfare of the Farmer," *The Outlook*, 100 (Apr. 20, 1912), 852-56.

30. Peter F. Dunne, "'Mr. Dooley' on Uplifting the Farmers," *American Magazine*, 67 (Nov. 1908), 95-97.

31. "Report of the Country Life Commission," S. Doc. 705, 60th Cong., 2d sess., 1-65; "Problems of Country Life," *World's Work*, 17 (Feb. 1909), 11195-96; "The American Farmer," *The Outlook*,

89 (Aug. 22, 1908), 876-77; for a good account of the commission's work see Clayton S. Ellsworth, "Theodore Roosevelt's Country Life Commission," *Agricultural History*, 34 (Oct. 1960), 155-62.

32. G. S. Dickerson, "The Drift to the Cities," *Atlantic Monthly*, 112 (Sept. 1913), 353; for a brief treatment of the back-to-the-land movement see Paul K. Conkin, *Tomorrow a New World: The New Deal Community Program* (Ithaca, N. Y., 1959), 17-21.

33. Earl Godwin, "Steps Back to the Farm," *Country Life in America*, 19 (Mar. 15, 1911), 399.

34. On Page see Burton J. Hendrick, *The Life and Letters of Walter H. Page* (3 vols.; New York, 1924), I, and also Mark Sullivan, *Pre-War America* (*Our Times*, III), 319-23; "Does Anybody Really Want a Farm?" *World's Work*, 23 (Nov. 1911), 119.

35. E. Godwin, "Steps Back to the Farm," 400.

36. A. P. Hitchcock, "The Joys of Being a Farmer," *Country Life in America*, 20 (July 1, 1911), 46-52.

37. E. Godwin, "Steps Back to the Farm," 400.

38. *Congressional Record*, 63d Cong., 3d sess., 426.

39. *Ibid.*, 61st Cong., 2d sess., 2574.

40. *Ibid.*, 2322.

41. *Postmaster General's Report*, 1931, 114.

42. Jacob Riis, "How We Found Our Farm," *World's Work*, 23 (Feb. 1912), 475-79; Ray Stannard Baker, *Adventures in Contentment*, by David Grayson [pseud.] (New York, 1907, 1910, 1929), 128.

43. George K. Holmes, "Movement from City and Town to Farm," in U. S. Department of Agriculture, *Yearbook*, 1915, 257-74.

44. Seaman Knapp, "An Agricultural Revolution," *World's Work*, 12 (July 1906), 7733.

45. Liberty H. Bailey, "Why Do Farm Boys Leave the Farm?" *Century*, 72 (July 1906), 410-16; Harvey W. Wiley, "Back to the Farm: Present Drawbacks and Future Prospects," *ibid.*, 83 (Feb. 1912), 624.

46. Theodore Roosevelt to Herbert Myrick, Sept. 10, 1908, in E. E. Morison (ed.), *The Letters of Theodore Roosevelt*, VI, 1226-27.

47. Roy Hinman Holmes, "The Passing of the Farmer," *Atlantic Monthly*, 110 (Oct. 1912), 519.

48. *Hutchinson News*, June 19, 1912, 6.

49. Bruce L. Melvin, *The Sociology of a Village and a Surrounding Territory* (Cornell University Experiment Station, Bulletin No. 523, 1931), 1-138.

50. H. Quick, *One Man's Life*, 217.
51. "The City Maligned," *The Nation*, 97 (Dec. 18, 1913), 584.

CHAPTER 12

1. J. L. Gillin, "Social Education of the Farm Population," *Proceedings of the Fifth National Country Life Conference* (Chicago, 1922), 82.
2. James Bryce, *The American Commonwealth* (2 vols.; New York, 1897), II, 294.
3. Hamlin Garland, *A Son of the Middle Border* (New York, 1917), 416; John W. Bookwalter, "The Farmer's Isolation and the Remedy," *Forum*, 12 (Sept. 1891), 50-51.
4. Rural Agent J. F. Grote to R. M. Fulton, n.d., Hardin County, Iowa, County Files, N. A.
5. Eldora Rt. No. 2, as amended effective Nov. 15, 1901, Hardin County, Iowa, County Files, N. A.
6. Rural Agent R. J. Martin to C. E. Llewellyn, Aug. 5, 1905, Sumner County, Kans., County Files, N. A.
7. E. V. Smalley, "The Isolation of Life on Prairie Farms," *Atlantic Monthly*, 72 (Sept. 1893), 378-82.
8. Viola Paradise, "By Mail," 477-78.
9. J. Stahl, *Growing with the West*, 101; Mari Sandoz, "The Wife of Old Jules," in *Roundup: A Nebraska Reader*, ed. Virginia Faulkner (Lincoln, 1957), 146.
10. *Congressional Record*, 64th Cong., 1st sess., 1383.
11. H. Quick, *One Man's Life*, 172 ff.; H. Garland, *Son of the Middle Border*, 120.
12. "Free Delivery Service," S. Doc. 92, 51; Allen Day Willey, "The Rural Free Delivery Service," *Review of Reviews*, 27 (Jan. 1903), 59.
13. From statistics drawn from the *Postmaster General's Reports*, 1898, 1903, and 1929, pp. 165, 614-17, and 135-38 respectively.
14. *Postmaster General's Report*, 1901, 143.
15. Charles Moreau Harger, "The Country Editor Today," *Atlantic Monthly*, 99 (Jan. 1907), 89-96.
16. *Congressional Record*, 61st Cong., 2d sess., 2903.
17. H. J. Ormsby, Report on Sumner County Service, Kans., April 7, 1902, County Files, N. A.
18. As quoted in Alfred M. Lee, *The Daily Newspaper in America*

(New York, 1937), 307; *Postmaster General's Report*, 1911, 613, and 1929, 135-38.

19. J. O. Rankin, *Reading Matter in Nebraska Farm Homes* (Nebraska Agricultural Experiment Station, Bulletin No. 180, 1922), 1, 11, 17; *U.S. Official Postal Guide*, 1920, 718; and Randall C. Hill, et al., *Social, Economic, and Homemaking Factors in Farm Living* (Missouri Agricultural Experiment Station, Research Bulletin No. 148, 1930), 32.

20. Comparison of figures drawn from George P. Rowell, *The American Newspaper Directory*, 1900, 21, and Nathan Wheeler Ayer & Son, *American Newspapers Annual and Directory*, 1930 (Philadelphia, 1880——), 12.

21. *Postmaster General's Report*, 1901, 300; G. P. Rowell, *American Newspaper Directory*, 1900, 967; N. W. Ayer, *Newspaper Annual*, 1903, 777; 1910, 804; 1920, 872.

22. William Allen White, "The Country Newspaper," *Harper's Magazine*, 132 (May 1916), 891.

23. W. A. White, *Autobiography*, 400.

24. *Postmaster General's Report*, 1901, 292; G. P. Rowell, *American Newspaper Directory*, 1900, 367; N. W. Ayer, *Newspaper Annual*, 1903, 309; and 1920, 334.

25. William W. Loomis, "People Do Love to See Their Names in Print," *American Magazine*, 94 (Nov. 1924), 42.

26. C. M. Harger, "The Country Editor Today," 94.

27. Carl C. Taylor, "The Country Newspaper as a Town-Country Agency," *Proceedings of the Fourth National Country Life Conference* (Chicago, 1921), 37.

28. "Periodicals Read in a Country Community," *World's Work*, 9 (Mar. 1905), 5926-27.

29. W. J. Spillman, "Relative Effectiveness of Different Means of Reaching the Farmer," n.d., received May 19, 1913, Bureau of Agricultural Economics, National Archives, 3, 7.

30. J. O. Rankin, *Reading Matter in Nebraska Homes*, 5, 11-13; R. C. Hill, *Social and Homemaking Factors*, 32; "Periodicals Read in a Country Community," 5927.

31. *Congressional Record*, 59th Cong., 1st sess., 5081.

32. Spillman, "Different Means of Reaching the Farmer," 10, 13, 14.

33. *Postmaster General's Report*, 1911, 373, and 1929, 135-36.

34. Robert J. Murray, "Getting the Farmer's Point of View Solved Our Sales Problems," *System*, 48 (Aug. 1925), 163.

35. *Congressional Record*, 61st Cong., 2d sess., 2903.

36. Edwin W. Lawrence, "Swindling Through the Post Office," *The Outlook*, 79 (Jan. 14, 1905), 121-26.

37. *Ibid.*, 123-24; "Mr. Hitchcock's War upon Swindles," *The Independent*, 69 (Dec. 1, 1910), 1221-22.

38. *Congressional Record*, 62d Cong., 1st sess., 2379; Arthur J. Cramp (ed.), *Nostrums and Quackery* (2 vols.; Chicago, 1912 and 1921), I, 40-41; on patent-medicine salesmanship see James Harvey Young, *The Toadstool Millionaires: A Social History of Patent Medicines in America before Federal Regulation* (Princeton, 1961), 165-89.

39. A. J. Cramp, *Nostrums and Quackery*, I, 210.

40. *Ibid.*, II, 169.

41. Edward Bok, "How Private Confidences of Women are Laughed at," *Ladies' Home Journal*, 21 (Nov. 1904), 18; A. J. Cramp, *Nostrums and Quackery*, II, 178.

42. A. J. Cramp, *Nostrums and Quackery*, II, 143, 482-88, and I, 100-33.

43. Edward Bok, "The Patent-Medicine Curse," *Ladies' Home Journal* (May 1904), 18; L. F. Kobler, *Habit-Forming Agents: Their Indiscriminate Sale and Use a Menace to the Public Welfare* (U. S. Department of Agriculture, Farmers' Bulletin No. 392, 1910), 1-19.

44. *Postmaster General's Report*, 1904, 27; Oscar E. Anderson, Jr., *The Health of a Nation: Harvey W. Wiley and the Fight for Pure Food* (Chicago, 1958), 154-59; see also "Investigation of Adulterated Foods, etc.," S. Doc. 270, 58th Cong., 2d sess., 1-4.

45. *Congressional Record*, 59th Cong., 1st sess., 1415.

46. *U.S. Statutes at Large*, 37 (1912), 416-17.

47. "Professor Samuels and His Eyewash," *The Journal of the American Medical Association*, 55 (Dec. 24, 1910), 2248.

48. A. J. Cramp, *Nostrums and Quackery*, I, 181-92, 287.

49. Victor I. Masters, *The Country Church in the South* (Atlanta, 1917), 40.

50. *Postmaster General's Report*, 1898, 237.

51. *R.F.D. News*, 3 (June 1905), 268.

52. *Congressional Record*, 57th Cong., 1st sess., 2447, and 58th Cong., 2d sess., 3359.

53. Charles H. Greathouse, "Free Delivery of Rural Mails," U. S. Department of Agriculture, *Yearbook, 1900*, 524.

54. A. L. Spencer to James Blakslee, Aug. 22, and Blakslee to Spencer, Sept. 7, 1920, Blakslee Correspondence, N. A.

55. *Postmaster General's Report*, 1903, 617, 620; 1911, 12, 373; 1929, 137-38.

56. *Postmaster General's Report*, 1911, 12, 373; 1929, 137-38.

57. *Congressional Record*, 61st Cong., 2d sess., 2530.

58. *Ibid.*, 2568.

59. *The National Rural Letter Carrier*, 46 (Jan. 25, 1947), 7.

INDEX

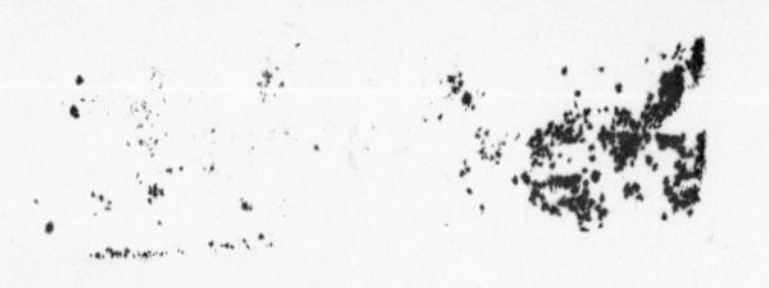